LIBRARY OF NEW TESTAMENT STUDIES
345

Formerly the Journal for the Study of the New Testament Supplement series

TEMPLE, EXILE AND IDENTITY
IN 1 PETER

ANDREW M. MBUVI

t&t clark

Published by T&T Clark International
A Continuum imprint
The Tower Building, 11 York Road, London SE1 7NX
80 Maiden Lane, Suite 704, New York, NY 10038

www.tandtclark.com

First published 2007

British Library Cataloguing-in-Publication Data
A catalogue record for this book is available from the British Library

ISBN-10: 0567-03142-X (hardback)
ISBN-13: 978-0-567-03142-6 (hardback)

Typeset by Free Range Book Design & Production Ltd
Printed on acid-free paper in Great Britain by Biddles Ltd, King's Lynn, Norfolk

CONTENTS

PREFACE

This book marks a significant point in a long journey that started in my home country, Kenya, where I began my theological training at Nairobi Evangelical Graduate School of Theology (NEGST) before coming to America to pursue further education at Westminster Seminary. Throughout, my life has been touched and enriched by teachers, students, church communities and family members who prodded me on and encouraged my endeavors even when they did not fully comprehend them. And so, as much as the book is my own product – including any shortcomings therein – it is an inspiration of a community of believers.

The primary focus of this work is on exegetical analysis of the temple imagery in 1 Peter in light of the Second Temple Jewish framework of the "lingering exile" as an interpretive matrix. Consequently, 1 Peter's use of cultic language in constituting the new identity of the Petrine community is scrutinized with the resultant conclusion that temple imagery in 1 Peter undergirds the entire epistle. This concern with the temple is then placed within the larger Second Temple rubric of *restoration eschatology* that anticipated the establishment of the eschatological temple, hope for the regathering of the scattered of Israel, the conversion (or destruction) of the Gentiles, and the establishment of God's universal reign, all of which are reflected in 1 Peter's discourse.

We anticipate that such a reading of 1 Peter would generate a fresh understanding of the main themes of 1 Peter, which include questions of identity, suffering, hope, holiness, and judgment. Central to 1 Peter's message is the assurance of hope that comes in light of the person of Jesus Christ, who in some mysterious way is the fulfillment of the Second Temple Jewish hope for national restoration.

Thanks are due to Mustard Seed Foundation, Africa Theological Initiative and Westminster Seminary for financial support. Earlier editorial assistance with the manuscript was offered by Melvin Peters of Duke University and my father-in-law Myron Beckenstein. My mother-in-law Charlotte Beckenstein organized a prayer group that kept bombarding heaven on my behalf. My parents, Jacob and Jane Musyoka, have always been supportive of my academic endeavors even when such dreams seemed daunting. My grandparents, Elisavethi Ngong'u and Éndélèa Ndũmũ have been lasting pillars of inspiration to my faith having faithfully served the Lord for over seven decades.

Finally, one person has borne the brunt of the whole process of earning a Ph.D. and now, getting a first book published – my beloved wife

Amanda! A scholar in her own right, her invaluable help in editing, focusing and encouragement throughout enabled me to finish the task with some sanity left in me. And now, even as I take my maiden step into the world of publication, she carries our first child who we pray will grow to come to appreciate the truth of the Gospel. To both, 'mother and child', this book is lovingly dedicated.

Soli Deo Gloria!

Andrew M. Mbuvi
Durham, NC
2006

ABBREVIATIONS

1 Clem.	*1 Clement*
1QH	*Hôdāyôt* (Thanksgiving Hymns) from Qumran Cave 1
1QM	*Milhǎmǎh* (War Scroll)
1QpHab	*Pesher Habakkuk* from Qumran Cave 1
1QS	*Serek hayyahad* (Manual of Discipline, Rule of Community)
1QSa	Appendix A (*Rule of Congregation)* to 1QS
4Q161–165	(4QpIsa) *Isaiah Pesher*
4Q166–167	(4QpHos) *Hosea Pesher*
4Q174	(4QFlor) *Florilegium*, also *Midrash on Eschatology*
4Q390	(4Qps Moses) *Pseudo-Moses*
4Q400–407	(4QShirshabb) *Songs of the Sabbath Sacrifice*
4Q434	*Barkhi Naphshi*
4Q504–506	(4QDibHam) *Words of the Luminaries*
4Q522	(4QapocrJosué) *Prophecy of Joshua*
4QMMT	*Miqsat Maaseh ha-Torah*
4QpIsa	*Pesher Isaiah* from Qumran Cave 4
4QpPs	*Pesher Psalms* from Qumran Cave4
4QShirShabb	*Songs of the Sabbath Sacrifice* from Qumran Cave 4
4QTest	*Testimonia* text from Qumran Cave 4
11QMel	*Melchizedek Scroll* from Qumran Cave 11
11QTemp	*Temple Scroll* from Qumran Cave 11
AB	Anchor Bible
ABD	D. N. Freedman (ed.), *Anchor Bible Dictionary*, 6 vols.
Abot R. Nat.	*Abot de-Rabbi Natan*
AJBI	*Annual of the Japanese Biblical Institute*
ANRW	*Aufstieg und Niedergang der römishen Welt: Geschichte und Kultur Roms im Spiegel der Neueren Forschung* (Berlin: W. de Gruyter, 1972–)
ANYAS	Annual of New York Academy of Sciences
Ant.	Josephus, *Antiquities of the Jews*
AOAT	Alter Orient und Altes Testament
2–3 Apoc. Bar.	Syriac, Greek *Apocalypse of Baruch*
ASNU	Acta seminarii neotestamentici upsaliensis
AsSeign	*Assemblées du Seigneur*

b.	Babylonian Talmud
b. Ber.	Babylonian Talmudic Tractate *Berishit*
b. Ketub.	Babylonian Talmudic Tractate *Ketubbot*
b. Sanh.	Babylonian Talmudic Tractate *Sanhedrin*
b. Shab.	Babylonian Talmudic Tractate *Shabbat*
b. Sot.	Babylonian Talmudic Tractate *Sotah*
b. Yoma	Babylonian Talmudic Tractate *Yoma*
BAGD	Bauer, Walter, W. F. Arndt, F. W. Gingrich, F. W. Gingich (2d. ed.: and, F. W. Danker, *Greek-English Lexicon of the New Testament*
BDF	F. Blass, A. Debrunner, and R. W. Funk, *A Greek Grammar of the New Testament*
Bar.	Baruch
Barn.	*Barnabas*
BASOR	*Bulletin of the American School of Oriental Research*
BCE	Before Common Era
Bib	*Biblica*
BT	*The Bible Translator*
BTB	*Biblical Theological Bulletin*
BVC	*Bible et vie chrétienne*
BZAW	Beihefte zur *ZAW*
ca.	*circa*, around
C. Ap.	Josephus, *Contra Apionem* (Against Apion)
CBQ	*Catholic Biblical Quarterly*
CBQMS	Catholic Biblical Quarterly Monograph Series
CD	Damascus Document (Cairo Geniza text)
CE	Common Era
DBSup	*Supplement au Dictionnaire de la Bible*
DJG	*Dictionary of Jesus and the Gospels*
DSS	Dead Sea Scrolls
DUB	Die Uhrchristliche Botschaft
EKKNT	Evangelisch-Katholischer Kommentar zum Neuen Testament
1–2–3 Enoch	Ethiopic, Slavonic, Hebrew *Enoch*
EQ	*Evangelical Quarterly*
Exod. Rab.	*Exodus Rabbah*
FOTL	Forms of the Old Testament Literature
Frag. Tg.	*Fragmentary Targum*
FRLANT	Forschungen zur Religion und Literatur des Alten und Neuen Testaments
HeyJ	*Heythrop Journal*
HTR	*Harvard Theological Review*
HUCA	*Hebrew Union College Annual*
ICC	International Critical Commentary

IEJ	*Israel Exploration Journal*
Int	*Interpretation*
j.	Jerusalem Talmud
j. Sot.	Jerusalem Talmudic Tractate *Sota*
JAAR	*Journal of the American Academy of Religion*
JBL	*Journal of Biblical Literature*
JETS	*Journal for the Evangelical Theological Society*
JJS	*Journal of Jewish Studies*
JNES	*Journal of Near Eastern Studies*
JR	*Journal of Religion*
JSNT	*Journal for the Study of the New Testament*
JSNTSup	Journal for the Study of the New Testament Supplement Series
JSOT	*Journal for the study of the Old Testament*
JSTS	Journal for the Study of Theology Supplememts
JTS	*Journal of Theological Studies*
Jub.	*Jubilees*
KLIO	*Klio: Beiträge zur Alten Geschichte (Akademie der Wissenschaften der DDR Zentralintitiut für Alte Geschichte und Archäologie)*
LXX	Septuagint
1–2–3–4 Macc.	1–2–3–4 Maccabees
m.	Mishnah
Midr.	*Midrash*
MT	Masoretic Text
NCBC	New Century Bible Commentary
NEA	*Near Eastern Archeology*
NedTT	*Nederlands Theologisch Tijdschrift*
Neot	*Neotestamentica*
NICNT	New International Commentary on the New Testament
NIDNTT	C. Bromiley, ed., *The New International Dictionary of New Testament Theology*, 3 vols. (Grand Rapids: Zondervan, 1975–8)
NT	New Testament
NovT	*Novum Testamentum*
NovTSup	Novum Testamentum Supplement Series
NthT	*Neue theologishe tijdschrift*
NTS	*New Testament Studies*
OTL	Old Testament Library
OTP	James H. Charlesworth, ed., *Old Testament Pseudepigrapha*, 2 vols. (Garden City, NY.: Doubleday, 1983)
p.	*Pesiqta*

Philo
Abr.	*De Abrahamo*
Conf. Ling.	*De Confusione Linguarum*
De Sob.	*De Sobrietate*
Flac.	*In Flaccium*
Leg. Gai.	*De Legatio ad Gaium*
Leg. All.	*Legum Allegoriae*
Migr. Abr.	*De migratione Abrahami*
Plant.	*De Plantatione*
Praem.	*Praemis et Poenis*
Provid.	*De Providentia*
QE	*Questionies et Solutiones in Exodum*
Spec. Leg.	*De Specialibus Legibus*
Vit. Mos.	*De Vita Mosis*
Pss. Sol.	*Psalms of Solomon*
Rab.	*Rabbah*
RB	*Revue biblique*
RE	*Review Expositor*
RestQ	*Restoration Quarterly*
RevQ	*Revue de Qumran*
RSPT	*Review des sciences philosophique et theologique*
RSR	*Religious Studies Review*
RTP	*Revue de théologie et philosophie*
SANT	Studien zum Alten und Neuen Testament
SBFLA	*Studii biblici franciscani liber annus*
SBL	Studies in Biblical Literature Series
SBLASP	*Society of Biblical Literature Abstracts and Seminar Papers*
SBLEJL	Society of Biblical Literature Early Judaism and its Literature
SBLMS	Society of Biblical Literature Monograph Series
SBLDS	Society of Biblical Literature Dissertation Series
SBS	Stüttgarter Bibelstudien
ScEccl	*Sciences Ecclésistiques*
Sib. Or.	*Sibylline Oracles*
Sir.	Sirach
SJ	Studia Judaica
SNTSMS	Society for New Testament Studies Monograph Series
SPB	Studia postbiblica
ST	*Studia Theologica*
SUNT	Studien zur Umwelt des Neuen Testament
TD	*Theology Digest*
TDNT	*Theological Dictionary of the New Testament*
T. Levi	*Testament of Levi*

T. Benj.	*Testament of Benjamin*
T. Sol.	*Testament of Solomon*
Tg. Neb.	Targum of the Minor Prophets
Tg. Onq.	Targum Ongelos
Tg. Ps.-J.	Targum Pseudo-Jonathan
THNT	Theologischer Handkommentar zum Neuen Testament
TL	*Theologie de Louvain*
TLZ	*Theologische Literaturzeitung*
Tob.	Tobit
TynBul	*Tyndale Bulletin*
VT	*Vetus Testamentum*
War	Josephus, *The Jewish War*
WBC	Word Biblical Commentary
WUNT	Wissenschaftliche Untersuchungen zum Neuen Testament
ZAW	*Zeitschrift für die alttestamentliche Wissenschaft*
ZNW	*Zeitschrift für die neuetestamentliche Wissenschaft*

All Scripture references, unless otherwise stated, are from the *New Revised Standard Version*, copyright 1989 by the Division of Christian Education of the National Council of Churches of Christ in the USA. Use by Permission. All rights reserved.

Unless otherwise noted, the Greek from the Apocryphal and Septuagintal texts is drawn from A. Ralfs, *Septuaginta*, 8th edn (Stuttgart: Württenbergische Bibelanstalt, 1965) reproduced in the *Bible Works for Windows: Hermeneutica Software* (© Mark Bushnel; Big Fork, Mont.: Hermeneutica, 1996)

MT refers to *Biblia Hebraica Stüttgartensia* (*BHS*) reproduced in *Bible Works for Windows: Hermeneutica Software* (© Mark Bushnel; Big Fork, Mont.: Hermeneutica, 1996).

Unless otherwise stated all quotations of Josephus, Philo, Epictetus and Seneca are from the Loeb Classical Library (Cambridge, Mass.: Harvard University Press, 1926–79).

Translation of Greek, Hebrew, and German and French works, by the author.

Chapter 1

INTRODUCTION

1.1. *Brief Survey of Previous Studies on Temple in 1 Peter*

While the clearest application of the temple imagery is found in 1 Pet. 2.4-10,[1] it is the aim of this study to investigate other possible temple allusions and imagery in the rest of the epistle, and their significance in the Petrine reinterpretation of the Israelite sanctuaries (e.g. 1.2; 4.17: 5.10).[2] Scot McKnight points out that

> 1 Peter uses a host of words to describe what has happened to those who enter the family of God. In particular, he draws deeply from the imagery of the temple with its rituals and worship to express this matter. They have been sprinkled with blood (1:2), they have been ransomed (1:18-19), they have been purified (1:22), they have tasted God (2:3), they have been healed (2:24), and they have been presented before God (3:18).[3]

1.   The use of stone *testimonia* in 1 Peter 2.4-10 has been identified as the largest of its kind in the NT, which has also been used to argue for Petrine authorship of the epistle. See C. F. D. Moule, 'Some Reflections of the Stone Testimonia in Relation to the Name of Peter', *NTS* 2 (1955/6) 56–9; Ceslas Spicq, 'La Ia Petri et le témoignage évangélique de saint Pierre', *StTh* 20 (1966) 37–61, 57, 56; Klyne Snodgrass, '1 Peter II.1-10: Its Formation and Literary Affinities', *NTS* 24 (1977) 97–106, 97; Thomas Lea, 'How Peter Learned the Old Testament', *Southwestern Journal of Theology* 22 (1980) 96–102, 101. Paul J. Achtemeier, *1 Peter: A Commentary on First Peter* (Hermeneia; Minneapolis: Fortress Press, 1996) 150, n. 18, dismisses the argument simply as an 'interesting suggestion, but it can be no more than that'.

2.   Allusion to Greek temple practices will also be investigated especially in the appropriation of the imagery of temple *sacral* manumission in 1 Pet. 1.18. Wider implications may be adduced for the Greek temple analogy at least from the point of view of the targeted recipients of the epistle who as we argue are made up of a majority of Gentile converts (who already have had connections to Jewish synagogues – God-fearers), and a minority group of Jewish converts. See the forceful and spirited argument for the role of the Judaizing Gentiles (God-fearers) in the life of the early church, especially in the Dispersion, by Irina Levinskaya, *The Book of Acts: Diaspora Setting*, vol. v (Grand Rapids: Eerdmans; and Carlisle: Paternoster, 1996). The variety of the God-fearers ranged from those who were one step from full conversion to those who simply added the Jewish God to their pantheon (78). Cf. also John J. Collins, *Between Athens and Jerusalem: Jewish Identity in the Hellenistic Diaspora* (2nd edn; Grand Rapids: Eerdmans, 2000) 264–72, who independently comes to the same conclusion as Levinskaya concerning the range of spectrum of the God-fearers in first-century Judaism.

3.   Scot McKnight, *1 Peter: The NIV Application Commentary* (Grand Rapids: Zondervan, 1996) 30.

While not meant to be comprehensive, McKnight's list omits what we consider the most important of temple imagery passages, including 2.4-10, 4.17, and 5.10. The prevalence of Exodus motifs, especially in the first two chapters of the epistle, also provides for the plausibility of the tabernacle imagery in the epistle (e.g. ῥαντισμὸν αἵματος, ἀμνοῦ ἀμώμου).[4] We will further propose that a structural development of the epistle, very roughly along the lines of the history of Israel (i.e. tabernacle, temple, judgment/ destruction, restoration/rebuilding), can be envisioned.[5]

Outside of commentaries, studies that have focused on the temple in 1 Peter are not that many. In fact, they tend to be part of broader studies of the temple in the New Testament or something of that nature. Bertil Gärtner's seminal study, perhaps the most important of the works we will be dealing with, compares the looming presence of temple symbolism both in the NT and Qumran writings, focusing on the eschatological reinterpretation and actualization in both communities.[6] The language and theology of both are shown to have been significantly shaped and colored by temple imagery. It probably stems from Gärtner's work that a common view has been presented concerning the Qumran community's view of itself as the new eschatological temple.[7] It is Gärtner's contention that the commonalities between 1 Peter's and Qumran's reinterpretation of the temple are 'so striking … that we are compelled to assume the existence of some common tradition'.[8] Without downplaying the significance of Gärtner's study, his focus was limited in scope, primarily engaging only Qumran literature and its relationship with the NT. A wider scope of the Second Temple field is needed in order to have a better idea of how 1 Peter's conceptualization fits within the larger framework of Jewish thought.

---

4.   It will be obvious from this observation that the reading of the text is different from that of McKnight, who perceives all the references to be to the temple.

5.   See Chapter 3 and Appendix below.

6.   Bertil Gärtner, *The Temple and the Community in Qumran and the New Testament: A Comparative Study in the Qumran Texts and the New Testament* (Cambridge: Cambridge University Press, 1965) 72–88.

7.   Gärtner's argument has not gone unchallenged and J. Baumgarten, *Studies in Qumran Law* (Leiden: Brill, 1977) 62–3, 67, holds an opposing view that the community did not hold their purity rituals at the same level as the temple sacrifices as evidenced by the lack of an altar in Qumran. However, most studies have continued to support the views espoused by Gärtner. See, for example, Hermann Lichtenberger, 'Atonement and Sacrifice in the Qumran Community', in W. S. Green, ed., *Approaches to Ancient Judaism*, II (Chico, Calif.: Scholars Press, 1980) 159–71.

8.   Gärtner, *Temple*, 78. *Contra* David Flusser, 'The Dead Sea Sect and Pre-Pauline Christianity', in C. Rabin and Y. Yadin, eds., *Aspects of the Dead Sea Scrolls* (Scripta Hierosolymitana 4; Jerusalem: Magnes, 1958) 215–66, esp. 233–66, who perceived possible literary dependence by 1 Peter on some Hebrew text very much like 1QS 8.4-11, Gärtner is not willing to go that far (72 n. 2). See William L. Schutter, *Hermeneutic and Composition in 1 Peter* (WUNT 2.30; Tübingen: J. C. B. Mohr, 1989) 122.

Several years later, Georg Klinzing took the argument one step further when he argued that the NT derives its notion of the community as the temple from the Qumran community: 'If the Christian community speaks of itself as the temple, no doubt about it can exist, that the conception originates from the Qumran community'.[9] Basically, arguing against the cleft between cultic and more spiritual forms, as maintained by Hans Wenschkewitz,[10] Klinzing found this distinction not exhibited in Qumran material which he envisioned to have subsequently influenced Christian theology on temple imagery. He perceived both groups as interpreting the temple from the point of realized eschatology such that the tendency in both is to elevate cultic motifs to a higher plane.[11]

Subsequently, both Gärtner's and Klinzing's conclusions were called into question by Elisabeth Schüssler Fiorenza, who maintains that the NT writers 'do not so much reinterpret the cultic institutions and terminology but express a new reality in cultic language'.[12] For Schüssler Fiorenza, any sense of interpretive equation between the Qumran understanding of the temple and cultic material, and the NT, is highly questionable. For the NT writers, including 1 Peter, the emphasis is on the use of language to describe a new reality premised on the person of Jesus Christ while for Qumran the expectation for the old reality is still at the center of their hermeneutic.

R. McKelvey's work does a commendable but brief analysis of the Temple imagery in 1 Peter showing awareness of the fact that the image/symbolism is present in more than just 1 Peter 2.4-10 (e.g. also in 1 Pet. 4.17), on which McKelvey primarily focuses.[13] He briefly notes the significance of the priesthood and sacrifice language but does not incorporate the role of the πνεῦμα and language of the δόξα (4.14), or the imperishable inheritance (1.4) as it relates to sacrifice (1.2), in his discussion, elements we perceive to be crucial in embracing the full scope of Temple imagery in 1 Peter. Significant though his study is, McKelvey's dealing with 1 Peter is understandably brief given that the focus of his monograph is on the temple in the entire NT. For this reason, it certainly appears that much more could be said on the matter of temple imagery in 1 Peter than is covered by McKelvey.

Another useful, but equally brief, analysis of the temple in 1 Peter is found in Marie-Joseph Congar's *The Mystery of the Temple*.[14] This study tends more

9.   Georg Klinzing, *Die Umdeutung die Kultus in des Qumrangemeinde und im Neuen Testament* (SUNT 7; Gottingen: Vandenhoeck & Ruprecht, 1971) 210.

10.   Hans Wenschkewitz, "Die Spiritualisierung der Kultusbegriffe Temple, Priester und Opfer im Neuen Testament", *Angelos* 4 (1932) 70–230.

11.   Klinzing, *Die Umdeutung*, 210.

12.   Elisabeth Schüssler Fiorenza, 'Cultic Language in Qumran and in the NT', *CBQ* 38 (1976) 159–77, 162 n. 12.

13.   Robert J. McKelvey, *The New Temple: The Church in the New Testament* (London: Oxford University Press, 1969).

14   Marie-Joseph Congar, *The Mystery of the Temple* (Philadelphia: Fortress, 1968).

towards a systematic theological approach to the temple in the NT with limited focus on exegetical appraisal of the passages. It is, therefore, not very helpful in terms of determining exegetical issues on temple imagery in 1 Peter.

The same can also be said of Craig Koester's *The Dwelling of God*, which is a significant study on the sanctuary.[15] It primarily focuses on the tabernacle and its imagery in the NT. Since it views the sanctuary imagery of 1 Peter as primarily temple imagery without any substantive reference to the tabernacle, little attention has been given to 1 Peter in this work.[16]

The otherwise extremely useful *Lord of the Temple* by Ernest Lohmeyer is primarily focused on the Gospel tradition and, therefore, pays no attention to the temple imagery of 1 Peter in its discussion.[17] However, significant points raised in the book are deemed to have a bearing in the study of the temple in 1 Peter, and so it is pertinent for our study.

Given the paucity of studies on the subject, it is our conviction that a comprehensive analysis of how the temple imagery functions in the epistle of 1 Peter, especially as it relates to the main concerns of suffering and identity within the matrix of Israel's restoration, has yet to be fully undertaken. The role that the concept of 'exile' plays in providing an interpretive background for the entire epistle (1.1, 17; 1.21-25; cf. Isa. 40.6-8), is another aspect of this study whose benefits have not previously been fully mined. The connection of the exile and the temple in the OT and in other Jewish literature prior to Christianity is an acknowledged fact but its significance for understanding the language of 1 Peter has yet to be fully realized. This is the lacuna in 1 Peter's studies that this work hopes to fill.

In essential accord with Schüssler Fiorenza, we intend to argue that the pervasive use of cultic language in 1 Peter is driven not simply by a reinterpretation of cultic institutions, but the use of cultic language in the description of a new reality.[18] The temple is no longer a physical structure awaiting re-establishment in Jerusalem; it is spiritual and cosmic.[19] The restoration of Israel is no longer political but of greater magnitude – it encompasses forgiveness of sin. The inheritance is no longer land, it is a heavenly inheritance (1.4).

---

15.   Craig Koester, *The Dwelling of God: The Tabernacle in the Old Testament, Intertestamental Jewish Literature and the New Testament* (CBQMS 22; Washington, D.C.: Catholic Biblical Association of America, 1989).

16.   In this study we intend to argue that the tabernacle imagery could be alluded to in 1 Peter's utilization of the exodus motif.

17.   Ernst Lohmeyer, *Lord of the Temple: A Study of the Relation between Cult and the Gospel* (trans. Stewart Todd; Richmond: John Knox Press, 1962).

18.   Schüssler Fiorenza, 'Cultic', 162 n. 12.

19.   David Hill, "'To Offer Spiritual Sacrifices . . .'' (1 Peter 2:5): Liturgical Formulations and Christians Paraenesis in 1 Peter', *JSNT* 16 (1982) 45–63, [59] commenting on this aspect of 1 Peter notes that it is by the 'means of a mythic language' that 1 Peter universalizes the message that was specific to Israel in the OT. And so the nations that were 'once relegated to inferior status now have access by faith to the dignity of the people of God' (2.10).

Cultic language thus provides the vehicle to communicate the active presence of God in the midst of the Christian community's struggles with ostracization, persecution and self-identity. Similar concerns facing the Jews at the time of exile had concretized a certain outlook on life that subsequently interpreted new adversities in light of the exile experience.[20] The language of exile then formed a matrix of self-expression that articulated a continuing psychological state of mind in the Second Temple Jewish communities that perpetuated what has been called an 'exile mentality'.[21]

Closely related to this 'exile mentality' was another metaphor that was born in the exile – the self-understanding of the community as the dwelling of God – the 'temple' (1 Pet. 2.5; 1QS 8.4). Estranged from the temple, the exiled community reinterpreted the function of the temple in their midst. To them, cultic language became a framework of articulating hope for restoration and also providing a vehicle for worship in the interim. Therefore, the imagery shifted the conception of the temple from that of a physical structure to one of, for a lack of a better term, a spiritual nature. This not only became a language of formulating or replacing the role of the cultic elements among the exile community, but it also became the means to articulate self-identity, in light of the old realities.[22] Language then becomes crucial not only in articulating the community's connection with the cultic elements of the past, but also in reconstituting a new reality in light of the old.[23]

Previous studies on 1 Peter such as Gärtner's, Klinzing's and McKelvey's listed above have rightly focused on the imagery of the temple as a most decisive imagery in the letter, and also have recognized the importance of the language of exile in the epistle. But to our knowledge, none of these studies have sought to read the epistle in light of the larger concerns of Israel's *restoration eschatology* as it is characterized by the concerns for '… a renewed, restored, or rebuilt temple … restoration of the people of Israel, …[and the] beginning of God's reign on Mt. Zion, …'.[24] It is the intent of this study to

---

20.   N. T. Wright, *The New Testament and the People of God*, Christian Origins and the Question of God, 1 (Minneapolis: Fortress, 1992) 268–72, 299–301; *idem, Jesus and the Victory of God*, Christian Origins and the Question of God, 2 (Minneapolis: Fortress, 1996) xvii–xviii, 126–27, 203–4, 248–50.

21.   Wright, *People*, 268–72.

22.   Schüssler Fiorenza, 'Cultic', 162.

23.   Espousing a similar understanding of the use of language John Lanci, *A New Temple For Corinth: Rhetorical and Archeological Approaches to Pauline Imagery* (SBL 1; New York: Peter Lang, 1997) 124, while discussing the temple imagery in 1 Corinthians 3, explains that a 'metaphor … was an important oratorical tool to grab the attention of an audience so that it attended to a rhetorical argument. A distinct, unusual metaphor could fix an image in the mind that would engage the audience's emotions and could powerfully anchor the speaker's developing claims'.

24.   E. P. Sanders, *Judaism: Practice and Belief, 63 BCE–66 CE* (London: SCM Press; and Philadelphia: Trinity Press International, 1994) 279–303; *idem, Jesus and Judaism* (Philadelphia: Fortress, 1985) 91–119; Andrew Brunson, *Psalm 118 in the Gospel of John* (WUNT 2 Reihe 158; Tubingen: Mohr Siebeck, 2003) 68.

subject the reading of 1 Peter, with its special focus on the temple (2.4-10; 4.14-17; 5.10), election and identity (1.1; 2.1-3, 4-10), holiness (1.6-7, 16; 4.12), and hope (1.3, 13, 21; 3.15) to these concerns.

1 Peter is said to have the highest concentration, relative to its size, of OT references in the entire NT, leaving little doubt as to the writer's intentionality in appropriating the current experience of his audience with that of the OT nation of Israel.[25] David Hill notes, without further explanation, that, 'The true Israel is formed by those who belong to the "spiritual temple" which is built upon Christ, the living stone.'[26] Paul J. Achtemeier explains further that, 'within the overall thought-world of the letter ... the identification of the readers with the history of Israel is best understood in terms of a metaphorical use of that material in relation to the Christian faith, whereby the Christian community has assumed the mantle of chosen people formerly worn by Israel'.[27]

The striking element is the fact that, as most recent commentators maintain, 1 Peter's epistle is addressed to a largely Gentile audience made up mostly of earlier Gentile converts to Judaism.[28] These Gentile 'God-fearers' had closely associated themselves with the Jewish faith and synagogues, but never quite went the distance of full proselytism, most likely for reasons of being averse to circumcision.[29] According to Acts, this category of mostly Gentile adherents to Judaism made up the largest portion of initial Gentile converts to Christianity (Acts 10.2, 22, 35; 13.6, 26; σεβομένοι τὸν θεόν – 13.50; 16.14; 18.6-7; σεβομένοι – 17.4, 17; σεβομένοι προσηλύτοι – 13.43).[30] The advent of the Jewish sect of Christianity (Acts 9.2; 18.25, 26; 19.9, 23) with its abolition of the requirement of circumcision (e.g. Acts 15; Gal. 5.6), was able to attract large numbers of the Gentile 'God-fearers' into its ranks.[31] Consequently, it is

---

25.   Schutter, *Hermeneutic*, 43, counts approximately 46 quotations and allusions 'not counting iterative allusions that would boost the total'.

26.   Hill, 'Sacrifices' , 59.

27.   Achtemeier, *1 Peter*, 51.

28.   So Achtemeier, *1 Peter*, 51; Wayne Grudem, *The First Epistle of Peter: An Introduction and Commentary* (Grand Rapids: Eerdmans, 1988) 38; John H. Elliott, *A Home For the Homeless: A Sociological Exegesis of 1 Peter, Its Situation and Strategy* (Philadelphia: Fortress, 1981); Ceslas Spicq, *Les Épîtres de Saint Pierre* (Paris: J. Gabalda & Cie, 1966) 13, 65; J. N. D. Kelly, *The Epistles of Peter and Jude* (BNTC; London: Adam & Charles Black, 1969) 4; Hill, 'Sacrifices', 59; F. H. Chase, 'Peter, First Epistle', in J. Hastings, ed., *Dictionary of the Bible* (Edinburgh: T&T Clark, 1900) 783; Scot McKnight, *A Light Among the Gentiles: Jewish Missionary Activity in the Second Temple Period* (Minneapolis: Fortress, 1991).

29.   Achtemeier, *1 Peter*, 51.

30.   Frederick W. Danker, '1 Peter 1:24-2:17 – A Consolatory Pericope', ZNW 58 (1967) 93–102, 95. I agree with Danker without assenting to his conclusion on pseudepigraphic authorship of 1 Peter. Danker, correctly in my opinion, identifies the οἱ φοβούμενοι of Ps. 118 (117).4 as proselytes equivalent to the proselytes in 1 Peter.

31.   Achtemeier, *1 Peter*, 51.

reasonable to assume that the vast majority of the recipients of the encyclical 1 Peter would have originated from this group.[32] Accordingly, all the references to Gentiles (ἔθνη) in 1 Peter (2.12, 4.3) do not mean non-Jews, rather, it is a stock-phrase for non-Christian.[33]

1 Peter also connects the identity of his audience with the commencement of the national restoration of Israel (2.9 quoting Exod. 19.6; 23.22). However, the contrast with old Israel is that, while for old Israel suffering was understood as 'motivated by their national and private sins,' in 1 Peter suffering is presented as God's purifying process (1.6-7; 4.11-12).[34] Therefore, in spite of their suffering, their calling as God's priestly community is assured.[35]

With the commencement of the Herodian persecution (Acts 12.1) the Christians in Jerusalem had been scattered to different regions separating them from the Temple and its *cultus*. It is, perhaps, with this remove from the Temple and the subsequent lingering desire for pilgrimage to Jerusalem in the background, that 1 Peter is written. Writing to those in διασπορᾶς ('Dispersion') distanced from the Jerusalem Temple and its *cultus*, 1 Peter communicates his confidence in the fact that the temple is not simply a physical building found in Jerusalem.[36] This is not to suggest that 1 Peter's audience were necessarily

32.   See further arguments in Achtemeier, *1 Peter*, 51-4. John H. Elliott, *1 Peter* (AB 37B; New York: Doubleday, 2000) 466, notes that: '… it is appropriated especially from Israelite usage where "Gentiles" (*ethnē* for Heb. *goyim* in contrast to '*am/laos*) is not merely a neutral term for "peoples" but, especially from the post-exilic period onward, designates all non Israelites, often as enemies (Isa. 24-27; Ezek. 38-39; Zech. 9-14; Dan 3:7, 37; 7:14; 8:22; 9:26…)…. However, in some cases, as here in 1 Peter, when *ta ethnē/hoi ethnikoi* is a foil to followers of Jesus, it becomes a designation for all non-Christians ….'

33.   Francis Wright, *The First Epistle of Peter: The Greek Text with Introduction and Notes* (3rd edn; Oxford: Blackwell, 1947) 101; Ernest Best, *1 Peter* (New Century Bible; London: Oliphants, 1971; repr. by Grand Rapids: Eerdmans, 1982) 111; Achtemeier, *1 Peter*, 177; *contra* J. W. C. Wand, *The General Epistles of St. Peter and St. Jude* (Westminster Commentaries: London: Methuen, 1934) 74–5, who maintains that the word must mean that 'the readers by contrast were Jews'. While indeed we acknowledge that some of the Petrine believers were Jewish, use of word ἔθνη is not dependent on such an understanding in 1 Peter.

34.   Danker, '1 Peter 1:24-2:17', 97: '… a further association is made with Isa. 43:14-21, where the deliverance of Israel is treated under the figure of the Exodus with stress on the declaration of God's ἀρεταί by the people of God's own περιποίησις (vs. 21)'.

35.   Danker, '1 Peter 1:24-2:17', 97: Given their geographical proximity (Asia Minor), 1 Peter's audience are dislocated from the Temple and possibly find themselves in the awkward position of desiring to fulfill their cultic roles at the Jerusalem Temple (in light of Jewish religious practice) but cannot because of, i) distance from Jerusalem, and/or, ii) persecution in their local areas, and iii) persecution of the Christians in Jerusalem not allowing them the possibility of making a pilgrimage. These possible reasons for the state of concern in relation to the matters of purity in 1 Peter can be deduced from the letter itself. 1 Peter writes both to warn about the dangers of negligence and the impending judgment, but also to encourage them not to be discouraged in spite of their present trials (1.6-7; 4.12).

36.   Victor A. Furnish, 'Elect Sojourners in Christ: An Approach to the Theology of 1 Peter', *Perkins Journal* 28 (1975) 1-11, esp. 2-3, recognizes that the term διασπορᾶς was used of the entire

literal exiles from Jerusalem, or Palestine in general, as F. Lapham has suggested,[37] yet it is plausible that within their numbers there might have been some Jewish people who literally were themselves in exile. However, they would compose a small minority.

1.2. *Structure of Study*

The primary focus of this book is an exegetical analysis of the metaphor of temple imagery (2.4-10) and other possible allusions to the temple imagery in the epistle of 1 Peter (1.18-19; 3.19-20; 4.14-17; 5.10) in light of the Second Temple Jewish framework of the 'lingering exile' as an interpretive matrix.[38] 1 Peter directly connects the community's identity with the temple when he describes them in vocabulary reminiscent of the temple structure as 'living stones' formulating an image that has been categorized as a 'Temple-Community'.[39] Such an image, as we will contend, would be best understood within the framework of other elements that characterize what has been referred to as a Second Temple Jewish anticipation of eschatological restoration of Israel from 'exile'.

We anticipate that such a reading of 1 Peter would generate a fresh and, even perhaps, a new understanding of the main themes of 1 Peter. Central to 1 Peter's message is to assure his audience of the hope that comes in light of the person of Jesus Christ who, according to 1 Peter, is in some mysterious way the fulfillment of the Second Temple Jewish hope for national restoration.

The overall structure of the study is thus to first establish the milieu out of which 1 Peter was writing. This will be done in the following chapter and is characterized by a number of things: the 'idea of exile' as a controlling metaphor, 'exile and the new exodus' as the background for reading 1 Peter,

---

dispersed community of Jews scattered in the Gentile world since the Babylonian exile. Harald Hegemann, 'The Diaspora in the Hellenistic Age', in W. D. Davies and Louis Finkelstein, eds, *The Cambridge History of Judaism* (3 vols; Cambridge: Cambridge University Press, 1999), 2.115–66.

37.   F. Lapham, *Peter: The Myth, the Man and the Writings* (Sheffield: Sheffield University Press, 2003) 127. He interprets the reference to 'she who is in Babylon' (5.13) as literal reference to sojourning in Asia Minor, understanding the reference to sojourning as literal migration of Christians from Palestine to Asia Minor. Therefore, the fact of their homelessness is in relation to the proximity to their Palestinian homeland. This forces Lapham to downplay such passages as 1 Pet. 1.4 and as such to see little significance in the metaphor. Thus, while he acknowledges the likelihood of a 'heavenly analogy' in 1 Peter 1.4 (128), it can only be used by the author if it reflects the true experience of the readers.

38.   Peter R. Ackroyd, *Exile and Restoration: A Study of Hebrew Thought of the Sixth Century B.C.* (Philadelphia: Westminster, 1968); Sanders, *Jesus and Judaism*, 91–113.

39.   Gärtner, *Temple*, 78; Best, '1 Peter', 111.

the question of immanence and transcendence of God in the OT taber-nacle/temple, development of the perception of the sanctuary in the history of Israel beginning with the prototypical Jewish sanctuary, Noah's ark, and culminating with the subsequent dissatisfaction with the so-called second temple within Judaism which partly spurred the anticipation of the eschatological temple in Jewish thought. We will also take a look at Qumran's development of the idea of community as the venerable temple (1QS 8.4) and Judaism's reaction to the destruction of the Herodian temple (e.g. *Avot de-Rabbi Natan* 4).

Chapter 3 will analyze the different understandings of the temple tradition in the Second Temple period with the hope of tracing the different streams of traditions from which the author of 1 Peter is most likely to have drawn, in the development of his temple imagery. We will also investigate how the larger context of exile can be brought to bear in our understanding of 1 Peter's development of temple imagery within the Second Temple milieu.

Chapter 4 then highlights how 1 Peter appropriates the elements that had been developed in the Jewish background of the temple into his own devel-opment and appropriation of temple imagery in relation to the Christian community. This involves 1 Peter's reinterpretation of the Jewish eschatological temple in light of the person of Jesus Christ, and Christian community as the 'Temple-Community'. 1 Peter also seems to have allowed for the historical development of the sanctuary in Israel to loosely structure the content of his epistle. 1 Peter's temple imagery is therefore investigated in light of the language of 'blood sprinkling' (1.2), 'holiness' (1.16), 'spiritual house' (2.5), 'Noah's sanctuary' (3.19), 'judgment that begins in God's house' (4.14-17), and 'restoration' (5.10).

Chapter 5 examines the implications of our investigation into 1 Peter's appropriation of temple imagery in light of the major themes of the epistle. This also involves a look at how temple imagery shaped the identity that 1 Peter constructs for his audience as the 'new Israel' that also comprises the 'new temple' (spiritual house) and a 'new priesthood' (holy and royal). The message of restoration (5.10) maintains the theme of hope in the epistle especially in light of the current state of the audience's persecution and ostracization. The study concludes with a section that surveys the overall significance of this study of temple imagery for subsequent studies of 1 Peter.

Chapter 2

'EXILE AND RESTORATION OF ISRAEL'
AS A BACKGROUND FOR READING 1 PETER

2.1. *Introductory Comments*

Julius Wellhausen perceived two major periods in the history of Israel – pre-exilic Israel and post-exilic Israel[1] – and he regarded with disdain the latter, primarily because of the limiting of the 'uncommon freshness of their impulses' by the institutionalizing of the Laws of Israel which had hitherto been free of the reigns of outward norms and establishments.[2] The exile, according to Wellhausen, marked the decline in Israelite religion, the demise of prophecy, and the narrowing of religious concerns to the temple and its *cultus*. This, he thought, was an unfortunate but necessary shift 'that changed the very character of the religion but at the same time helped to preserve the community'.[3] However, subsequent scholarship has shown the vitality and creativity of the exilic period to be significant and crucial for understanding Second Temple Judaism.[4]

Before the exile, Israelite social identity was based on clans and family ties, as well as on the monarchy.[5] With the return from exile, Jewish identity was

---

1. John Barton, 'Wellhausen's Prolegomena to the History of Israel: Influences and Effects', in Daniel L. Smith-Christopher, ed., *Text and Experience: Toward a Cultural Exegesis of the Bible* (Sheffield: Sheffield Academic Press, 1995) 316–29 (328), even suggests that Wellhausen might have, in fact, 'discovered the exile' which helped him ground the late date of P, a central element of Wellhausen's redefinition of the Documentary Hypothesis.

2. Julius Wellhausen, *Prolegomena to the History of Israel* (London: A & C Black, 1885; repr. Grand Rapids: Baker, 1993) 412.

3. Ibid., 424–5; cf. Douglas A. Knight, 'Foreword to the Scholars Edition' of Julius Wellhausen's *Prolegomena*, xiv. As Abraham Kaplan, 'Identity and Alienation: Zionism For the West', in Étan Levine, ed., *Diaspora: Exile and the Contemporary Jewish Condition* (New York: Steimatzky, 1986) 327–52, 328–9, explains regarding the situation of the exile: 'The lesson had been learnt in the First Exile. The Babylonian captives carried with them a book and a tradition which could endure as long as the Jews, however widely dispersed, would cherish them.'

4. See David. N. Freedman, *The Unity of the Hebrew Bible* (Ann Arbor: University of Michigan, 1991) 1-40, for a discussion of scholarship from Wellhausen to the present.

5. Norman K. Gottwald, *The Tribes of Yahweh* (New York: Maryknoll, 1979) 285ff; Daniel L. Smith, *The Religion of the Landless: The Social Context of the Babylonian Exile*

tied to the Torah and faithful adherence to it (Nehemiah 8.2ff). So significant were the events of the exile that they became paradigmatic for the description of the later spiritual journey of the post-exilic Jewish community.[6] These matrices of distinction became so ingrained within the psyche of post-exilic Jews that they became the primary determinants of who the 'true' Jew was.[7]

As it turns out then, the very acts of institutionalization that Wellhausen was negatively inclined towards seem to have been the very means for the Jewish community to reconstitute itself and re-imagine its existence, not only in terms of the past (Exodus) but also in terms of a future (eschatological apocalypticism). Such reformulation created new possibilities within a renewed understanding of the community's relationship with YHWH.[8] And while some of the biblical writings seem to suggest that the full restoration from exile came with the establishment of the second temple (e.g. Malachi, Haggai), a lingering dissatisfaction persists in many documents from the period (Ezra-Nehemiah; Philo, *Provid.* 2.64; Josephus, *War* 6.267; *m. Baba Bathra* 4a).

(Bloomington, Ind.: Meyer Stone, 1989) 93–126. While some level of continuity was maintained in certain areas (e.g., continuous presence of elders in the pre-exilic *Bēt Āb* and post-*Bēt Ābôt*) there were profound alterations in the social structures of the community where criteria other than 'blood' lineage were used in organizing society. For example, the pre-exilic structure of the society, according to Josh. 7.16ff, was three-tier with the smallest unit being the family unit (*Bēt Āb*) several of which made up each of the *Mišhpᵉhôt* (Clans?) and several of the *Mišhpᵉhôt* made up a tribe. The post-exilic structure was primarily based on the *Bēt Ābôt* which included more than family units. Determination of the 'true Israelite' (or the 'purified sons of Exile') then shifted from a family unit base to 'social adaptation to the conditions of the group', an example of which can be seen in the Golan List of Ezra 2.59-63. For example, the Hakkoz priests initially could not find their names on the list, but later on appear functioning as priests, meaning that at some point they were incorporated into society on a criterion other than family 'blood' relations. Daniel L. Smith (aka Smith-Christopher) adopts the 'Citizen-Temple-Community' model laid out by the Latvian historian Joël Weinberg, 'Das Beit Avot im 6-4 Jh. v. u. Z.', *VT* 23 (1973) 400-14; *idem*, 'Der *'am hā'āres* des 6.-4. Jh. v. u. Z.', *KLIO* 22 (1974) 325–35, who argues that 'combination of Temple concerns with the *Bēt Ābôt*, as a "collective of the returnees from exile", (*hāôlîm, habbāîm, haśśābîm mišᵉbî haggôlâ*)' allows him to postulate the existence of a post-exilic 'Citizen-Temple-Community' based on the leadership of the various *Bāttim 'Ābôt*, which are distinct and larger social units than the pre-exilic *Bēt Āb*, and so essentially a post-exilic development which was quite distinct from the pre-exilic *Bēt Āb*.

    6.   See Michael A. Knibb, 'The Exile in the Literature of the Intertestamental Period', *HeyJ* 17 (1976) 253–72, and Donald E. Gowan, 'The Exile in Jewish Apocalyptic', in Arthur L. Merrill and Thomas W. Overholt, eds., *Scripture in History and Theology: Essays in Honour of J. Coert Rylaarsdam* (Pittsburgh, Pa.: Pickwick, 1977) 205–22, who built on the concept of the 'idea of exile' to investigate intertestamental literature and Jewish apocalyptic literature, respectively.

    7.   D. L. Smith-Christopher in 'Translator's Foreword' to Joël Weinberg, *The Citizen-Temple Community* (Sheffield: Sheffield Academic Press, 1992) 4.

    8.   Knibb, 'Exile', 253–72; Gowan, 'Exile', 205–22. According to Knight, 'Foreword', xiv, it is also clear that Wellhausen did not have in his purview the later Jewish literature of the Talmudic period.

2.2. The Event of Exile and Its Historical Significance

The period of exile has been characterized as one of 'unparalleled importance for Israel. It was a period that witnessed the death and resurrection of a nation.'[9] It was a disruptive event in the life of the Jewish community with a significant impact on all spheres of life.[10] The *event* of exile involved geographical, spiritual, psychological, moral, social, and cultural displacements.[11]

The institutions and frameworks of Israel (and Judah) were transformed, interrupted and eradicated by the exile event. Some examples include,

(a) the political structure witnessing the disappearance of sovereignty;
(b) religious life being dealt a blow by the ending of the cultic life following destruction of the Jerusalem temple – the seat of God amidst the people;
(c) the people being displaced from the homeland of God's promise;
(d) the exiles especially, losing their Jewish Hebrew language and replacing it with Persian Aramaic (e.g. 2 Kgs 18:26; Ezra 4:7; Isa. 36:11; Daniel);
(e) the Israelite culture being greatly reconfigured from the way the pre-exilic society was ordered into a structure that had to incorporate the scattering abroad of the peoples.

All these elements were central to the national identity of the 'people of God', and with the demise of their political independence came what one could refer to simply as an identity crisis, especially for the exiles.[12] Myriad questions germinated: Were they still considered the chosen people of God or had God abandoned them? Was God ever going to accept them back, and restore them to their promised land? Would the temple be rebuilt and the Šekinah presence of God inhabit the sanctuary as in days of old? These, and other concerns, became the primary focus of the exilic and the post-exilic prophets.[13]

---

9.   Carol L. Meyers and Eric M. Meyers, *Zechariah 9–14* (AB 25C; New York: Doubleday, 1993) 18. We use the term 'exile' in this work to presuppose the whole period from 587/5 BCE to the restoration that commenced in 538 BCE. Thus, it incorporates the notions of 'judgment' and 'restoration'.

10.   Joel Weinberg's works show the exile's serious impact on the Jewish community's social life. Smith, 'Foreword', in Weinberg, *Citizen-Temple*, 14, notes that '[w]hether one agrees or not with the specific line of the "temple community" concept when applied to the post-exilic Judean community, Weinberg argues convincingly that the post-exilic community underwent significant social and ideological changes, and the basic social formation ... is in fact an entirely new social structure in the Persian period that is helpfully outlined in the "temple community" concept'.

11.   Ralph W. Klein, *Israel in Exile: A Theological Interpretation* (Philadelphia: Fortress, 1979) 2, explains that exile 'meant death, deportation, destruction, and devastation'.

12.   Smith, *Landless*, 50–68.

13.   Bustenay Oded, 'Judah and the Exile', in *Israelite and Judean History* (John H. Hayes and J. Maxwell Miller, eds.; Philadelphia: Westminster Press, 1977) 485, points out: 'Without doubt, the prophetic activity in the diaspora and particularly the prophetic explanations and reinterpretation of the difficult national and ideological issues raised by the massive national

In short, almost all of the old system symbols had been rendered useless. Almost all of the old institutions no longer functioned. What kind of future was possible for a people which traced its unique election to a God who had just lost a war to other deities? What kind of future was possible for a people who had so alienated their God that categorical rejection was his necessary response?[14]

To these questions of identity and God's sovereignty the prophets sought to reassure the people that YHWH was still God and that the exile was only a temporary measure out of which God would redeem a more pure people following the divinely allotted period of exile. In this regard, Bustenay Oded reasons:

> The national religious identity survived because of the celebration of such traditional customs as Sabbath observance (see Isa. 56.2-4; 58.13; Ezek. 44-6) and circumcision, and because of the activities of prophets like Jeremiah, Ezekiel and the so called Second Isaiah or Deutero-Isaiah (Isa. 40-55). The prophets preached that the tragedies that befell the people – the destruction of the temple and Jerusalem, the destruction of the land of Judah, the loss of political independence, and the exile – were not a result of the triumph of the Babylonian over the Israelite religion. Rather, everything stemmed from the will of the God of Israel, the one and only God on earth....The prophets encouraged the people's belief in the God of Israel and cultivated among the exiles a hope in future redemption and salvation (i.e. Jer. 23:7f.).[15]

With the destruction of the city of Jerusalem and the temple, resulting in the cessation of the sacrificial cult and bringing an end to the monarchy, these events began to effect a transformation in the Israelite religion. This transformation provided various contours and frameworks within which the different forms of Judaism, including Christianity, were to emerge.[16] Nickelsburg's view provides further evidence of the centrality of the exile as a formative element of all the subsequent developments in Israel. He puts it thus:

> The destruction of Jerusalem and the exile meant the disruption of life and the breaking up of institutions whose original form was never fully restored. Much of post-biblical Jewish theology and literature was influenced and sometimes governed by the *hope for such a*

calamity ... saved the people from complete despair ... and prevented complete assimilation of the exiles which would have led to the loss of national identity and religious uniqueness....'. Cf. also Enno Janssen, *Juda in Exilzeit: ein Beitrag zur Frage der Entstehung des Judentums* (FRLANT 69; Göttingen: Vandenhoeck & Ruprecht, 1956) 57-71.

14.   Klein, *Israel in Exile*, 5.

15.   Oded, 'Judah', 435–538, 484.

16.   Rosenburg, Roy A. 'Exile, Mysticism and Reality', in Étan Levine, *Diaspora: Exile and the Contemporary Jewish Condition* (New York: Steimatzky, 1986) 37–42, 41. A. Kraabel, 'Unity and Diversity among Diaspora Synagogues', in Lee I. Levine, ed., *The Synagogue in Later Antiquity* (Philadelphia: American Schools of Oriental Research, 1987) 49–60, 49; Ralph W. Klein, *Israel in Exile: A Theological Interpretation* (Philadelphia: Fortress, 1979) 6.

restoration; a return of the dispersed: the *appearance of a Davidic heir* to throw off the shackles of foreign domination and *restore Israel's sovereignty*: the *gathering of one people around a new and glorified temple.*[17]

As James Sanders observes, '… it was the Exile that had formed the crucible from which Judaism arose as God's New Israel, no matter what expression one form of Judaism, or another, eventually gave it thereafter'.[18]

Thus, the *event* of exile marks a significant turning point in the history and welfare of the nation of Israel, and the Jewish people's self-perception *vis-à-vis* their relationship to God and to the surrounding nations. As Norman Gottwald states, 'there can be no doubt that the sequence of happenings from 597–538 were among the most fateful in all Hebrew-Jewish history', enforcing new matrices for articulating reality.[19]

2.3. *Second Temple Literature and the Lingering 'Exile'*

N. T. Wright has recently argued that in the Second Temple period the general prevailing perception in the national psyche of Israel was of a persistent 'exile'.[20] Pinkhos Churgin had pointed out the significant premise of the

---

17.   George W. E. Nickelsburg, *Jewish Literature Between the Bible and the Mishnah: A Historical and Literary Introduction* (London: SCM Press, 1981) 18 (emphasis added).

18.   James Sanders, 'The Exile and Canon Formation', in James M. Scott, ed., *Exile: Old Testament, Jewish and Christian Conceptions* (Leiden: Brill, 1997) 37–61, 61.

19.   Norman Gottwald, *Studies in the Book of Lamentations* (London: SCM Press, 1954) 19.

20.   Wright, *People*, 268-72, 299-301; *idem*, *Victory*, xvii–xviii, 126–7, 203–4, 248–50. This is analogous to what Ackroyd earlier perceived in his development of the 'idea' of exile (Ackroyd, *Exile*, 237–47). Craig A. Evans, 'Aspects of the Exile and Restoration in the Proclamation of Jesus and the Gospels', in Scott, ed., *Exile*, 305-12; *idem*., 'Jesus and the Continuing Exile of Israel', in C. C. Newman, ed., *Jesus and the Restoration of Israel: A Critical Assessment of N. T. Wright's Jesus and the Victory of God* (Downers Grove: Inter-Varsity Press, 1999) 77–100; D. J. Verseput, 'The Davidic Messiah and Matthew's Jewish Christianity', *SBLASP* 34 (1995) 105–16; Daniel G. Reid, 'Jesus: New Exodus, New Conquest', in Tremper Longman III and Daniel G. Reid, *God is a Warrior* (Studies in Old Testament Biblical Theology; Grand Rapids: Zondervan, 1995) 91-118; all espouse agreement on the significance of the concept of 'exile' in the Second Temple period and its relevance to understanding the New Testament. Opposition to this perspective has recently been articulated by Steven Bryan, *Jesus and Israel's Traditions of Judgement and Restoration* (Cambridge: Cambridge University Press, 2002) 12–20, and by Maurice Casey, 'Where Wright is Wrong: A Critical review of N. T. Wright's Jesus and the Victory of God', *JSNT* 69 (1998) 95–103. Klyne Snodgrass, 'Reading and Overreading the Parables in *Jesus and the Victory of God*' and Richard Hays, 'Victory Over Violence: The Significance of N. T. Wright's Jesus for New Testament Ethics', in Newman, ed., *Jesus and Israel*, 142–58, also expresses caution concerning the exile theory, feeling that Wright might have overstated his case on this point. In the same volume ('In Grateful Dialogue: A Response', 252–61), Wright responds to these objections.

theory of persistent exile as the absence of an official festival to mark the end of exile.[21] Swarup forthrightly states that, 'Even after Israel had returned from exile physically, the promises of restoration seemed to have been only partially fulfilled.'[22] Michael Knibb surmises that, 'According to this pattern, Israel remained in a *state of exile* long after the return in the last decades of the sixth century', constantly anticipating a regathering.[23] Even, with a good amount of the 'exilic' literature actually produced in Palestine,[24] Wright elaborates further that the 'exile' persisted as an ingrained state of mind that governed the outlook of the reality of first-century Jews, basically designating the present an 'evil age' which anticipated 'the age to come' – the 'Kingdom of God'.[25] Such a perspective of 'exile' has less to do with provision of exact dates of the exile than with the articulation of its theological significance and implications.[26]

Otto Plöger's articulation of the optimism of eschatological hope in Second Temple Judaism is apt in this regard:

> Insofar as it was not possible to determine the exact significance of the eschatological hope in the exilic and early post-exilic period because of the uncertainty as to what was to become of the defeated Israel in the future, it was probably chiefly the picture of restoration eschatology, a *restitutio in integrum*, that exercised an attractive and formative influence … . The transmission and arrangement of hopes of a restoration of the old Israel, hopes which historically belong to an earlier epoch, not only implies that surviving pieces of tradition should not be rejected, but it is also the expression of opposition to the view that the present position was definitive and final.[27]

The general trend in the Second Temple period continued to be one of dissatisfaction or unenthusiastic cultic involvement. The result was a predisposition

---

21.   Pinkhos Churgin, 'The Period of the Second Temple: An Era of Exile' [Hebrew], *Horeb* 8 (1944) 1–66, in Paul R. Eddy, 'The (W)right Jesus: Eschatological Prophet, Israel's Messiah, Yahweh Embodied', in Newman, ed., *Jesus and Israel*, 45 n. 2.

22.   Paul N. W. Swarup, 'An Eternal Planting, a House of Holiness: The Self Understanding of the Dead Sea Scroll Community', synopsis of a Ph.D. thesis, University of Cambridge, 2002, in *TynBul* 54 (2003) 151–6.

23.   Michael Knibb, *The Qumran Community* (Cambridge: Cambridge University Press, 1987) 20 (emphasis added).

24.   Janssen, *Exilzeit*, 20–22. According to Janssen's construction Ezra/Nehemiah, Zechariah 1-8, Haggai, Isaiah 56-66, Malachi, etc., are all products of Palestine while Isaiah 1-55, Jeremiah, Ezekiel, Daniel, are exilic books.

25.   Wright, 'Dialogue', 260.

26.   Wright, 'Dialogue', 259: 'When I use the word *exile* in this sense, then, it refers to *a period of history with certain characteristics*, not to a geographical situation. To the objection that this is somewhat misleading, since exile inalienably refers to geography, I reply that our task as historians is not to dictate to our subjects how they ought to have thought and spoken, but to think ourselves into the thoughts of the period' (emphasis original).

27.   Otto Plöger, *Theocracy and Eschatology* (trans. S. Rudman; Richmond, Va.: John Knox, 1968) 115–16.

to articulate a future that would abound with God's action of restoration and blessing culminating with the reestablishment of Zion as the center of the World. It is in this regard that E. P. Sanders opines:

> In general the visionaries looked forward to *the full restoration of Israel*. Just what that meant would have varied from group to group and even from person to person, but there was a lot of common ground, and the main lines can be clearly discerned. The chief hopes were for the re-establishment of twelve tribes; for the subjugation or conversion of the Gentiles; for a new, purified, or renewed and glorious temple; and for purity and righteousness in both worship and morals ... These hopes ... were widely held among Jews ... The general hope for the restoration of the people of Israel is the most ubiquitous hope of all ... in any case the reassembly of the people of Israel was generally expected.[28]

Thus, 'failure' of the second temple to live up to expectation only served to fuel the eschatological apocalyptic outlook reflecting the lack of enthusiasm with which reports on the restoration of the second temple in the Jewish apocalyptic literature betray dissatisfaction with the restoration experienced thus far – the problem of the exile was still perceived as unresolved.[29] Such a general trend of thought undoubtedly spearheaded the articulation of a superior resolution within apocalyptic literature seeking to reconstitute a final resolution in light of a *restoration eschatology*.[30]

According to Knibb, restoration eschatology is characterized as the 'situation where the exile is understood as a state that is to be ended only by the intervention of God and the inauguration of the eschatological era'.[31] A brief survey of Second Temple literature helps solidify this outlook.

The prayer of Daniel in Babylon (Dan. 9) reinterprets the prophecy of Jeremiah such that *'the exile is extended beyond the time of Israel's actual sojourn in Babylon'*. This happened when Daniel interpreted Jeremiah's seventy years of exile as seventy *'weeks of years*, subdivided into seven, sixty two, and one (Dan. 9.24-27) ... [which meant that] the Babylonian exile was simply the beginning of a longer period of history, *one in which the same political and theological conditions applied to which the same word* – exile – *could therefore appropriately be given'*.[32] Therefore, in spite of the rebuilding of the temple, the return of some of the exiles to the homeland, and the re-institution of cultic life – including the Hasmonean establishment of some aspects of independent monarchy – the full extent of the promises of YHWH was not perceived to have been fulfilled in the Second Temple period.[33]

---

28.   Sanders, *Judaism*, 289–90, 294. Daniel R. Schwartz, 'Introduction: On the Jewish Background of Christianity', in *Studies in the Jewish Background of Christianity* (Tübingen: Mohr, 1992), 5.

29.   Gowan, 'Exile', 205–23.

30.   Sanders, *Judaism*, 279–303; *idem, Jesus*, 81–113.

31.   Knibb, 'Exile', 253–72.

32.   Wright, 'Dialogue', 258–9 (emphasis original).

33.   Ibid., 259.

Ben Sira (*ca.* 180 BCE) maintains that Israel is still under oppression, particularly those in the διασπορά who are still in literal exile (Sir. 36.6, 11, 14-16; 48.10); Tobit (2nd century BCE) pictures in chapter 13 the present state of the scattering of the Jewish people and articulates a futuristic hope of regathering that is tinged with apocalyptic expectation (Tob. 13.5, 10-11, 13; 14.5-7)[34] – the *Song of Moses* (Deut. 31–32) at the end of Tobit reflects the expectation of an imminent return to the promised land, just as it happened to the biblical ancestors before;[35] Baruch 2.7-10 (160–150 BCE) reflects the same perspective as Ben Sira and Tobit in its interpretation of the current state of Israel with a clear picture of restoration hope reflected in its address (cf. Bar. 4.36-37; 5.5).[36] O. H. Steck concludes that for Baruch, the 'present Israel should see itself still in a condition of exile';[37] and 2 Maccabees sees little hope of the recovery of the tabernacle, the ark, and the altar before the gathering of the scattered people by God (2.7). In a passage that clearly alludes to Exod. 19.6 (cf. 1 Pet. 1.4; 3.4-5, 9), 2 Macc. 2.17 describes the κληρονομία ('inheritance')/βασίλειος ('reign'), ἱεράτευμα ('priesthood'), and ὁ ἁγιασμός ('holiness') in light of later Hasmonean rulership.[38]

Although, according to Maccabees, the fire from the Solomonic temple was miraculously kept burning in the second temple – allowing for the understanding of a continued presence of God even during the time of the temple's desecration – the second temple marked only 'an important abatement of God's wrath' but definitely not the end of the exile.[39] As Jonathan Goldstein explains, 'the writer correctly refrained from having Judas Maccabeus and his contemporaries claim that in their time God had restored the three attributes promised at Exodus 19.6. Rather, he made them express their confidence, using the future tense, that the attributes would be restored in the near future'.[40]

This subtle but significant shift of tenses reflects the author's view of the present state of Israel as a continuing state of bondage, which is also evidenced in the prayer made earlier in 2 Macc. 1.24-29, where the author beseeches God

34. Steve Weitzman, 'Allusion, Artifice, and Exile in the Hymn of Tobit', *JBL* 115 (1996) 49–61.

35. Ibid., 60.

36. Bar. 5.5: 'Arise, O Jerusalem, stand upon the height and look toward the east, and see your children gathered from west and east, at the word of the Holy One, rejoicing that God has remembered them'.

37. O. H. Steck, *Das apokryphe Baruchbuch: Studien zu Rezeption und Konzeption 'kananischer' Überlieferung* (Göttingen: Vandenhoeck & Ruprecht, 1993) 267.

38. Jonathan A. Goldstein, 'How the Authors of 1 and 2 Maccabees Treated the "Messianic" Promises', in Jacob Neusner *et al.*, eds., *Judaisms and Their Messiahs at the Turn of the Christian Era* (Cambridge: Cambridge University Press, 1987) 69–96.

39. Ibid., 83.

40. Ibid., 83–4.

to 'guard Israel', 'make her holy', 'gather her dispersed exiles', and 'free those enslaved in the nations'.[41]

3 Maccabees (6.36; 7.19) presents the new festival instituted by the Egyptian Jews (whose self-identify as παροικία aligns with 1 Peter 1.1; 2.11) celebrating the rescue and victory of God which was to become a festival for generations to come.[42] The passage is marked with a cry that clearly understands the present condition of Israel as one of exile: 'Even if our lives have become entangled in impieties in our exile (ἀποικία), rescue us from the hand of the enemy, and destroy us, Lord, by whatever fate you choose' (6.10). The antic-ipation of a restoration is mixed up with a grievance over the gloating of Gentile enemies on misfortunes of the people of God (6.11-13).[43]

Turning to the Dead Sea Scrolls, the Qumran covenanters viewed themselves as the exclusive seed of Israel (CD 11.21-2), the holy remnant (CD 11.11-12; 1QH 17.14), the true biblical Israel. They appropriated the role of Babylonian exile returnees (שבי ישראל) as found in the post-exilic biblical accounts (Ezra-Nehemiah, 2 Chronicles, Haggai, Zechariah and Malachi)[44] making their withdrawal into the Judean desert a reenactment of 'the paradigmatic events that had determined and enfolded Israel's history in the biblical period of Exile – Egypt and Babylon rolled into one'.[45]

---

41.   Ibid., 84–5. Nevertheless, this is not a hopeless situation because, as he explains in 2.18, 'We have hope in God that he will soon have mercy on us and will gather us from everywhere under heaven into his holy place, for he has rescued us from great evils and has purified the place.' This is an anticipation of a quick end to the 'Age of Wrath' as part of the fulfillment of Exod. 15.17; 'i.e., a new exodus by which the exiles will return to be planted again in God's Holy place'. Note also the centrality of the temple, 'God's holy and purified place' where the regathered would assemble.

42.   3 Macc. 6.36: (ἐπὶ πᾶσαν τὴν παροικίαν αὐτῶν εἰς γενεάς); 3 Macc. 7.19: (τὰς ἡμέρας ἐπὶ τὸν τῆς παροικίας αὐτῶν χρόνον εὐφροσύνους).

43.   James M. Scott, 'Exile and Self-Understanding of the Diaspora in the Greco-Roman Period', in Scott, ed., *Exile*,173–218, 192, sees the anticipation of the 'ingathering of the exiles', but Eric S. Gruen, *Diaspora: Jews amidst Greeks and Romans* (Cambridge, Mass.: Harvard University Press, 2002) 242 n. 84, argues that such an ingathering is not part of the purview of this text.

44.   Martin G. Abegg, Jr., 'Exile and the Dead Sea Scrolls', in Scott, ed., *Exile*, 111–25: 'Although it is wise not to be too dogmatic in light of the ambiguous nature of the expression, I suggest that the translation "Israelite returnees" best satisfies the contexts of all the passages in which it occurs and the emphasis on exile imagery in the Qumran corpus' (114). CD 8.16; 1929; 4Q166 1 i 16(?); 4Q171 1-10 iv 24; 4Q266 6 i 13 (cf. also 4Q171 1-10 iii 1 – שבי המרבר). Samuel Iwry, 'Was there a Migration to Damascus? The Problem of שבי ישראל, *Eretz-Israel* 9 (1969) 86–8; *idem.*, 'The Exegetical Method of the Damascus Document Reconsidered', in Michael O. Wise *et al.*, eds., *Methods of Investigation of the Dead Sea Scrolls and the Khibet Qumran Site: Present Realities and Future Prospects* (ANYAS 722; New York: New York Academy of Sciences, 1994) 329–38.

45.   Shemaryahu Talmon, 'Waiting for the Messiah: The Spiritual Universe of the Qumran Covenanters', in Neusner *et al.*, eds., *Judaisms*, 97–137, 120. Cf. also Knibb, *Qumran*, 20.

Numerous references to the exile are appropriated by the Qumran community to describe its present status (CD 1.3-11= Ezek. 4.4-6; CD 7.13-14 = Zech. 6.8; CD 7.20-21= Zech. 11.11) with the sojourn in the wilderness interpreted in light of prophetic pronouncements of the Babylonian exile. In her analysis of the Damascus Document (CD), Ellen Christiansen discusses the place of covenant (ברית) in the Qumran community and its relation to the OT community, concluding that the exile is the point of departure for the characteristic features of CD (1.4-12 and 6.2-11).[46] In CD 2.14-16, 5.20-21 and 3.10, the disobedience of Israel as a whole – in contrast to the Qumran covenanter's obedience – is described in terms of the exilic situation where Israel (primarily priests) have breached the covenant and thus are being punished for it.[47]

As 'exiles' (in 'Damascus' – CD 6.4-5)[48] anticipating the establishment of a new covenant (CD 6.19; 8.21), the Qumran community looked forward to a time when they would march into Jerusalem (1QM 1.2-3; 4QpIsa[e] 5.6) and 'bring to a climax the historical cycle of the biblical days: Exile – Sojourn in the Wilderness – Settlement'.[49] Reminiscent of Ezekiel's war of Gog and Magog (Ezek. 38–39), this battle is anticipated in the War Scroll (1QM; cf. 4Q390) – a war that would shake the foundations of the universe, and in which God would judge the nations. Afterwards, the way would be paved for the covenanters to seize Jerusalem, rebuild the temple (note here a lack of recognition for the legitimacy of the second temple), and reinstall the rightful Zadokite priesthood from among the covenanters themselves.[50]

---

46.   Ellen Christiansen, 'The Consciousness of Belonging to God's Covenant and What it Entails according to the Damascus Document and the Community Rule', in Frederick H. Cryer and Thomas L. Thompson, eds., *Qumran Between the Old and the New Testament* (Sheffield: Sheffield Academic Press, 1998) 69–97.

47.   Ibid., 76–7: 'Hence, the motivation for keeping the law is found in God's punishment of those who disregard the divine will. Moreover, CD ties the motivation for law obedience to the command to separate clean and unclean, holy and profane, by means of which covenant is interpreted narrowly as *priestly* covenant (CD 6.17; 7.3)' (emphasis original).

48.   There are at least three different views as to the referent 'Damascus': 1) it is a reference to 'Babylon' – Jerome Murphy-O'Connor, 'The Essenes and Their History', *RB* 81 (1974) 215–44; J. A. Fitzmyer, 'The Dead Sea Scrolls and The New Testament after Thirty Years', *TD* 29 (1981) 357–8; 2) it is 'literal Damascus' – Frank Moore Cross, *The Ancient Library of Qumran and Modern Biblical Studies* (Garden City, NY: Doubleday, 1958) 81–2 n. 46; 3), it is the 'desert of Qumran' – Cross, *Library*, 81–2.

49.   Shemaryahu Talmon, 'The "Desert Motif" in the Bible and in Qumran Literature', in A. Altmann, ed., *Biblical Motifs, Origins and Transformation* (Study and Texts of the Philip L. Lown Institute of Advanced Judaic Studies 3; Cambridge, Mass.: Harvard University Press, 1966) 31–63.

50.   Yigal Yadin, *The Scroll of the War of the Sons of Light Against the Sons of Darkness* (trans. B. and C. Rabin; Oxford: Clarendon Press, 1962). That all these things are a future anticipation (4QMMT; 4Q434 3 ii 2-3; 4Q504-506) is a clear indication that the present status of the community in the second century BCE is viewed as a state of 'exile' awaiting eschatological redemption.

Paul Garnet concludes as much in his study when he states that an 'exile theology' plays an important role in Qumran's self-understanding.[51] Swarup has argued that the metaphors of 'eternal planting' and 'house of holiness' reflect a 'deep yearning of the DSS community for a complete restoration of Israel, for a return to Edenic conditions before the Fall, and for a temple which is pure'.[52] The longing for restoration marks a strong perception that the covenanters were still in exile.

In sum, a fairly widespread expectation of an eschatological restoration of Israel in the Second Temple period, which perceived the present condition of Israel as 'exile' awaiting God's glorious eschatological intervention, prevailed. It encompassed the reestablishment of the temple (Isa. 11.11-17; Ezek. 29.21-29; Hag. 1.1-5; *Jub.* 1.15-17; *T. Benj.* 9.2) and the coming of God to reign in Zion, creation of a new community of faithful Israel (Jer. 33.31-33), the regathering of the twelve tribes (2 Macc. 1.27ff; 2.18; *Pss. Sol.* 11.17–28: 31; 17.50; 11QM 2.2-7; 11QTemp 18.14-16; Sir. 48.10), the forgiveness of national sin (*Pss. Sol.* 17.26), and the defeat of the enemies of Israel (Bar. 4–5; Sir. 36).[53] These estimations seem to have lingered well into the NT period influencing even the Jewish socio-political conceptualization of the Palestinian occupation by the Greco-Roman empires.[54]

2.4. *Peter Ackroyd's 'Idea of Exile'*

In the Hulsean Lectures of 1960–2 at the University of Cambridge – later published under the title *Exile and Restoration* – Peter Ackroyd developed his argument about the creativity of the exilic period and its significance for understanding the institutions of Israel, including the temple, prophecy, and priesthood. In Ackroyd's estimation, the events of the exile 'exerted a great influence upon the development of theological thinking' in the Second Temple period.[55] As detailed above, we can identify two distinct components concerning the exile – the historical *event* itself and of the *idea* of exile.[56] The

---

51.   Paul Garnet, *Salvation and Atonement in the Qumran Scrolls* (WUNT 3; Tübingen: Mohr-Siebeck, 1977).

52.   Swarup, 'Planting', 152.

53.   Brunson, *Psalm 118*, 40.

54.   N. H. Taylor, 'Jerusalem and the Temple in Early Christian Life and Teaching', *Neot* 33 (1999) 445–61, 452. While it is probably impossible to determine precisely how widespread were any of the specific expectations identified from the surviving literature, we can nonetheless assume a fairly widespread belief among eschatologically minded Jews during the Roman period that Jerusalem and the temple would be the focal point of fulfillment of their hopes and expectations, and the anticipated epicenter of eschatological delivery ... We need therefore to reconstruct our understanding of Jesus and the first Christians against this background.

55.   Ackroyd, *Exile*, 237.

56.   Ibid.

former (the forced removal of the Jewish people from their homeland in Palestine and deportation to a foreign land – Northern Kingdom to Assyria in 722 BCE and the Southern kingdom to Babylon in 587/6 BCE) forms the premise on which the latter (the symbolic and theological articulation of it) is built.

For Ackroyd, with the 'idea' of exile, '[t]he understanding of exile is clearly enlarged far beyond the temporal considerations of seventy years [Dan. 9.24] and the precise period covered by Babylonian captivity in the stricter sense'.[57] He further points out that:

> It is in this that we may see the truth of the type of interpretation of the post-exilic age which points out that the exile came to be seen as of paramount importance, a great divide between the earlier and later stages, but one which is necessary to traverse if the new age was to be reached. Only those who had gone through the exile – whether actually or spiritually – could be thought of as belonging. The rebuilt Temple was dedicated by the returned exiles and those who, forsaking the abominations of the land, joined themselves to them.[58]

Several points need to be highlighted. First, the 'idea' of exile transcends the *event* of exile providing a matrix within which to understand events such as Antiochus Epiphanes' desecration of the Jerusalem temple 'as a continuation of that desecration which belongs to the exilic age'.[59] Second, the exile gained symbolic value beyond the physical experience, so that one could experience the exile 'spiritually'.[60] Third, the temple remained the central focus of the anticipated restoration from exile.

The 'idea' of exile is characterized by Ackroyd as the use of the concept of 'exile' in defining and shaping a literary expression that 'reflects outlooks arising from the consideration of [their] particular situation' of displacement.[61] The 'idea' of exile is rooted in history, no matter how nebulous the details, for the 'exile was a historic fact, though its precise description in detail is a matter of great difficulty'.[62] The exile is not simply a challenge in 'historical reconstruction' of Israel, but also a 'matter of understanding an attitude, more properly a variety of attitudes, taken up towards that historic fact'.[63] This

---

57.   Ibid., 243.

58.   Ibid.

59.   Ibid.

60.   Ibid., 243–4: Ackroyd postulates that, '… the experience of the exile, the experience of judgment, can be appropriated either by virtue of having gone through it … or by accepting its significance by the abandonment of what belongs to it namely uncleanness, pollution of the land'.

61.   Ibid., 237. Peterson describes the idea of exile as the provision of 'a theological perspective relevant to a new situation, that of Yahwism without the independent territorial state'. David Peterson, 'Zechariah's Vision: A Theological Perspective', *VT* 34 (1984) 195–206, 205.

62.   Ibid.,

63.   Ibid., 238-9. Michael Fishbane, *Biblical Interpretation In Ancient Israel* (Oxford: Clarendon Press, 1985) 19: 'Is it possible that the origins of the Jewish exegetical tradition are

reasoning accords with what Jacob Neusner articulates in relation to the Torah, when he points out that only a minority of 'Israel' underwent the whole experience of the 'exile, atonement, reconciliation, restoration and renewal of the covenant'.[64] The majority were those who either were never deported or never returned from exile, who, nevertheless, 'under the Judaic system of the Torah made normative that experience of alienation and reconciliation'.[65] Thus, the experience of only a few became a defining element of the entire community.

Even with the physical exile over for some, a majority of the Jews remained in the διασπορά (Dispersion) and the anticipation of full restoration of the glorious prophecies remained unfulfilled (Isa. 42; 60; 61). The awesome temple of Ezekiel (40–48) had yet to be realized. Armed with this evidence Ackroyd concluded that the 'idea of exile' continued to dominate the thinking of Second Temple Judaism.[66] How does all this connect with the concepts of exile in 1 Peter?

2.5. 'Idea *of Exile*' *as a Controlling Metaphor*

2.5.1. *Earlier Proposals*
Richard Earl has recently questioned the hermeneutical validity of the concept 'controlling metaphor' in explaining 1 Peter's 'view, strategy and message'. Rather than use a 'controlling metaphor', Earl argues that instead the theme of suffering should be considered as the primary concern in 1 Peter and the 'theology of suffering' as what 1 Peter is intent on developing.[67] While Earl

---

native and ancient, that they developed diversely in ancient Israel, in many centres and at many times, and that these many tributaries met in the exile and its aftermath to set a new stage for biblical culture which was redirected, rationalized, and systematized in the lively environment of the Graeco-Roman world? To ask the question this way is almost to answer it. What remains are the details …'.

64.   Jacob Neusner, *Understanding Seeking Faith: Essays on the Case of Judaism* (vol. I; Atlanta Ga.: Scholars Press, 1986) 139.

65.   Ibid., 1.137–41, 138. Neusner's main point is to highlight what he perceives to have been the 'minority view' (primarily of the priests) that assumed the privileged position of the dominant perspective and emerged as the dominant paradigm of the self-definition for 'true Israel' '… But we grasp the fact of the matter only when we remind ourselves that that particular experience *itself* happened, to begin with, in the minds and imaginations of the authorships of Scripture' (139–40: emphasis original) We maintain, however, *contra* Neusner, that only the *event* could have produced the *idea*.

66.   Ackroyd, *Exile*, 237–47; Brunson, *Psalm 118*, 40. The universality of these expectations in Second Temple Israel is articulated in Brunson's conclusion: 'To sum up: End-of-exile hope, whether it be for renewed, restored or rebuilt temple, for the restoration of the people of Israel, and/or for the beginning of God's reign on Mount Zion, is not limited to a few sectarian groups.'

67.   Richard Earl, *Reading 1 Peter, Jude and 2 Peter: A Literary and Theological Commentary* (Macon, Ga.: Smyth and Helwys, 2000) 16ff. Karen Jobes, *1 Peter*, (Baker Exegetical

may be correct about the centrality of suffering in 1 Peter, his argument against the use of a 'controlling metaphor' misses the point. The controlling metaphor is meant to provide a useful and meaningful mental backdrop or context within which the author's use of certain linguistic expressions is to be understood.[68] A useful heuristic tool, a 'controlling metaphor' is helpful in harnessing the diverse elements found within a writing such as 1 Peter, which, on occasion, may appear disjunctive. As such, it provides the framework within which to analyze the author's (sometimes unstated) connections and allusions, allowing for a fuller grasp of the message.[69]

In the mid-twentieth century Heinrich Rendtorff published his study on 1 Peter entitled *Getrostes Wandern*. As seen from the title of his work, he identified the significance of the status of the audience as 'aliens' and 'strangers' as the central compositional element for the entire letter.[70] However, Rendtorff did not seem to see the implications of this for the structure of the epistle, as he proceeded to employ the motif of 'hope' (*Hoffnung*) instead of exile (*Exil*) as the central organizing element for his analysis of the entire epistle. While exile and hope are not mutually exclusive, only exile provides a suitable background in which to understand such a hope. John Piper later also argued for 'hope' as the final motivating fact in 1 Peter.[71] Nevertheless, the relevance of 'hope' for the structuring of the whole epistle has been called into question, especially since it cannot explain 'how hope is designed to create willingness to act according to the commands' in the paraenetic sections.[72] Also, as we will see, hope is only relevant when understood in light of the anticipated *eschatological restoration*.

More recent scholars have chosen to focus on exile rather than hope as central to the epistle. J. Ramsey Michaels' designation of the genre of 1 Peter, as an 'apocalyptic Diaspora letter' addressed to Israel, combines the two elements that most scholars have noted are the key to interpretation of the epistle: its apocalyptic nature (1.5, 7), and the title applied to its audience as those of the διασπορά ('Dispersion').[73] While highlighting the importance of

Commentary on the New Testament; Grand Rapids: Baker Books, 2005) 24–5, points at lack of consensus on controlling metaphors in essentially agreeing with Earl.

68. Troy W. Martin, *Metaphor and Composition in 1 Peter* (SBLDS 131; Atlanta, Ga.: Scholars Press, 1992) 144.

69. Our intent is to understand how 1 Peter articulated his message by utilizing the Scriptures of Israel – like most NT writers, 1 Peter's OT quotations mostly follow the Septuagint (LXX) – and how the Jewish milieu out of which he wrote nuanced his message.

70. Heinrich Rendtorff, *Getrostes Wandern: Eine Einführung in den ersten Brief des Petrus* (DUB 20; Hamburg: Furche, 1951) 7–8, 10–18.

71. John Piper, 'Hope as the Motivation of Love: 1 Peter 3:9-12', *NTS* 26 (1980) 221–31.

72. Lauri Thurén, *Argument and Theology in 1 Peter: The Origins of Christian Paraenesis* (JSNTSup 114; Sheffield: Sheffield Academic Press, 1995) 203.

73. J. R. Michaels, *1 Peter* (WBC 49; Waco, Tx.: Word, 1988) xlvi. He used the *Epistle of Barnabas* 78-87 (*ca.* 80 CE) as the primary basis of the creation of this particular genre.

exile, Michaels does not, however, incorporate the larger restoration hope and continuing exile as a rubric for reading 1 Peter. Troy Martin, building somewhat on Michael's work, identifies 'Diaspora' as the controlling metaphor in the epistle of 1 Peter.[74] It is introduced in the prescript (1.1) and restated in the farewell section (5.13) with a different word 'Babylon', which, for Martin, is simply another term for diaspora.[75] Martin suggests that the explicit use of the term 'Diaspora' (1.1) at the beginning of the epistle marks it out as significant metaphor in the compositional structure of the letter.[76]

Martin's 'Diaspora' metaphor has been criticized for being too broad and open-ended on the one hand, [77] and on the other, as too restrictive in its focus on 'diaspora images'.[78] Paul Achtemeier suggests that 1 Peter's appropriation of the language of Israel for the Christian community is unique among Christian canonical writings, so that 'Israel as a totality has become for this letter the controlling metaphor'.[79] McKnight describes it as language of fulfillment and replacement, in this case being more of displacement than fulfilment.[80] Yet, neither is Achtemeier's suggested metaphor any more specific than Martin's. Indeed, not the entire history of Israel is in perspective in 1 Peter, but rather a more specific period of instability and homelessness could be said to characterize the concern of this epistle.[81] William Schuster's theme of

74.	Martin, *Metaphor*, 144–61. He builds on the work of Pseudo-Euthalius, 'Elenchus Capitum septum Epistolarum Catholicarum', *Patrologia Graeca*, ed. J. P. Migne, vol. 85, 680, who identified 1 Peter as 'an instructional letter written to the Diaspora Jewish converts into Christianity'.

75.	Martin, *Metaphor*, 144; Michaels, *1 Peter*, 311. See Von Claus-Hunno Hunzinger, 'Babylon als Deckname für Rom und die Datierung des 1 Petrusbriefes', in Graf Henning Reventlow, ed., *Gottes Wort und Gotttes Land: Hans-Wilhem Hertberg zum 70. Geburstag am 16. Januar 1965 dargebracht von Kollegen, Frueden und Schülern* (Göttingen: Vandenhoech & Ruprecht, 1965) 67–77. Parallels to Babylon as a metaphorical reference to Rome include *Sib. Or.* 5.143, 149 and Rev. 14.8; 16.19; 17.5.

76.	Max-Alain Chevallier, 'Condition et vocation des chrétiens en diaspora: Remarques exégétiques sur la 1er Épître de Pierre', *RSR* 48 (1974) 387-98, 390, notes that the three significant concepts in 1 Peter in relation to the addressees is that they are the 'new people of God', by virtue of their 'election', and that they currently are in 'Diaspora'. Cf. Martin, *Metaphor*, 144-7.

77 .	Ramsey Michaels' review of Troy Martin, *Metaphor and Composition in 1 Peter*, in *JBL* 112 (1993) 358–60.

78.	Achtemeier, *1 Peter*, 70 n. 709. 1 Peter simply addresses the Petrine community in language and expressions reserved for Israel in the OT assuming a direct correspondence between Israel and the Christian believers.

79.	Achtemeier, *1 Peter*, 69. Thurén, *Argument*, 201: 'We have seen that one of the central goals of the letter (1.1-2.10) is to make the addressees appreciate their [new] status to the degree that they become willing to act in a way which the status implies ... Thus the description of the new status belongs without doubt to the most important motifs in the Letter.'

80.	McKnight, *1 Peter*, 24.

81.	Elliott, *Home*, 21–30.

'God's call to holiness', suffers the same fate of being too general and too broad to help us appropriate the specificity of the Petrine OT utilization.[82] Indeed, the whole of Israel's religion could be characterized as 'God's call to holiness'. While 1 Peter selects OT language that is fully applied to Israel and applies it to the Christian community, it seems that he also focuses on their state of 'exile' as a defining characteristic of their current existence.[83]

J. N. D. Kelly points out that 'just as the Jews of the Dispersion were a scattered people cut off from their country but with the prospect of ultimately going back, so Christians are bound, wherever they are, to be transitory sojourners yearning for a home'.[84] The home that Christians hope for is heaven, which 1 Peter 1.4 describes as the locus of Christian inheritance. However, Kelly does not specifically point to the exile metaphor as central or controlling. Francis Beare, while recognizing exile as a significant point of departure in reading 1 Peter, like Kelly, does not bring the overarching concerns of restoration and the continuing exile to bear on the interpretation of the letter.[85] As we will seek to show, not only is the exile specific – in light of the use of OT passages in 1 Peter (Isa. 40–55; Hos. 6; Ezek. 9.6) – but it is also crucial in locating 1 Peter within historical, theological, and ideological developments in Second Temple Jewish thinking.[86] The focus on exile by John H. Elliott is on the social dimension of the believers as presently living away from their homeland, and also as a reality of their pre-conversion political status.[87]

Such an argument, while downplaying the metaphoric sense of 'exile', does not necessarily eliminate it, as Elliott himself concedes.[88] And as Achtemeier maintains, the use of the comparative particle ὡς in introducing the terms πάροικος and παρεπίδημος is characteristic of the introduction of metaphors in 1 Peter (cf. 2.2, 5).[89]

Marc Kohler singled out the significance of the concept of 'exile' in the interpretation of 1 Peter as central to the entire message of the letter: 'For Peter, the notion of Christians as "strangers/aliens" is not simply at the beginning and the end [of his letter], but throughout his message.'[90] Kohler argued that the use

82. Schutter, *Hermeneutic*, 80.
83. Elliott, *Home*, 21–100.
84. Kelly, *Peter and Jude*, 41.
85. Francis Wright Beare, *The First Epistle of Peter: The Greek Text with Introduction and Notes* (3rd edn; Oxford: Blackwell, 1970) 47–9. Our use of the exile motif is specifically distinct from Beare, who perceives the concept of the Jewish Diaspora as simply 'a symbol of the Christian Church' (48), with little or nothing to do with restoration eschatology.
86. Daniel L. Smith-Christopher, 'Reassessing the Historical and Sociological Impact of the Babylonian Exile (597/587–539 BCE)', in Scott, ed., *Exile*, 7–36; William G. Dever, 'Will the Real Israel Please Stand Up? Archeology and Israelite Historiography: Part 1', *BASOR* 297 (1995) 61–80.
87. Elliott, *Home*, 21–100, 131, 226.
88. Elliott, 'Peter, First Epistle', 273-4.
89. Achtemeier, *1 Peter*, 56.
90. M.-E. Kohler, 'La Communauté chrétienne selon la première Épître de Pierre', *RTP* 114 (1982) 1–21, 5.

of the term 'exiles' to address the community of believers in 1 Peter was a clear contrast to the Pauline use of ἐκκλησία.[91] This may be due to the reasoning of the author of 1 Peter that the Hellenistic concept of ἐκκλησία maintained the meaning 'association' in which case it would also signify dissociation from the world, i.e. those not part of the church gathering.[92] A similar view was espoused ten years later by Reinhard Feldmeier in his *Habilitationschrift* – whose work investigated the metaphor of 'stranger' in 1 Peter in light of its use in antiquity and in early Christianity[93] – only for Elliot to call the study into question for overlooking the clear use of communal collective identity and the solidarity with the suffering Christ even if 1 Peter does not use the term ἐκκλησία.[94]

1 Peter prefers vocabulary that indicates preference for the Christians to remain involved in the world and 'exile perfectly fits the bill. Irrespective of the suffering this would cause, the believers are not to abandon their relation to the world around them, for ultimately it will result into glory to God (1.6-9; 2:12)'.[95] As the believers bear witness to the world, God's presence through their lives is acknowledged by the nonbelievers (3.1-17).

To support his argument, Kohler references the allusion to Gen. 23.4 in 1 Peter 2.11, and the story of Abraham as a παροίκος καὶ παρεπιδήμος (cf. also Ps. 38.12).[96] Like Abraham, the Christians live a life under constant suspicion from the surrounding peoples and face animosity as they choose to discontinue the past modes of conduct (1.14), reject the sinful ways of their fathers (1.18), and seek to live more responsible and righteous lives (2.24; 4.2-4). The

---

91. Ibid., 4–5. Chevallier, 'Diaspora', 390. For a general analysis of the relationship between 1 Peter and Pauline writings see Norbert Brox, *Der erste Petrusbrief* (EKKNT; Zurich: Benziger, 1979) 47–51, who agues that the language of 1 Peter is more Pauline than the content of the letter is, and that the evidence is not sufficient to establish a case for dependence either way.

92. Kohler, 'Communauté', 2.

93. Reinhard Feldmeier, *Die Christen als Fremde: Die Metaphor der Fremde in der antiken Welt, in Urchristentum und im 1. Petrusbrief* (WUNT 64; Tübingen: J. C.B. Mohr Siebeck, 1992). This remains the basic framework for his recent work on 1 Peter, *Der Erste Brief des Petrus* (ThHK 15/1; Leipzig: Evangelische Verlagsanstalt, 2005).

94. John H. Elliott, 'Book Review of Reinhard Feldmeier's *Die Christen als Fremde*', *CBQ* 56/4 (1994) 792–3.

95. J. L. Villiers, 'Joy in Suffering in 1 Peter', *Neot* 9 (1975) 64–86; W. Nauck, 'Freude im Leiden, Zum Problem einer urchristlichen Verfolgungstradition', *ZNW* 46 (1955) 68-80, argued for a Judeo-Christian tradition of 'joy in suffering' whose origins he traced back to the Maccabees (cf. 4 Macc. 16.1ff) and their willingness to joyfully give their lives in martyrdom for the sake of their faithfulness to God. The believers to whom 1 Peter is writing are urged to endure suffering with joy for the sake of being joined to Jesus who also suffered on their behalf (2.20-25). They should count it as joy to partake of, and complete, the work started by Jesus, their redeemer (1.6-9); David Hill, 'On suffering and Baptism in 1 Peter', *NovT* 18 (1976) 181–9; J. Butler, 'Grace and Suffering: A Study in 1 Peter', *Notes on Translation* 10 (1996) 58–60; T. P. Osborne, 'Guidelines for Christian Suffering in 1 Peter: A Source-Critical and Theological Study of 1 Peter 2:21-25', *Bib* 64 (1983) 381–408.

96. Kohler, 'Communauté', 5.

assurance they have is that the God of the exodus is with them along their pilgrimage of righteousness. For Kohler, the reference to Babylon (5.13), irrespective of its association with Rome by commentators, maintains the idea of exile.[97]

More could be added to Kohler's argument. Ps. 38.12 echoes Gen. 23.4 with the psalmist identifying himself as a foreigner and alien 'just like all my ancestors' (καθὼς πάντες οἱ πατέρες μου). By connecting himself with the experience of Abraham the psalmist not only situates himself as a true Israelite, but also perceives his experiences as parallel to those of the patriarch, giving him special status. While in Genesis Abraham's state of alienation and sojourning is related to geographical boundaries, for the psalmist the concern is with the fleeting nature of human life before God and the encompassing suffering that entails it. In 1 Peter the two aspects are also reflected: the reality of social ostracism, on the one hand, and the idea of pilgrimage towards a heavenly inheritance (1.4), on the other.

T. P. Osborne identified what he perceived to be three groupings of the Isaianic passages in 1 Peter and classified them according to some semblance of historical developments in Israel during the time of the Isaianic prophecies. In the first group he saw parallels of the advance of the Assyrians upon Israel (Isa. 8.12-13.14), in the second group, reflections on the return from the Babylonian exile (Isa. 40.6-8; 43.20-21; 52.3), while the third group focus on the four songs of the Suffering Servant in Isa. 53 (Isa. 53.4, 5, 6, 9, 12).[98] The last set of passages are used by 1 Peter to relate to Christ's suffering, which in turn becomes a model for the Christians in their 'justified suffering'. However, against Osborne's argument, 1 Peter does not use the OT to appeal to its authority but to explicate Scripture. If the former was his purpose, he would have appealed to the Pentateuch which was more authoritative for the Jews.[99] For example, rather than use Isa. 53 in 2.22-23 to prove that Jesus is the Messiah, 1 Peter uses it to exhort the Christians to follow the example of their Lord.[100]

The use of the OT in 1 Peter serves more than just exhortational purposes. It involves the application of Scripture to a different situation which nevertheless continues themes that originate in the OT – actualization of the reality of the 'old Israel' in the 'new Israel'. It is not strange, for example, for Paul to address the ἐκκλησία, which for him is usually made up of Gentiles, as part of the chosen race and as having inherited the promises of Israel (e.g. Rom.

---

97. Ibid.
98. T. P. Osborne, 'L'utilisation des citations de l'Ancien testament dans la première épître de Pierre', *TL* 12 (1981) 64–77, 76.
99. Ibid., 76.
100. Pierre Lestringant, *Essai sur l'unité de la révélation biblique* (Paris: Editions 'Je sers', 1942) 142.

9-11; 1 Cor. 10).[101] However, Paul, in contrast to 1 Peter, would not have used the term ἔθνη. As such, the distinction between 1 Peter's use of Isa. 53 and Isa. 40 creates an artificial distinction between the Isaianic passages within the larger section of Isa. 40-55 and its collective focus on the Babylonian exile.

Ultimately, even the application of Isa. 53 in 1 Peter has to be understood in terms of the exile motif, keeping in mind that the suffering Servant-Messiah of Isa. 53 is understood as a collective identity for Israel (Isa. 49.6; 52.13).[102] This aspect of the collective, in and of itself, invites 1 Peter's audience to envision itself as the new covenant community that fulfills the Isaianic expectations for a post-exilic restoration reflected in the image of the suffering Servant.[103] Alternately, the versatility of the suffering servant image in Isaiah allows 1 Peter to apply it both to the individual (Jesus' suffering) and to the collective (the suffering of the community of believers).[104]

2.5.2. 'Idea of Exile' in 1 Peter

Something of a compromise is suggested here in comparison to the positions discussed above. It is our opinion that the controlling metaphor for the letter should be the 'idea of exile', primarily as it also remains a useful metaphor in delineating the contemporary state of Second Temple Judaism.

In contrast to Martin, who puts the emphasis on 'dispersion' or 'diaspora' in the phrase ἐκλεκτοῖς παρεπιδήμος διασπορᾶς,[105] we should place the emphasis

---

101. Richard Hays, *Echoes of Scripture in the Letters of Paul* (New Haven: Yale University Press, 1989) 95-121. Cf. James Sweeney, 'Jesus, Paul and the Temple: An Exploration of some Patterns of Continuity', *JETS* 46 (2003) 605-31.

102. Isa. 52.13–53.12 refers to an individual figure while, in the MT, Isa. 49.6, the servant is addressed as 'Israel'.

103. Paul Hanson, 'The World of the Servant of the Lord in Isaiah 40-55', in William H. Bellinger, Jr., and William R. Farmer, eds., *Jesus and the Suffering Servant: Isaiah 53 and Christian Origins* (Harrisburg, Pa.: Trinity Press International, 1998) 9–22.

104. R. E. Clements, 'Isaiah 53 and the Restoration of Israel', in Bellinger, and Farmer, eds., *Suffering Servant*, 39–54: while the NT applied the passages of the suffering servant to Jesus (an individual) they were not original in this regard. Already, the figure of Isaiah fluctuated between individual (king, prophet, Moses) and collective (Israel) as both intercessor and victim. Cf. also Israel Kohl, *The Messiah before Jesus: the Suffering Servant of the Dead Sea Scrolls* (Berkeley: University of California Press, 2000), 19–24, who points out that the evidence supports an individual interpretation of Isaianic suffering servant in Qumran, of an expected Messiah. However, whether any link exists with the Qumran messianic figure as Kohl argues (47), is doubtful. See also Morna Hooker, 'Did the Use of Isaiah 53 to Interpret His Mission Begin with Jesus?', in Bellinger and Farmer, eds., *Suffering Servant*, 103, n. 17, who does not think the echo in 1 Peter 2.24 of Isa. 53 implies a sharing of the suffering with Christ: 'The author does not say or imply that Christ shared our human death, or that we share his righteousness – simply that Christ dealt with our sins by his death so that we might live for righteousness.' However, 1 Peter 4.13 seems to imply more than just a connection of Christ's death and our sin. We become partakers of Christ's suffering in order to also be recipients of his glory.

105. The use of διασπορᾶς in 1 Peter 1.1 can be classified as either epexegetical or qualitative genitive. In the LXX διασπορᾶς (διασπείρω, διέσπειρα) is used in relation to exile as judgment (Deut.

on the concept of 'exile', 'alien' (παρεπιδῆμος; cf. also 1.17 – παροικία, and 2.11– παροίκος καὶ παρεπιδῆμος) for a number of reasons, but one is primary.[106] 'Exile' conjures a state of affairs where the 'exiled' have no choice in the matter, yet somehow are intricately entwined in God's future plan for his people.[107] On the other hand, 'Diaspora' simply refers to the reality of living outside of the homeland – whether voluntarily or forcibly – without necessarily any theological ramifications to it.[108] Given that 1 Peter deals with the suffering

28.35; 30.4; Jer. 14.14; 15.7; Ezek. 36.19; Ps. 106.27), or as a promise of the eschatological ingathering of Israel from the nations (Isa. 11.12; 49.6; Ps. 147.2[146.2 – LXX], Neh. 1.8-9; Jdt 5.19; 2 Macc. 1.27). The terminology thus captures the two dimensions of the exile – judgment and restoration hope. In effect, without actually using the terminology, 1 Peter understands the Christian community as the 'new Israel', elect by God through the saving work of Jesus Christ. As such, the two concepts of 'judgment' and 'restoration hope' are reflective of the Jews both as an elect people before the exile, *in toto*, but more so, as the people of God who live outside the promised land.

106.   *Contra* L. Goppelt, *A Commentary on 1 Peter* (Grand Rapids: Eerdmans, 1993) 67–8, who argues that 1 Peter uses Hellenistic terms rather than Hebrew terms in presenting the imagery of the dispersion: 'even with respect to the points of contact ... [1 Peter] expresses these concepts not according to Hebrew terminology, but in the conceptual language of the LXX, of Hellenistic Judaism, finally in that of Hellenistic Christianity: It calls life in a foreign land διασπορᾶς and not exile (גולה) or residence in the desert. It speaks not of repentance but of second birth ... it is evident the field of conceptual references has not been appropriated directly from the Essene tradition, but has been mediated through Christian tradition'. Nevertheless, even though use of the term נדה קצה (outskirts, edge, extremity; impel, drive away, banish) Deut. 30.4; Zech. 1.9; Ps. 147.2 (LXX Ps. 146.2); זעוה (object of horror) Deut. 28.25; Jer. 34.17 (LXX 41.17); נכה (strike, smite) Ezek. 32.15; רוק (make empty) Isa. 32.16; זרה (scatter) Jer. 15.7; 25.16; Ezek. 20.23; 22.15; פוץ (scatter) Gen. 49.7; Deut. 4.20; 28.26; Isa. 24.1; 41.16; Jer. 18.17; Ezek. 29.1; 30.23, 26; פרש (spread out, stretch, break to pieces) Deut. 30.4 translated as διασπορά in LXX as a term of judgment not specifically against Israel but even against nations that God judges, e.g. Egypt. The use of the concept is more vague and unclear in the LXX than Goppelt presumes. In *Pss. Sol* 8.29 and 9.1 there is specific reference to 'the dispersion of Israel' (ἡ διασπορὰ τοῦ Ἰσραήλ) which God will gather from the nations. Cf. also 2 Macc. 1.27. In Isa. 49.6 the Hebrew is נצר (to *watch over* Israel) while the LXX reads 'the *diaspora* of Israel', perhaps a misreading of נצר for זרה. LXX Dan. 12.2 adds the term 'diaspora' to the verse where it is missing in the MT.

107.   Christian Wolff, 'Christ und Welt im 1 Petrusbrief', *TLZ* 100 (1975) 334. Wolff identifies the language of exile in 1 Peter as reflective of the dispersion of Jews and Christians after the destruction of the temple in 70 CE, which retrospectively reflects the Babylonian exile of 587 BCE. Wolff focuses on the metaphor of stranger (*Fremde*) rather than exile (*Exil*) as primary, patterning the lives of the Petrine believers to that of Christ who was a stranger in the world. So Feldmeier, *Fremde*.

108.   Ackroyd, *Exile*, 234. Note, however, that the argument made by Martin, *Metaphor*, 212-17, based on 2 *Apoc. Bar.*, states that 'the Diaspora, like the Exile, was a time of tribulation in which God's people suffer afflictions as a punishment for their sins' (213). Scott, 'Greco-Roman', in Scott, ed., *Exile*, 173–218 (in essential agreement to Kraabel, 'Unity', 49-60) refers to Thomas Kraabel's argument that '[a]fter the return from Babylonia, "exile theology" remained a part of the Jewish religious thought, although it was gradually transformed into a more positive 'Diaspora theology', as more and more Jews either voluntarily stayed outside of the Jewish homeland or purposely moved there' (175).

of the believers *vis-à-vis* hostile surroundings, the term 'exile' better captures this state of affairs.[109]

Abraham Kaplan, in discussion of a contemporary use of the terms, distinguishes between 'dispersion/diaspora' (*tfutost*) and 'exile' (*galut*) and notes that,

> ... diaspora is a neutral, geographical concept. Exile implies something involuntary and undesirable. It connotes alienation and longing, a life whose meaning lies in the past or in the future but never in the present. Diaspora is experienced as exile unless there is a systematic self-deception or else scarcely a self to be deceived ... Exile is alienation when the exile has become a 'marginal man' ... At best, being a member of a minority is like ... being poor: it's no shame, but it's no great honor either.[110]

In a similar vein, Ackroyd reasons that,

> The Exile is seen as judgment upon the people's life, but more than that it is understood as lying within the purposes of God not simply as judgement but in relation to what he is doing in the life of the world. The response to it must be acceptance, ... not merely a repentant attitude ... [since] the effect and acceptance of disaster [bring] an understanding of restoration in terms of God's action ... [for] only in divine action can there be hope.[111]

Thus, *exile* quite fittingly encrusts two dialectical elements central in the OT prophetic messages which are also central in 1 Peter – *judgment* and *restoration hope*. Both ἐλπίδα (1.3, 21) and κρίμα (4.17; cf. also δοκίμιον – 1.7; πειρασμός – 4.12) are key elements of the 'end-of-exile' motif that anticipated the restoration of Israel and the judgment of the nations.[112]

The exile motif as used in 1 Peter also incorporates the exodus motif so that the quotations from Exodus have to be understood in light of their reinterpretation within the Second Temple Jewish exile matrix, which is subsequently reinterpreted in light of the Christian understanding of the person of Jesus Christ. Thus, the two elements of exodus and exile are intricately entwined by 1 Peter into a complex utilization of OT themes and concepts to

---

109. Brox, *Petrusbrief*, uses *Hoffnung* as the central theme in structuring the entire letter just like Rendtorff does. But if, as we argue, the 'exile' should be the overarching metaphor of reading 1 Peter, then the hope becomes meaningful only under the larger interpretive matrix of 'sin-exile-restoration'. See discussion below.

110. Kaplan, 'Identity', 327–52, 328–9.

111. Ackroyd, *Exile*, 234; Willem Cornelius van Unnik, *Das Selbstverständnis der jüdischen Diaspora in der hellenisch-römischen Zeit* (AGJU 17; Leiden: Brill, 1993) 95, 101, distinguishes between Diaspora and exile where exile denotes a horrible situation while Diaspora reflects an even worse situation (based on the use of the word διασπορά by the LXX to translate זעוה – 'horror', in Deut. 28.34 and Jer. 41[34].17).

112. James Scott, '"For as many as are works of the law are under a curse" (Galatians 3.10)', in C. A. Evans and J. A. Sanders, eds., *Paul and the Scriptures of Israel* (JSNTSup 83; SSEJC 1; Sheffield: JSOT Press, 1992) 195–213. Brunson, *Psalm 118*, 170.

communicate the message of hope and grace that 1 Peter offers. 1 Peter, therefore, freely mixes exile and exodus motifs so well that one author refers to a 'deliberate theological crafting'.[113]

Perhaps even more telling is 1 Peter's quotations of, and allusions to, the OT (especially Isaiah 40–55) which, apart from the allusion to Hosea 1.6, 9 (2.10), Ezekiel and Jeremiah (4.17), provides practically all the references to the prophetic literature in 1 Peter.[114] Other references and allusions include, among others, Daniel (4.1 [*Theodotus* 6.26] in 1 Pet. 1.2; 6.27 in 1 Pet. 1.23), and those that reflect the exodus theme (1 Pet. 1.2 – Exod. 24.7; 1 Pet. 1.16 – Lev. 11.44; 19.2; 20.7, 26), and those that reference the *Writings* (1 Pet. 1.17 - Ps. 89.26; 1 Pet. 2.7 – Ps. 118.22; 1 Pet. 3.10-13 – Ps. 34.12-16; 1 Pet. 4.18 – Prov. 11.31; 1 Pet. 5.5 – Prov. 3.34).

While identification of 1 Peter's audience with the language of the covenant formula in 2.4-10 (Exod. 19.6 – 'you shall be for me a *priestly kingdom* and a *holy nation*') recalls a central point in Israelite history – the beginning of the sojourn to Sinai[115] – likewise, the reference to Isa. 40.6-8 and the use of Isaiah 53 (1.10f, 18f; 2.21-25) also locates the readers at another significant juncture in the history of Israel – the beginning of the Babylonian exile.[116] The Christology of the epistle, which is heavily premised on the Servant-Messiah of Isaiah 53 (see 1 Pet. 1.18-20; 2.22, 24-25), adds weight to the preference for exile imagery as the background for reading 1 Peter.[117]

This then situates both the author and the readers in the context of 'exile', meaning, the author perceives himself as writing to fellow 'exiles' very much as did the OT exilic prophets, on whom he so heavily depends and to whom

---

113. Mark Dubis, *Messianic Woes in First Peter: Suffering and Eschatology in 1 Peter 4:12-19* (New York: Peter Lang, 2002) 50. The exodus motif functioned in at least two ways in the OT prophets: first, it connected the present experiences of Israel to the events of redemption from Egypt, confirming God's activity in the current events, and second, it was an actualization of the earlier events in light of the present as a basis of hope of redemption.

114. Osborne, 'L'utilisation', 76. (1 Pet. 1.11= Ps. 22.1; Isa. 53; 1 Pet. 1.12 – *Enoch* 1.2, 16; 1 Pet. 1.18 – Isa. 52.3; 1 Pet. 1.24-25 – Isa. 40.6-8). Rikki Watts, 'Consolation or Confrontation: Isa. 40–55 and the Delay of the New Exodus', *TynBul* 41/1 (1990) 31-59.

115. Rolf Rendtorff, 'Der Text in seiner Endgestalt: Überlegungen zu Exodus 19', in *Ersten, was man sät: Festschrift Klaus Koch* (Neukirchen-Vluyn: Neuchirkner Verlag, 1991) 459–70, 461. Exod. 19.1 begins what Rendtorff calls the 'Sinaiperikope' (Exod. 19 – Num. 10.10).

116. The meturgeman in *Targum Isaiah* 40.2 makes the connection to exile explicit when it cries out: 'Speak to the heart of Jerusalem and *prophesy* concerning her that *she will be filled with the people of her exiles* (גלותהא מעם), that her *sins* have been *forgiven her*, that she has received *the cup of the consolations from before* the Lord as *if she suffered two for one* for all her sins'.

117. It is not merely that Christians are antitypes of Israel as Albert R. Jonsen, 'The Moral Theology of the First Epistle of St. Peter', *ScEccl* 16 (1964) 93–106, 95, claims. They are, rather, rightfully assumed to bear the promises of Israel as the recipients of the eschatological expectations of Israel.

he appeals for prophetic vision (1.10-12).[118] Such an image fits well with the picture that emerges concerning the state of suffering of 1 Peter's audience (1.6-7; 4.12) reinforcing the emphasis on the concept of being elect – based on God's free will and covenant faithfulness – just like it was for OT Israel.[119] This fact is clearly reflected in the prescript (1.1 – ἐκλεκτοῖς παρεπιδήμοις) and the postscript (5.13 – ἐν Βαβυλῶνι συνεκλεκτή) which bracket a present reality as a transient evil anticipating a more glorious future.[120]

While *exodus* and *exile* remain references to two distinct events in the story of Israel, they retain common themes – pilgrimage and restoration hope.[121] Utilizing the rubric formulated by Rikki Watts, in his analysis of the 'New Exodus' in the Gospel of Mark, the following pattern of the 'New Exodus' in 1 Peter emerges.[122]

Exodus:	Deliverance from Egypt	Journey through the desert	Sinai
Isaianic NE:	Deliverance from Babylon	Journey along the 'way'	Jerusalem
1 Peter:	Deliverance from the Devil	Sojourn in 'exile'	Heaven

Considering 'exile' a temporary phenomenon, Second Temple Jews anticipated the termination of the social *descripta*, διασπορά, with the arrival of the Messiah, who would unite all exiles under a united Israel.[123] Reference to Jesus' sacrificial death as an echo of the Passover sacrificial lamb (1.19 – ἀμνός ἀμώμος) invests the death of Jesus with a 'New Exodus' theme where Jesus' death resolves, once and for all, the 'Sin-Exile-Restoration' conundrum.[124] As

---

118. Walter Zimmerli, 'Der "Neue Exodus" in der Verkündigung der beiden grossen Exilspropheten', in *Gottes Offenbarung: Gesammelte Aufsätze zum Alten Testament* (Munich: Chr. Kaiser, 1963) 192–204. Manuscript Sinaiticus as well as the *Peshitta* and the Vulgate add the word ἐκκλησία or its equivalent in 5.13, which most commentators explain as a later addition of scribes who were eager to supply the implicit term. Michaels, *1 Peter*, 311, is probably correct when he asserts that '*Babylon* at the end of the epistle is simply the counterpart to *Diaspora* at the beginning'.

119. Elliott, *Elect*, 54.

120. Watts, 'Consolation', 58–9.

121. Shmuel Safrai, 'Relations Between the Diaspora and the Land of Israel', in S. Safrai and M. Stern, eds., *The Jewish People in the First Century* (2 vols.; Philadelphia: Fortress, 1974) 1.193–4, points out that there were inscriptions in Palestine that mentioned Jews from the Diaspora buried in Palestine. This indicates the regard for the homeland that Jews of the 'Dispersion' had and it might also indicate some evidence of the practice of pilgrimage. The Egyptian Jewish writing *Sibylline Oracle* 3.545–72 (2nd century BCE) equates reverence for God with sacrifices at the Jerusalem temple.

122. Rikki E. Watts, 'Jesus' Death, Isaiah 53, and Mark 10.45: A *Crux Revisited*', in Bellinger and Farmer, eds., *Suffering Servant*, 129. Cf. also Zimmerli, 'Der neue Exodus', in *Gottes Offenbarung*, 195, who notes that 'Die Königserweis des neuen Exodus wird in weiteren mit dem Vokabular des alten Exodusgeschehnisses' (192).

123. Wolfson, *Philo*, 402. Sanders, *Judaism*, 279–81; *idem*, *Jesus*, 89.

124. It is this theme that was the basis for the publication of F. L. Cross's *1 Peter: a Paschal Liturgy* (London: Mowbray, 1954) in which the argument is put forth that the epistle of 1 Peter

such, the exodus references in 1 Peter do not preclude our contention that the primary framework for 1 Peter is the exile. Even passages that seem to be dominated by the exodus motifs still have exilic parallels that they echo, e.g. 1 Pet. 1.13-25, girding up [ἀναζωσάμενοι] your loins (Exod. 12.11 = Isa. 43.11; Job 38.3; 40.7); 1 Pet. 1.17, dwelling as exiles (Exod. 15.13 = Isa. 43.14-21; Jer. 1.17), and 1 Pet. 1.19, the Passover sacrificial lamb [ἀμνὸς ἀμώμος] (Exod. 19.2, 22 = Isa. 57.11; Jer. 11.19).

Both the author's contemporary experiences (5.13) and those of his audience (1.1; 1.17) in 1 Peter, are portrayed in light of the exile (διασπορά, πάροικος and παρεπίδημος) which colors the entire epistle, warranting the appropriation of the exile metaphor.[125] This language of exile in 1 Peter is most meaningful when apprehended in light of Ackroyd's 'idea of exile' and of Second Temple Jewish *restoration eschatology* with its anticipation of eschatological regathering of the διασπορά, reestablishing the temple, forgiving of national sin, eradicating or converting the Gentiles, and implementing measures to maintain purity and holiness.[126] A tripartite rhetorical parallel – εἰς ἐλπίδα (1.13, 21), εἰς κληρονομίαν (1.4) and εἰς σωτηρίαν (1.5) – not only reinforces the exodus/exile theme in 1 Peter but also locates primary elements of the epistle within the larger framework of the Second Temple period.[127]

2.6. 'Idea of Exile' and Select OT Passages in 1 Peter

2.6.1. *Exod. 24 in 1 Peter 1.2b*
The clear point is that the metaphor ῥαντισμὸν αἵματος Ἰησοῦ Χριστοῦ refers to the sacrificial death of Jesus Christ which ratified the new covenant with the 'new Israel'.[128] The combination of the genitive (Ἰησοῦ Χριστοῦ) with the objective (ὑπακοή) and the subjective (αἵματος) is difficult to maintain since the obedience is the human response to the divine act of redemption through the blood of Jesus Christ. The possible OT background passages that have been suggested for the phrase ῥαντισμὸν αἵματος can be split into two categories: those within the context of atonement (Num. 19; cf. Lev. 16.11-19), and those

should be understood as a baptismal liturgical writing used in the Passover celebration, owing to Cross's theoretical interplay between πάσχω and πάσχα. The liturgical view has, however, fallen out of favor, and Kelly, *Peter and Jude*, 15–20, makes a sustained argument against it.

125. Lapham, *Peter*, 126. He agrees to as much concerning the importance of the πάροικος and παρεπίδημος terminology for the entire epistle, despite his reluctance to utilize the vocabulary of 'exile'.

126. Ackroyd, *Exile*, 247–9. Cf. Sanders, *Judaism*, 279–303; *idem, Jesus*, 91–119; Wright, *People*, 268–72, 299–301; *idem, Victory*, xvii–xviii, 126–7, 203–4, 248–50; Schwartz, 'Introduction', 8–7; Evans, 'Aspects', 305–12; *idem, Jesus and Judaism*, 77–100.

127. Achtemeier, *1 Peter*, 67.

128. 1 Peter never uses the term 'New Israel' even though the application of the promises of Israel to the Petrine community betrays such an understanding on his part.

within the context of covenant ratification (Exod. 12 and 24). The question of whether these OT passages in any way draw a connection to the cult in the tabernacle/temple depends on how we understand 1 Peter's use of the term. Does he simply equate the sacrificial death of Christ with the animal sacrifices in the OT? And if so, how? In light of the rest of the imagery in the epistle, could this phrase be pointing beyond just the sacrificial imagery to a more specific sacrificial event? to a cultic edifice?

Well, for the author of 1 Peter, what is true of Jesus is equally applicable to the body of believers. They are at once 'a holy priesthood' who offer spiritual offerings, and at the same time also the new temple cleansed with sprinkling of the blood of Jesus Christ (1.2; 2.4-5). In light of the 'sin-exile-restoration', the death of Jesus is presented as the fulfillment of the expectation of the eschatological restoration of Israel that would bring an end to exile. This language leaves little doubt as to the significance of the sanctuary imagery, not just in the language 1 Peter chooses to use but also in the thought frame of the entire letter. The imagery of the sanctuary looms large in shaping Peter's understanding of the believers in relation to Christ (2.4-10; 4.14, 17), to each other (2.5; 3.7), and to the world that is often hostile to them (4.12-17). It is in this context that the ῥαντισμός αἵματος in 1 Pet. 1.2 has to be understood.

While we agree with Goppelt that 'these terms are not used in the few OT passages in which the sprinkling of persons with blood is mentioned, and consequently not even in the passages that deal with the institution of the covenant at Sinai (Exod. 24:8; cf. Exod. 29:20f.; Lev. 14:14)', we see no need to have recourse to the epistle to the Hebrews to explain the blood sprinkling in 1 Peter, similarities notwithstanding.[129] This is because 1 Peter's focus is on the analogy between the tabernacle/temple image and the 'new temple' – the believers. In this regard, the comparison of the sprinkling would be more accurately applied, not primarily to the sprinkling of the people in the OT passages (cf. however, Num. 19.9-10), but to the sprinkling of the tabernacle as the consecrated sanctuary of God.

2.6.2. Isa. 40.6-8 in 1 Pet. 1.21-25 and echo of Isa. 43.14-21 in 1 Pet. 1.13-25
Isaiah 40, a passage of God's reassurance of hope to the exiles and out of which these passages arise, became a classic expression of God's comfort and salvation in Judaism and Christianity (*Tg. Isa.* 40.1-10; 1QS 8.12-20; Bar. 5.7; Pesiqta Rabbati 29-33; Mk 1.2-3; Mt. 11.10; Lk. 1.17, 30-31, 76-79; 3.3-6; 7.27; 9.52; Jn 1.23; 3.28). The section of Isaiah 40.1-10 starts with pronouncement of YHWH's comforting words to the people ('Comfort, Comfort my people, says your God. Speak tenderly to Jerusalem.' 40.1)

---

129. Leonhard Goppelt, *Typos: The Typological Interpretation of the Old Testament in the New* (Grand Rapids: W. B. Eerdmans, 1982) 155.

followed by the announcement that the people have paid their dues (even double)[130] for their sins and now it is the time to return from the foreign land back to the promised land. And so the majestic pronouncement to 'prepare the way of the Lord' and to 'make straight the paths' (Isa. 40.3) is sent forth by the prophet to indicate the way from Babylon back to Jerusalem.

Rolf Rendtorff has argued that the so-called 'Second Isaiah' (40-55) is foundational for understanding the Isaianic corpus.[131] If this is the case, then it seems strategically expedient for 1 Peter to quote Isa. 40.6, 8 early on in the epistle (1 Pet. 1.24-25) since it helps set the 'exile' background that is crucial in interpretation of the epistle. Note the distinctly different use of the same Isaianic passages in Jas 1.10-12 where they function simply as illustrations while in 1 Peter they act as texts that must be taken seriously both as proof-texts and as exegetical texts of the OT.[132]

As Robert Davidson points out, Isa. 40.6-8 has had at least three possible interpretations, especially in regard to the meaning of the phrase 'all flesh'. These are that all flesh could be 1) the entire human race (cf. Isa. 49.22-26; 51.12-16) or 2) a more specific reference to God's enemy, e.g. Egypt or Assyria (cf. Isa. 37.27) or 3) a specific reference to Israel (cf. Isa. 28.1, 3).[133] Davidson reports that each of these three has continued to find supporters throughout the tradition of biblical interpretation well into the present day. The context for the Isaianic passages being Babylon allowed for the association of 'all flesh' with the greatness of Babylon, 'the threat to the continued existence to the people of God'.[134]

However, for those who would understand 'all flesh' as the people of God the attack would be to the transience and frailty of the institutions of Israel which fall under the rubric of 'flesh'; 'human constructions that can no longer bear the burden of Israel's present needs or future hope'.[135] Such a position is adopted by Claus Westermann who concludes that:

---

130. 'Double' (διπλος; כֶּפֶל) here probably means 'corresponding quantity' rather than 'twice as much', in spite of *Tg. Isa.*'s interpretation of it in terms of quantity.

131. Rolf Rendtorff, 'Zur Komposition des Buches Jesajas', *VT* 34 (1984) 295–320.

132. Peter Ackroyd, 'Isaiah 36-39: Structure and Function', in *Von Kanaan bis Kerala* (Festschrift J. P. M. Van der Ploeg; AOAT 211; Neukirchen-Vlyn: Neukirchener Verlag, 1982) 1–6; Christopher R. Seitz, 'The Divine Council: Temporal Transition and New Prophecy in the Book of Isaiah', *JBL* 109 (1990) 229–47. F. L. Cross, 'The Council of Yahweh in Second Isaiah', *JNES* 12 (1953) 274–323, 276, takes vv. 6–8 as an address to the prophet by some 'anonymous herald' whom Christopher Seitz, 'Council', 229–47, identifies as the 'divine council' based on his understanding of the plural imperative in Isa. 40.1. The passages quoted by 1 Pet. 1.24, 25 fall within this larger context of Isaiah (40-55), which announces the return of the exiles from Babylon.

133. Robert Davidson, 'The Imagery of Isaiah 40.6-8 in Tradition and Interpretation', in Craig A. Evans and Shemaryahu Talmon, eds., *The Quest For Context and Meaning: Studies in Biblical Intertextuality in Honor of James A. Sanders* (Leiden: Brill, 1997) 37–55.

134. Ibid., 54.

135. Ibid.

The answer is that the exiles' greatest temptation ... was precisely to thinking of themselves as caught up in the general transience of all things, to believe that nothing could be done to halt the extension of their national existence, and to say 'just like countless other nations destroyed before our time, in our time and after our time, we are a nation that perishes: all flesh is grass'.[136]

1 Peter seems to adopt the first interpretation by identifying 'all flesh' with the 'perishable seed' – the human race in all its frailty. Nevertheless, it is hard not to see associations with Babylon being drawn, especially considering 1 Peter's use of the word 'Babylon' in 5.13.

A second significant element is the focus on the theme of life and death in 1 Pet. 1.24–2.4. The promise of Isaiah's prophecy was an anticipation of an eschatological deliverance of Israel by YHWH through the death of the servant (53.8). Out of death would spring life. For this reason, the eschatological prophecy was begun with a new word of the Lord (ῥῆμα τοῦ θεοῦ – 40.8) that brings life, in contrast to God's judgment (word) that brings death (Isa. 53.9-10). Therefore, while Isaiah's hope for life was premised upon the suffering servant (Isa. 51–53), 1 Peter identifies Jesus Christ with the suffering servant, the 'Word of the Lord' (ῥῆμα κυρίου) – the Messiah.[137] Note especially the change of ῥῆμα τοῦ θεοῦ in Isa. 40.8 to ῥῆμα κυρίου in 1 Pet. 1.25 which actualizes the hope of Israel within the audience of 1 Peter.[138] *Contra* Martin Scharlemann who thinks that the ῥῆμα κυρίου is a 'specific reference to the time when the newly baptized persons to whom this epistle addresses itself made their confession of faith', ῥῆμα in 1 Peter is a *terminus technicus* referring specifically to the preaching of the gospel of Jesus Christ (1 Pet. 1.25b).[139] Similar to its use in Heb. 6.4, it here retains eschatological ramifications that are central to the message of salvation that 1 Peter preaches. (The synonymous λόγος is used in 3.1 to refer to the gospel message, the source of salvation.)

The exile, as separation from God, meant death. The return from exile then came to be understood as a return to life – a resurrection.[140] Such language

---

136. Claus Westermann, *Isaiah 40-66* (OTL; Philadelphia: Westminster, 1969) 41.

137. Danker, 'Consolatory', 93–102. He does not relate the thought of vanity in human life to the exile event, though this would probably be the most relevant scenario for Isaiah's words and therefore, inferentially, the backdrop of 1 Peter's OT quotations.

138. Cf. Ernst Käsemann, *The Wandering People of God: An Investigation of the Letter to the Hebrews* (trans. Ray A. Harrisville and Irving L. Sandberg; Minneapolis: Augsburg, 1984 [German 1957]) 27–37.

139. Martin Scharlemann, 'Why the Kuriou in 1 Pet. 1. 25?', *Concordia Theological Monthly* 3 (1959) 354.

140. R. P. Gordon, 'The Targumists as Eschatologists', in *Congress Volume: Göttingen, 1977* (VTSup 29; Leiden: E. J. Brill, 1978) 113–30. See *Tg. Isa.* 38.16 as the explicit targumic statement on resurrection where only interment in the land of Israel was the guarantee for the blessing of resurrection. As Gordon reports: 'Israel was, in an eschatological sense, "the land of the living", the land of the everlasting life. Some obscure Hebrew in Hos. xiv 7 (Heb. 8) becomes

of life and death is echoed in 1 Peter's passages that use the language of life, e.g. living stones, and the metaphor darkness to light (2.9). Ultimately, it is fulfilled in Jesus Christ, who is the 'living stone' and to whom all the believers must now be attached (2.4-9). As such, the current exile of 1 Peter's audience (1.1; 2.11) serves only to remind them of the anticipated eschatological transition that gives hope in spite of the unfavorable current state of affairs. Suffering with and for the sake of Christ would only produce glory to God and resurrection life (2.19-25).

2.6.3. Exod. *19.6*; Isa. *28.16; 42.20; 43.20-21*; Hos. *1.6, 9 in 1 Pet. 2.6-10*

1 Peter 2.4-10 is the central passage on temple imagery and identity in 1 Peter. A mosaic of OT passages utilizing temple cultic language is presented with intertwining elements of the exodus and exile in a formulation that captures the imagination of the readers. The believers are given a new identity that is premised on the temple and its function within Israel as the physical representation of the presence of God. The OT passages affirm both the continuity and the discontinuity of the frames and images that 1 Peter points to, reshaping and re-appropriating the institutional elements of the OT *cultus* within a new framework of Christian experience. This passage of 1 Peter is subjected to greater exegetical analysis in Chapter 4 below.

2.6.4. Isa. *53 in 1 Pet. 2.21-25*

1 Pet. 2.22-25 quotes from LXX Isa. 53 in the paraenetic context addressed to slaves. The significant verb πάσχω (used in the NT 42 times) usually refers to the suffering of Christ and in 1 Peter πάσχω and πάθημα occur 16 times with about 6–8 of the references focusing on the suffering of Christ and about 10 on the suffering of the Christians.[141] Use of πάσχω in 1 Peter also reflects the influence of Isa. 53 and the motif of suffering servant with 1 Peter simply standing in a tradition that favored its use for Jesus' death.[142] 1 Peter, nevertheless, takes the tradition a step further when he equates the current sufferings of the believers with those of Christ (2.21).[143]

---

the vehicle for expressing this conviction … But it also came to be regarded as "the land of the living" in the sense that only there could the dead entertain the hope of being raised from their graves. Some authorities held that even a righteous Israelite could be denied a part in the resurrection if he had been buried beyond the borders of Israel (so R. Eleazer in *b. Ketub.* 111a). Conversely, the hope of resurrection was extended to the non-Israelites whose only merit was their interment within the holy land (117)'. *Tg. Ezekiel* 37.1-14 seeks to 'correct the view which denied the blessing of resurrection to those who died beyond the borders of Israel' (121).

141. The count may be up to 18 times depending on how one accounts for the textual problem in 1 Pet. 2.21.

142. Vernon Solomon Olson, 'The Atonement in 1 Peter' (Th.D. diss., Union Theological Seminary, 1979) 84–101, 85.

143. ὑπὲρ ὑμῶν in 1 Pet. 2.21 may also reflect LXX Isa. 53.4.

1 Pet. 2.22-25 recalls the innocence of the lamb whose blood saves us (1.19) and clearly echoes Isa. 53.5-7 (remember the silence of Jesus before Caiaphas – Mk 16.61, Pilate – Mk 15.5 and before Herod – Lk. 23.9). Rather than being a case of passive resignation 'to one's fate', 1 Peter reworks the aspect of the suffering servant imagery to encourage his readers to have patient confidence in God just like Jesus, who when he was silent was committing himself completely to God rather than to humans.[144] The motivation is that they would share in the glory of God with Christ.

2.6.5. Ps. 34.12-16 in 1 Pet. 3.10-13

The overall significance of the lengthy paraphrase of Psalm 34 in 1 Pet. 3.10-13 has been exaggerated in the past. Several attempts have been made to find in Psalm 34 an overriding biblical passage that controls the entire epistle. W. Bornemann was the first to suggest that the whole epistle of 1 Peter is a baptismal homily based on Psalm 34 (33).[145] Retaining a positive regard for Bornemann's hypothesis, Snodgrass toned it down somewhat when he argued that while the Psalm may possibly have served as a 'catalyst for attraction of other OT texts' it, nevertheless, cannot account for the use of the OT in the whole epistle.[146] Yet, Snodgrass proceeds to affirm the following:

> ... Ps. xxxiv does play a formative role in the composition of 1 Peter and especially of ii.1-10. I would go as far as to say that the author of 1 Peter attempted to convey the consolation and exhortation of the righteous sufferer in Ps. xxxiv to his readers and that he used explicit quotations, allusions, and themes from Ps. xxxiv to do so.[147]

Note, however, the caution of Schutter who, following a thorough analysis of Bornemann's theory, concludes that the purported references to Psalm 34 in 1 Peter – which are 'exactly one explicit quotation, one explicit allusion, one very weak implicit allusion, and a handful of iterative allusions' – are not sufficient to support the kind of claim that Snodgrass makes.[148] So Danker's

---

144. Hill, 'Sacrifices', 55.

145. W. Bornemann, 'Der erste Petrusbrief – eine Taufrede des Silvanus?' *ZNW* 19 (1920) 143–65, 146: 'It seems to me however, that of all OT sections, one that is used in 1 Pt the most and stands in special relation to the entire epistle is indeed Psalm 34.'

146. Snodgrass, 'Affinities', 103. He identifies themes present in 1 Peter but not reflected in Psalm 34 including the stone *testimonia*, emphasis on election, holiness, and people of God. He also identifies the words in Ps. 34 that are reflected in 1 Peter including παροικία (Ps. 34.5; 1 Pet. 1.17); φοβέω/φόβος (Psa 34.10; 1 Pet. 1.15-17); χρηστὸς ὁ κύριος (1 Pet. 2.3) as a reminder of χρηστὸς ὁ κύριος (Ps. 34.9).

147. Snodgrass, 'Affinities', 103, does identify some themes present in 1 Peter that are not reflected in Psalm 34, including the stone *testimonia*, emphasis on election, holiness, and people of God.

148. Schutter, *Hermeneutic*, 48-9. For a complete listing of the passages, phrases, words or allusions in 1 Peter identified as paralleled in Psalm 34 see the listing in Bornemann, 'Taufrede', 149f.

remarks make sense when he states that, 'The baptismal notes scattered in the epistle are more probably the normal theological reinforcement found in passages such as Rom. 6:1-4; Gal. 3:27; Eph 4:24; Col 2:12.'[149]

At this point, it is prudent to conclude that while the importance of Ps. 34 as a classic expression of OT themes for 1 Peter should be recognized – the psalm deals with suffering and with salvation over the enemies who are the cause of suffering (cf. 1QH 7.19-22), themes that are also present in other OT passages that are used by 1 Peter (e.g. Isa. 53) – it should not be exaggerated, especially not to the level of the literary dependence asserted by Bornemann and Snodgrass.[150]

2.6.6. Ezek. 9.7 in 1 Pet. 4.16-17

The judgment that begins in the 'house of God' (LXX – οἶκος τοῦ θεοῦ) is central to understanding the place of the temple imagery in 1 Peter's concern for the eschatological restoration of Israel.[151] Such an understanding elicits a transformation of the readers' understanding of their current afflictions, from one of *retribution* to one of *purification* (1.6-7; 2.11). It is an eschatological purification of the 'temple of God' that is part of the final judgment which, unusual though it might seem, is not lacking in OT support (Isa. 10.11-12; Jer. 25.29; Zech. 13.7-9).[152]

2.7. Exile and Identity in 1 Peter

There are only two places in the OT where the terms πάροικος and παρεπίδημος are combined in similar fashion to 1 Peter 2.11 – Gen. 23.4 and Ps. 39.12 (LXX – 38.13).[153] Abraham applies both terms 'stranger' and 'sojourner' (πάροικος καὶ παρεπίδημος ἐγώ εἰμι μεθ' ὑμῶν) to himself when negotiating with the Hittites about a place to bury his wife Sarah in their land where he had settled (Gen. 23.4). As a foreigner he lacked inherited rights and did not have a place to bury his dead wife.[154] Not only were the believers in 1 Peter

---

149. Danker, 'Consolatory', 101.

150. Cf. Schutter, *Hermeneutic*, 48ff.

151. Typically in the LXX, οἶκος τοῦ θεοῦ refers to the temple or sanctuary and not the 'people of God'. However, we see that 1 Peter's transference of the imagery of the temple to the people (2.4-10) necessitates our combining the two in this passage. Furthermore, it also precludes the idea of social concept of 'household of God' as the primary focus.

152. Achtemeier, *1 Peter*, 315.

153. Eph. 2.19 combines ξένοι and πάροικοι both of which are used by LXX to translate the Hebrew גר. Πάροικος is also used in the LXX to translate נכרי ('Gentile') and תושב ('resident alien').

154. Abraham is called a sojourner (Gen. 17.8; 28.4) and so are the Israelites while in exile. Paul Achtemeier, 'John H. Elliot, 1 Peter: An Appreciation', *BTB* (2002) 150–3, 152, has argued that based on the fact that the words 'stranger and alien' are applied to Abraham 'exclusively', the phrase

addressed as members of the lowest social stratum (foreigners/aliens and sojourners could not own land or property), but the same terminology also denotes the characteristic of 'exile', both literally and metaphorically (1 Pet. 1.17).[155]

In exile, two seemingly contrasting concerns become primary: *propagation* of the faith, and retaining intact national *identity*.[156] 1 Pet. 1.1 anticipation of the ingathering of the 'Dispersed exiles', reminiscent of Second Temple sentiments,[157] is mirrored in James 1.1 where specifically mentioned is the restoration of the twelve tribes (Ἰάκωβος θεοῦ καὶ κυρίου Ἰησοῦ Χριστοῦ δοῦλος ταῖς δώδεκα φυλαῖς ταῖς ἐν τῇ διασπορᾷ χαίρειν).[158] The fulfillment of previously exclusively Israelite promises in the commencement of a 'new eschatological community' as anticipated by Isa. 56.7-8 also marks a turning point – the inclusion of foreigners into the house of God, which would become the 'house of prayer for all nations'. What is presented as an Isaianic promise in the MT לכל־העמים ('all peoples') appears to be transposed specifically to 'all Gentiles' (πᾶσιν τοῖς ἔθνεσιν) in the LXX. The *Targum Isaiah* makes this interpretation even more explicit when it elaborates:

> And the sons of the Gentiles who *have been added to the people of* the LORD, to minister to him, to love the name of the Lord, and to be his servants, every one who *will keep the* sabbath from profaning it, and hold fast my covenants – these I will bring to *the* holy mountain, and make them joyful in my house of prayer; their burnt offerings and their *holy* sacrifices will *even go up* for [*my*] *pleasure* on my altar; for my *sanctuary will be* a house of prayer for all the peoples. Thus says the LORD *God* who *is about to* gather the outcasts of Israel, yet will I *bring near their exiles, to* gather *them*.[159]

Two primary points can be drawn from this targumic rendering of Isaiah. First, the meturgeman is still anticipating a future eschatological restoration of Israel that will entail a gathering of the people from exile.[160] Second, he

---

as used in 1 Peter has to be understood as metaphorical within what he identifies as the larger controlling metaphor 'Israel as a chosen people'. Cf. Achtemeier, *1 Peter*, 69-72, 244ff.

155. Elliott, *Home*, 21–100.

156. Raymond S. Forster, *The Restoration of Israel: A Study of Exile and Return* (London: Darton, Longman and Todd, 1970) 57.

157. The *Psalms of Solomon* (first century BCE) look forward to this event when Israel would be restored by imploring God to 'Bring together the dispersed of Israel with mercy and goodness, for your faithfulness is with us' (*Pss. Sol.* 8.28). See also *Pss. Sol.* 11.1-4; 17.4, 21, 26-28, 44.

158. Michaels, *1 Peter*, xlvii, considers the epistle of James as the second part of a doublet with 1 Peter, which parallels another doublet 2 Peter and Jude ('brother of James') forming two pairs of letters connected to the two significant leaders of the early Church (cf. Gal. 2.7-10). 1 Peter is addressed to Jews who are in fact 'Gentiles' while James is addressed to scattered messianic Jews (i.e. Christians) who are in fact Jews.

159. Bruce Chilton, *The Isaiah Targum* (The Aramaic Bible, 11; Wilmington, Del.: Michael Glazier, 1987) 109. Cf. *idem*, 'Salvific Exile in the Isaiah Targum', in Scott, ed., *Exile*, 239–47.

160. On the notes of this passage, Chilton points out the significance of the association of the *Šekinah's house* and *Gentiles* '... especially in the context of Jesus' reputed citation of v. 7 during his occupation of the Temple (... Lk. 19:46 ...). But the emphasis of the passage falls on

expects the ingathering to also involve Gentile proselytes in ministry to the Lord. So while 1 Peter retains the promises of Israel on one hand, on the other hand, it expands their application to include non-Israelites reconstituting the basis of identity as faith in Jesus Christ.

Jews in the Dispersion found it necessary not to draw a line between one's moral life and one's identity, so that one's Jewishness was premised on his or her faithfulness to the Jewish moral code (cf. Josephus, *Ant.* 4.114; Philo, *Spec. Leg.* 4.179-180; *Leg. Gai.* 3-5).[161] This same sentiment can also be said to be true of 1 Peter, where the emphasis on the 'moral conduct' (ἀναστροφή) is placed side by side with the focus on identity (1.15, 17; 2.12).[162] In this respect, the epistle continues the Jewish maxim that 'who one is' cannot be separated from 'how one lives' even as it applies it to the Gentile-inclusive Petrine community.

The first call to exercise responsibility ἀναστροφή in 1 Peter is anchored to the believers' identification with God. Since God is holy, they too must exercise holiness in their conduct (Lev. 11.44). The second concern for conduct (ἀναστρεφω – 1.17) has to do with their status as 'exiles' (παροικία). It is primarily because of their status as aliens that their conduct should help guard their identity. It is the only way to keep themselves from being consumed by the surrounding cultures, risking loss of their distinctive Christian identity.[163] The danger of assimilation is a constant threat that they have to live with occasioning focused scrutiny (2.12).

Only in exercising responsible Christian conduct would they find justification following any negative accusations from the ἔθνη. This, is true not just in the general community, with whom they must maintain a clear conscience (συνείδησις – 3.16) to avoid any traducement propagated against them, but more so within mixed marriages where one partner is not a Christian (3.2).

---

the return of the "*exiled*" (v. 8) and on the concomitant victory of Jerusalem over the hapless Gentile "*kings*" (v. 9, cf. 54.15b)' (emphasis original).

161. Allan Bevere, *Sharing in the Inheritance: Identity and the Moral Life in Colossians* (JSNTSup 226; Sheffield: Sheffield Academic Press, 2003) 29.

162. Ibid., 30.

163. See discussion in David L. Balch, *Let Wives Be Submissive: The Domestic Code in 1 Peter* (SBLMS 26; Atlanta: Scholars Press, 1981) 108–9, 133–6; *contra*, Elliott, *Home*, 42, 74–5, 476–7. For Balch, the adaptation of the Hellenistic Code in 1 Peter was not because eschatological hopes had faded and Christians felt more at home in society. Rather, 'the Code has an apologetic function in the historical context; the paraenesis is given in light of outside criticism'. If we adopt the larger rubric of exile to read 1 Peter, the eschatological anticipation cannot be narrowed to one of failed expectation or fading importance within the Christian experience. Instead, it serves to reassure the readers of God's faithfulness (that this is the eschatological restoration anticipated) which the believers ought to feel comfortable defending against any that may question them in regard to their exuberance (3.15). The ἀπολογία here is not a defense but a positive counter-claim that seeks to establish the validity of the believers' faith in light of any questioning by outsiders.

In such situations the ἀναστροφή becomes the ῥῆμα (1.25) of Christian witness to the unbelieving partner.[164] And so the question of whether the purpose of the letter is apologetic (Balch) or missionary (Elliott) becomes moot, since both seem to be present in 1 Peter. It is no surprise since both aspects characterize the very essence of exile concerns of maintaining faith and identity in a bid to survive in the 'foreign' world.[165]

1 Peter is able to use the Exodus 'echoes' to explain the work of Christ as the final liberation from bondage (1.1-4, 5-7, 18-25) for the Christian believers. The placing of these 'echoes' at the beginning of the epistle signifies the centrality of the redemptive work of Christ parallel to YHWH's promise of redemption to the nation of Israel in the midst of their travail.[166] It also reminds the readers of God's redemptive acts in the redemption of Israel from bondage, commemorated in the Passover and now finding its eschatological fulfillment in Jesus' death on the tree (1 Pet. 1.19-24). Coupled with this, the pilgrimage motif in the epistle (1.1, 17) enforces the Christian community's connection to OT Israel by highlighting:[167] i) the pattern of desert wanderings (1.3-12), ii) the settlement in the land and eventual exile from the land following God's judgment (4.17), and iii) the constant expectation of a restoration reflected in the structure of the whole epistle (cf. 5.2-4 which alludes to the image of wicked shepherds in *Ezek. 34.*[168]

Such Petrine designations as 'exiles of the Dispersion' (1.1, 17), 'a time of exile' (2.11-12), and 'foreigners/aliens in exile' scattered and suffering anew (5.10) draw comparisons with Qumran documents, which also combine elements of election, sojourning in a foreign land, and exodus/exile motifs.[169] For example, CD 3.21–4.6 opines:

> The *Priests* are the converts of Israel who are departed from the land of Judah, and (the *Levites* are) those who joined them. The sons of *Zadok* are the *elect of Israel*, the men called by name who shall stand at the end of days. Behold, the exact list of their names according to their generations, and the time when they lived, and the number of their trials, and the years of their *sojourn*, and the exact list of their deeds ...[170]

---

164. Elliott, *Home*, 42, 74–5, 476–7.

165. Feldmeier, *Fremde*, 201-10, concludes that the two dimensions put forth by Elliott as distinct ('social aspect' and the 'cosmological') cannot be held in contrast, since the hope of the divine future (*Gottes Zukunft*) is based on the latter in supplanting the former.

166. Bevere, *Inheritance*, 30.

167. See Käsemann, *Wandering*, for pilgrimage in Hebrews. Similarities with 1 Peter would venture useful comparisons, especially the use of the OT cultic symbols to interpret their respective Christian communities.

168. Chevallier, 'Diaspora', 391. W. C. van Unnik, 'The Redemption in 1 Peter 1:18-19 and the Problem of the First Epistle of Peter', in *Sparsa Collecta: The Collected Essays of W. C. van Unnik* (NovTSup 30; Leiden: Brill, 1980) 31, asks and responds to his own query: 'How must they behave in this world, where they are like exiles? That the author was particularly concerned with this appears from the frequent use he makes of the word.'

169. Dubis, *Woes*, 48.

170. Emphasis added. Cf. also CD 6.4ff; 1QM 1.2-3.

Utilizing a hermeneutic akin to that of the Qumran covenanters (and contemporary Jewish literature, e.g. *2 Apoc. Bar.*; *Pss. Sol.*; *Jub.*), 1 Peter employs the exodus motif to recast the exilic writings by providing a matrix for understanding the exile experience as a 'Second/New Exodus' (Isa. 40–55; Ezek. 40–48) rather than a reflection on the literal exodus from Egypt.[171]

The exodus provides the linguistic framework within which the present situation of the believers can be reinterpreted and actualized, just as prophets like Isaiah were able to recast the anticipated restoration from Babylonian exile as a 'New Exodus'. Thus the exodus 'echoes' in 1 Peter are subsumed into the exile imagery, which itself is expressed in light of the Second Temple mindset of the 'continuing exile'.[172] Note that their being 'exiles in Dispersion' does not necessarily mean that the people of God are scattered in disorderly fashion with no sense of unity.[173] On the contrary, it is the designations of restoration, i.e. 'spiritual house', 'new Israel', which provide the bond of unity. That is why to simply understand the designation 'exiles' from a sociological point of view obscures the spiritual/theological significance of the metaphor's analogy of oneness – both with Israel of old and with other believers who also suffer (5.9).[174]

Furthermore, for 1 Peter, the people of God can only be described in terms of their being united by faith in Christ which provides the central element of the imagery of the 'Temple-Community' as a chosen race and a royal priesthood (2.4-10).[175] It is only in the communal aspect, based on their election by God, premised on their faith in their redeemer Jesus Christ, that his audience can be pictured as the 'Temple-Community'. Their unity is a spiritual unity which changes their status in relation to the world, making them

---

171. M.-E. Boismard, 'Liturgies Baptismale dans Pierre (1re Épître)' (*DBSup* 7; Paris, 1966) col. 1431, points out that the letter is shaped by the idea of the 'nouvel Exode' with the Christians forming the new people of God and the expectation that they are journeying through a new exodus that would culminate at Sinai. The strength of his argument lies less with the individual passages he discusses, some of which are questionable, than with the argument as a whole. Cf. Goppelt, *1 Peter*, 64.

172. Walter Brueggemann, 'Preaching to Exiles', *Journal for Preachers* 16 (1993) 3–15, 8: 'It is the need to somehow maintain the essence of the presence of the God in the midst of all the "contrary reality" by drawing upon the imagery of wilderness wanderings of the Exodus that are in turn recounted and actualized in the current experience of the exiles (cf. Ezekiel 40–48). Most important, the *tabernacle* is an imaginative effort to form a special place where God's holiness can be properly hosted and therefore counted upon (Exodus 25–31, 35–40)' (emphasis original).

173. Chevallier, 'Diaspora', 392.

174. Elliott, *Home*, 21ff.

175. The warning by Norbert Brox, 'Sara zum Beispiel …'. Israel im 1. Petrusbrief', in P.-G. Muller and W. Stegner, eds., *Kontinuität und Einheit: Fur Franz Mussner* (Freiburg: Herder, 1981) 484–93, 489, that the OT quotes in 1 Peter do not serve as continuation of 'Heilgeschichte', needs to be kept in mind, since for 1 Peter the promises of Israel are applied directly to the Petrine community.

'strangers' and 'sojourners' since their heritage is 'in heaven' (1.4). They have a shepherd of their souls (2.25) who, through the elders (the shepherds of the flock 5.2-4), provides the rallying point for the community of believers, uniting them into a vibrant and living community.[176]

2.8. *Temple and Restoration from Exile*

Restoration from exile was to be epitomized by the reestablishment of the temple and the *cultus* (Isa. 11.11-17; Ezek. 29.21-29; Hag. 1.1-5; *Jub.* 1.15-17; *T. Benj.* 9.2). Given that Isaiah provides the largest share of OT passages quoted, echoed or alluded to in 1 Peter, it is significant to note that Isaiah closely associates the eschatological temple with Gentiles who stream into the temple, are gathered with the scattered of Israel, and bring their wealth to adorn the temple (Isa. 2.2; 56.7; 60.4-13).[177] 1 Peter takes over this Isaianic theme and not only allows for the possibility of Gentiles entering the eschatological temple but also goes a step further to integrate Gentiles into the 'spiritual eschatological temple' (2.4-10).[178] In so doing, 1 Peter reshapes and reconstitutes both the identity of the temple and that of the believers, merging '... two strains of Jew and Gentile ... into a new body'.[179]

Because a major part of the Jewish community lived outside of the homeland,[180] three annual pilgrimages to Jerusalem provided the opportunity for a dynamic and concrete participation in the cultic experience.[181] As McKelvey reports:

176. Chevallier, 'Diaspora', 392.

177. Notice the parallel between τοὺς διεσπαρμένους Ισραηλ (Isa. 56.7) and παρεπιδήμοις διασπορᾶς (1 Pet. 1.1). 4QFlor 1.3-4; *T. Benj.* 9.2; *Sib. Or.* 3.616-34, 715-20; *1 Enoch* 90.32-33 all anticipate Gentile participation in the eschatological temple's worship. However, note also Isa. 44.6-9 and *Sib. Or. 5*, which only foresee the coming judgment of the Gentiles.

178. Beare, *First Peter*, 101.

179. Ibid.

180. L. Rost, 'Erwangen zum Kyroserlass', in A. Kuschke, ed., *Verbannung und Heimkehr* (Tübingen: J. C. B. Mohr, 1961) 305: Rost's primary point is that the temple cult had been significant to the Jews in Dispersion because it was a requirement of the Torah to make a contribution to the temple.

181. Philo gives his own description of a personal pilgrimage to the temple in Jerusalem 'to offer prayers and sacrifices' (*Provid.* 2.64). Cf. also Wolfson, *Philo*, 1.242 n. 28. However, this positive view must be tempered with the observation by Neusner, 'Judaism After the Destruction of the Temple', in Neusner *et al.*, eds., *Judaisms and their Messiahs*, 666, that, '... for large numbers of the ordinary Jews outside of Palestine, as well as substantial numbers within, the temple was a remote and, if holy, unimportant place. For them, piety was fully expressed through synagogue worship', Elliot's objections to the use of the term pilgrim notwithstanding (*Home*, 47). On pilgrimage and procession as two forgotten themes of the return from exile, see Merrill, 'Pilgrimage and Procession: Motifs of Israel's Return', in G. Avraham, ed., *Israel's Apostasy and Restoration: Essays in Honor of Ronald K Harrison* (Grand Rapids: Baker, 1987) 261–72.

The annual pilgrimages to Jerusalem became occasions of great sentiment. The journey to Zion was the chief joy of life (Isa. 30.29; 35.10; Psa. 42.1ff; 43.3ff; 122.1ff; 137.6) ... One must go to Jerusalem because that is where God is. To be away from the temple is to be away from God (Psa. 137.4; cf. 1 Sam. 26.19; Ezek. 11.15; Jonah 2.4); to go up to the temple is to go up to God (Psa. 42.2; 63.2; 65.1f., etc.).[182]

Indeed, pilgrimage to the Jerusalem temple to offer sacrifice became part of the requirements for a proselyte to enjoy full acceptance into the Jewish community.[183] For those who could not make the pilgrimage, both Jew and Gentile God-fearer (Acts 8.27–39.13),[184] an alternative means for continued connection to the Jerusalem *cultus,* recognized both in Palestine and the Diaspora, availed: an annual half-shekel temple tax – probably of post-exilic provenance[185] – which became a central part of diaspora Jewish experience in the Second Temple period (cf. Neh. 10.32; 2 Chron. 10.32; Mt. 17.24), gaining even atonement value in its identification with the ransom money of Exod. 3.13.[186] (R. Eleazer said, 'While the temple stood, a man paid his shekel and made atonement for himself' *Baba Batra* 9a.[187])

1 Peter's re-appropriation of the temple into a 'spiritual Temple-Community' (2.4-10) is likely constructed within a framework of similar concerns. In lieu of a pilgrimage to Jerusalem, God has come to dwell in their midst, transforming them into the cultic equivalent of the physical

---

182. McKelvey, *Temple*, 4; Harald Hegemann, 'The Diaspora in the Hellenistic Age', in W. D. Davies and Louis Finkelstein, eds., *The Cambridge History of Judaism* (3 vols.; Cambridge: Cambridge University Press, 1999) 2.115-66, 154.

183. Michael Fishbane, 'The "Exodus" Motif/Paradigm for Renewal', in *Text and Texture: Close Readings of Selected Biblical Texts* (New York: Schocken Books, 1979) 121–51, and *idem*, *Biblical Interpretation*, 356–68. Cf. also van Unnik, 'Redemption', 44. In the Rabbinic tradition, three things were required for a proselyte to be considered a full Israelite: baptism, circumcision, and sacrifice (*m. Keritot* 2.1; cf. Gemara of *Tosefta Keritot* 9a [81a]). The last requirement presupposes a trip to Jerusalem where the sacrifices were offered before the destruction of the temple. Since it was the case that purification could not be complete without sacrifice, pilgrimage to Jerusalem became mandatory for any proselyte seeking full status as an Israelite. Whether these customs were prior to or followed the destruction of the temple is unclear.

184. See Levinskaya, *Acts*, 19–34, 120–6; Collins, *Between Athens and Jerusalem:* 264–72; Albert Bell, Jr., *Exploring the NT World* (Nashville, Tenn.: Thomas Nelson, 1998) 21–6, on 'Diaspora'.

185. Alfred Edersheim, *The Temple: Its Ministry and Services as they were at the Time of Jesus Christ* (London: F. H. Revell, 1874) 72–4.

186. Willam Horbury, 'The Temple Tax', in Ernst Bammel and C. F. D. Moule, eds., *Jesus and the Politics of His Day* (Sheffield: Sheffield Academic Press, 1984) 281. The ransom element might have been part of the veiled rejection of Jesus in his response about temple tax in Mt. 17.24-27.

187. Hegemann, 'Diaspora', 154. While Nehemiah's levy was regarded as temporary, that of 2 Chronicles is understood to correspond to Exod. 25.1f and not the half-shekel of ransom. In Tobit 1.6-8 and in *Jubilees* the amount is not specified. See also Horbury, 'Tax', in Bammell and Moule, eds., *Jesus and Politics* 265–86.

temple, where 'spiritual sacrifices' can be offered (v. 9). Not only is the national sanctuary of Israel replaced by the eschatological sanctuary of the 'new Israel' but maintenance of national unity in the exile motif is replaced by the eschatological unity of the Church.[188]

188. Fishbane, *Text*, 129-30.

Chapter 3

'TEMPLE', 'EXILE', AND 'IDENTITY' IN SECOND TEMPLE LITERATURE

3.1. *Introductory Comments*

In this chapter we examine Second Temple Jewish literature in an effort to locate 1 Peter within the stream of theological reflection that emanated from this period. We begin by analyzing select biblical writings (Daniel, Zechariah, Haggai, Malachi) and then look at several non-biblical Jewish writings (*1 Enoch, Testaments of the Twelve Patriarchs, Jubilees*, Qumran, Philo and Josephus).

One of the reasons given in the OT – why the ten tribes were wiped out – is their failure to honor the prescribed pilgrimage to Jerusalem for the cultic practices (2 Kgs 17.28-34; cf. also 1 Kgs 12.1–14.31 and Jer. 25.9) resulting in judgment that eliminated them from the history of Israel.[1] Realizing, as we have seen in the previous chapter, that pilgrimage had become so central for the Second Temple Jews in the Dispersion, it makes sense to assume that a possible concern for some of the readers of 1 Peter was whether, having become Christians, the pilgrimage to Jerusalem still mattered. In fact, it is plausible, that some might even have been postulating that missing the pilgrimage might be a part of the reason for their current suffering.

As a result, suffering for 1 Peter's audience might have been interpreted as follows:

i) that God had abandoned them, and/or

ii) that they had sinned (possibly by failing to make the pilgrimage to the Jerusalem temple, the dwelling of God) and therefore were being punished for their sin. With this as a plausible background for understanding the larger concern of suffering in 1 Peter, the letter seems to be partly a response to these kinds of interpretations of suffering by some in the Petrine community. By relating suffering instead to purification and by re-appropriating the *locus divinitus* from the physical temple to the Temple-Community (the 'spiritual house') 1 Peter counters such sentiments. The resultant affirmation is a reassurance of God's abiding presence even in their current 'exile' and pilgrimage (cf. Ezek. 10–11).

---

1. See discussion in Tudor Parfitt, *The Lost Tribes of Israel: The History of a Myth* (London: Weidenfeld & Nicolson, 2002) esp. 1–24.

3.2. Biblical Writings

3.2.1. *Daniel 9*

Daniel 9 is a difficult passage which reflects a significant reinterpretation of the exile period as earlier presented by Jeremiah (vv. 2, 24-25) by placing the reason for the exile squarely on the people's sinfulness – thus exonerating God for this act of judgment (vv. 14-15) – in refusing to entreat God. Depending on one's dating of Daniel, this chapter might be reflective of the Second Temple period's sense of the ongoing 'exile' with a Jerusalem provenance or a Second Temple gloss into a sixth-century writing.[2] J. J. Collins distinguishes three attitudes to the temple in the Second Temple period, designating them as *priestly* (positive, e.g. Chronicles), *sectarian* (negative, e.g. *1 Enoch* 89.73; 93.9; *T. Levi* 16), and *non-priestly mainstream* (between the two extremes, e.g. Dan. 9).[3] Overall, central to Daniel's prayer for the restoration of Israel from exile is the restoration of the sanctuary (vv. 16-17).[4] However, that Daniel's attitude is less positive than, say, Ezra 9 or Neh. 1.9 is questionable, putting at stake its non-priestly designation.[5] The expectation is for the people to turn to God, love and keep his commandments (v. 4). Only on the basis of these 'right deeds' (צדקת) would they be able to appeal to God (v. 18) and the prayer presupposes that these expectations have not been met.[6] The 'restoration and restitution are now different experiences from those envisaged in the older expressions of covenant theology. Now, in the apocalyptic setting, they are cosmic in scope and eternal in consequence'.[7]

3.2.2. *Zechariah, Haggai, Malachi – Second Temple and the Apocalyptic Uprising*

These three post-exilic books give a glimpse of the lives of the returning exiles and of the remnants in the land of Palestine. The Mishnah presents these books together as a unified coda to the OT revelation indicating the possibility that they circulated as a corpus in the Second Temple period. With these prophets, a more eschatological vision of the temple, the priesthood, and the Davidic royal line emerge. Their appropriation of the tabernacle rather than temple motif evidences what we have seen earlier as the fascination with the

---

2.   John. E. Goldingay, *Daniel* (WBC 30; Dallas, Tex.: Word Books, 1989) 237, and André Lacocque, 'The Liturgical Prayer in Daniel 9', *HUCA* 47 (1976) 119–42, respectively.

3.   John J. Collins, *Daniel: With an Introduction to Apocalyptic Literature* (FOTL 20; Grand Rapids: Eerdmans, 1984) 90–5.

4.   The significance of the 'holy mountain of God' (הר קדש) is in relation to the 'sanctuary' (מקדש) (v. 17).

5.   Goldingay, *Daniel*, 238: 'Unlike Ezra 9; Neh. 9, however, it includes neither positive nor negative references to the priesthood...'

6.   Goldingay, *Daniel*, 249.

7.   W. Sibley Towner, *Daniel: A Bible Commentary for Teaching and Preaching* (Interpretation; Atlanta: John Knox Press, 1984) 135.

Mosaic tent as the ideal 'dwelling place of YHWH' in opposition to the permanent stationary temple, which, though recognized as the legitimate successor to the tabernacle, still remained inconclusive as to its ability to 'house' YHWH (1Kgs 8.27: 'But will God indeed dwell on the earth? Even heaven and the highest heaven cannot contain you, much less this house that I have built!').[8]

Recourse to tabernacle imagery also reflects a harking to the exodus theme as a template for analyzing the exile experience, the 'new exodus'. As such, the designation of YHWH as 'Lord of Hosts' envisions the universal power of YHWH over the nations and creation as a whole, ushering in a new age.[9] No doubt at the center of their messages of hope and restoration was the rebuilding of the temple that had lain in ruins for half a century or so during the period of exile. Continued neglect of the temple by the remnants was thus proffered as the reason for the people's continued hardships. And in spite of the Isaianic prophecies of a glorious restoration of the temple Haggai 2.3 reports that the anticipated majesty and glory spoken of the rebuilt temple was not in any way met by the edifice that was built under Zerubbabel;[10] and neither was the Davidic monarchy restored as expected (the glory and majesty of the first temple had been associated with the wealth of Solomon and the magnitude of his power, now missing). The restoration of the temple had fallen short of the prophetic expectations and could not be counted as the actual fulfillment of these prophecies.[11]

Following this disappointment there grew an eschatological expectation that foresaw yet a greater future time when there would be a majestic temple in Jerusalem which would be filled with wealth from the nations (Hag. 2.6-7; Mic. 4.1-5). Historically, however, Israel neither really prospered nor was politically powerful in intervening years, enough for any nation of the world to bring offerings to its temple. The eschatological expectations were not met by the second temple, nor was the Davidic monarchy restored through Zerubbabel. Therefore, it seemed clear that the prophetic words of the exilic prophets were unfulfilled and, therefore, had to await a later fulfillment.

---

8.   In *b. Yoma* 9b it is reported that, 'after the death of the last prophets Haggai, Zechariah and Malachi the Holy Spirit (of prophecy) departed from Israel, but they still availed themselves to the *bath qôl* (lit. 'daughter of a voice', 'echo' – trans. 'heavenly voice'), to be the continuing means, albeit inferior, by which God spoke in the post-exilic period.

9.   Paul L. Redditt, *Haggai, Zechariah, Malachi* (NCBC; London: Marshall Pickering; and Grand Rapids: William B. Eerdmans, 1995) 12, notes that the name appears 14 times in Haggai, 53 times in Zechariah, and 24 times in Malachi. 'Lord of Hosts' was initially connected with God at Shiloh in the pre-monarchical period (1 Sam. 1.13).

10.   According to Carol L. Meyers and Eric M. Meyers, *Haggai, Zechariah 1-8* (AB 25B; Garden City, NY: Doubleday, 1987) 73, the term כבוד here carried both economic and political connotations.

11.   The LXX also evinces this tendency to downplay the significance of the second temple by preferring to use the terms οἶκος (Zech. 6.9ff) to the commonly used cultic term for temple (ναός). Cf. W. von Meding, 'ναός', *NIDNTT* 3.782. The exception is Ps. 45(44).15.

3.3. *Extra-Canonical Jewish Writings*

3.3.1. 1 Enoch *83-90: Dream Visions/Animal Apocalypse*

The final great judgment looms large in *1 Enoch*, bringing 'to full expression the eschatological viewpoint that has been developing in the exilic and post exilic prophets, notably Jeremiah, Ezekiel, Second and Third Isaiah, Deutero Zechariah, Haggai and Malachi'.[12] In this early eschatological apocalypse (*ca.* 3-2 cent. BCE), claims are made concerning the impurity of the sacrifices offered on the altar of the temple as the basis for its destruction (89.73).[13]

In this '"zoomorphic" history of the world'[14] the concept of house is earlier used of God's heavenly abode – 'a house within a house' (*1 En.* 14.10-17; 71.5-9) and later, of the nation of Israel with the temple within it metaphorically referred to as the 'lofty tower' (89.50):[15]

> And that house was made large and wide; a lofty tower being built upon it by the sheep, for the Lord of the sheep. The house was low, but the tower was elevated and very high; and the Lord of the sheep stood on that tower and they offered a full table before him.

While it is possible to understand the reference here as epexegetical, so that both the house and the tower refer to the same object, it is unlikely given the distinction made in 89.76-77. All the sheep occupy 'the house', and there is the rebuilding/repairing of 'the tower' after the initial destruction, which fits well with the historical description of the exile (89.55-58) and the destruction (89.72-73) and eventual reconstruction of the temple and city, as recorded in the biblical books of Ezra-Nehemiah.[16]

---

12. George W. E. Nickelsburg, *1 Enoch 1* (Hermeneia; Minneapolis: Fortress Press, 2001) 55.

13. This section contains the oldest extant mss of *1 Enoch* dated as far back as 175 BCE by J. T. Milik, *The Books of Enoch, Aramaic Fragments of Qumran Cave 4* (Oxford: Oxford University Press, 1976) 41. More recently, Patrick A. Tiller, *A Commentary on the Animal Apocalypse of* 1 Enoch (SBLEJL 4; Atlanta, Ga.: Scholars Press, 1993) 61–79, has argued for a date closer to 165 BCE. Matthew Black, *The Book of Enoch or 1 Enoch: A New English Edition* (Leiden: E. J. Brill, 1985) 1–23. Nickelsburg, *1 Enoch 1*, 55, also dates the Dream Visions around 165 BCE, 'although a prior form *may* date to the end of the third century or beginning of the second century' (emphasis original).

14. Black, *Enoch*, 19.

15. The identity of the lofty tower with the Jerusalem temple is in accord with August Dillmann, *Das Buch Henoch: Übersetzt und erklärt* (Leipzig: F. C. W. Vogel, 1853; repr. New York: Unger, 1955) 257, and Nickelsburg, *1 Enoch 1*, 384; *contra* Black, *Enoch*, who identifies it as the 'Heavenly Temple', and James VanderKam, *Enoch and the Growth of an Apocalyptic Tradition* (Washington, D.C.: Catholic Biblical Association of America, 1984) 169–70, who identifies it as 'paradise'. Milik, *Books of Enoch*, 43, wants to combine the heavenly temple and the mountain-throne of God.

16. Nickelsburg, *1 Enoch 1*, 385.

More poignant is the subsequent description of the problem that follows the building of the temple after the exile.[17] They [priests] began to place before the table that stood in front of the tower 'every impure and unclean kind of bread' (89.73; cf. Isa. 28.7-21). It would seem from this evaluation that the priesthood and its *cultus* are blamed for the resultant extreme situation that befalls the sheep.[18] The defiling of the altar by the priests culminates in the destruction of the tower and, as such, blame for the exile is placed squarely on the priesthood of Israel.

In a 'pleasant land' (90.20), another throne is erected upon which the Lord of the sheep sat, opening up the books before the sheep. It is the judgment throne and the Lord of the sheep proceeds to judge the Shepherds who had killed more sheep than they should have. And following the destruction of this 'old house' (90.28) which is described in great detail, there is a new building which is constructed. As such, the new house that is built by 'the Lord of the sheep' himself is the new city of Jerusalem (90.29):

> And I saw until the Lord of the sheep brought a house, new and larger and loftier than the former, and he erected (it) in the place of the former one which had been rolled up. And all of its pillars were new and its beams were new and the ornaments were new and larger than the former old one which he had taken out. And all the sheep were in the midst of it.[19]

While the sheep were in this new house, other animals also came in subjection to it – the cosmic dimension. This could indicate a reaching out to the Gentiles to bring them into the Jewish faith or, more likely, their subjugation. Also, the Lord of the sheep does not seem to be living *above* in the lofty tower like he did in the previous temple, implying that he could be living *with* the sheep.

3.3.2. Testaments of the Twelve Patriarchs
From its use of the LXX, this is possibly the original work of a Hellenized Jew *circa* 250–150 BCE, in spite of the dozen or so Christian interpolations. The Christian interpolations betray a close affinity to Johannine thought, while the rest of the document evidences an openness to non-Jewish cultural insights and influences well beyond those being laid out by Josephus, *Ant.* 3.171-3.[20] For

---

17.   Frederic Manns, '"La maison où réside l'Esprit."1 P 2,5 et son arrière-plan juif', *SBFLA* 34 (1984) 207–24, 209. Nickelsburg, *1 Enoch 1*, 47.

18.   Jonathan A. Goldstein, *I Maccabees: A New Commentary with Introduction and Commentary* (AB; Garden City, NY: Doubleday, 1976) 42: 'Unlike the author of the Testament of Moses, the author of Enoch lxxxv–xc believed that the Second Temple was as much God's temple as the First, though the priests of the Second Temple did not properly observe the laws of purity, so that all offerings there were ritually impure (lxxxix 73)'.

19.   M. Black, *Enoch*, 82, translates the last sentence: 'And the Lord of the sheep was in the midst of it.'

20.   Howard Clark Kee, 'The Testaments of the Twelve: A New Translation and Introduction', in James H. Charlesworth, ed., *The Old Testament Pseudepigrapha I: Apocalyptic Literature and Testaments* (2 vols.; New York: Doubleday, 1985) 778.

example, the ethical exhortations are not presented to encourage obedience to the Law as is presented in the Torah, but in terms very similar to Stoicism.[21] The emphasis in this document is on the holiness of God (*T. Levi* 4.1; 18.1ff) and his wrath (*T. Levi* 6.11). While God is the one who executes judgment, he is also merciful and gracious. The temple is destroyed as a judgment of the people's sin – particularly the priests (*T. Levi* 10.3; 15.1; 16.4-5) and only later, in *T. Benj.* 9.2, are we told that the temple is rebuilt.

3.3.3. Jubilees

Scholarly consensus dates *Jubilees* to about the second century BCE and agrees that it was originally written in Hebrew.[22] *Jubilees,* the product of a priestly author, is a composite work made up of history, testament, apocalyptic, ritual law and chronology.[23] Presented with the authority of the 'normative orthodox position', *Jubilees* purports to contain the revelations to Moses during his forty days on Mount Sinai in Exod. 24.18. However, while exercising much freedom in omitting, condensing, and enlarging the different parts of the biblical story, the author is largely retelling the biblical narrative from Genesis to the early part of Exodus.[24] More importantly *Jubilees'* post-exilic retelling of Exodus in light of the Babylonian exile reflects in the former the current experiences of the latter event. The author uses the recurring cycles of seven-day weeks to structure his writing with periods of seven years being represented by what he calls a 'week of years' or simply 'week', e.g. 50.1-5. The period after the seven weeks of years (forty-nine years) is designated the year of Jubilee.

Abram is presented as a sojourner in the land of Canaan after being called out of Ur by God. He reaches the land around Bethel and builds an altar and makes a burnt offering to God after a promise of receiving the land from God (13.1-9). This happens again when he comes back to the area of Bethel and God, once again, promises to give land to Abram and his seed. After sacrificing another burnt offering, Lot separates from Abram to dwell in Sodom (13.15b-18).

The indication seems to be that the author wants to create a clear contrast between the symbolic House of God (Bethel) – the safe haven to which

21.   Kee, 'Testaments', 779.

22.   R. H. Charles, *The Ethiopic Version of the Hebrew Bible of Jubilees* (Oxford: Oxford University Press, 1895) had earlier argued for the Hebrew provenance but the matter was largely put to rest by the discovery of the Hebrew texts in Qumran and Masada. *Jubilees,* whose earliest mention is in Qumran text of CD 16.2-4 also uses the book of *1 Enoch* in 7.38-39. Nevertheless, unlike the Qumran writings, *Jubilees* does not reflect any significant break with the larger Jewish establishment that viewed the temple in Jerusalem as still valid.

23.   Michel Testuz, *Les Idées religieuses du livre des Jubilées* (Geneva: E. Droz, 1960) 11. Priestly authorship can be accounted for by the interest in festivals, sacred times and ritual details (e.g. 21.7-8).

24.   O. S. Wintermute, 'Jubilees: A New Translation and Introduction', in *OTP* 2.37.

Abram is brought by God 'in peace' – and Sodom, the place of sin outside of God's presence. In *Jubilees*, 'sanctuary' refers to the temple since the tabernacle is specifically named and identified (מֹשׁכָּן). Only after 49.18 does the author talk of the sanctuary being built and replacing the 'tabernacle of the Lord' (which is in the midst of the land and also called 'house of God') built 'in the name of the Lord in the land of their inheritance'. Thus, the instructions on eating the Passover meal (49.16-17), which appear before the instructions concerning the building of the temple (49.18ff), seem to be out of place.

Again, he talks of the 'house which is sanctified in the name of the Lord' in 49.20. In 49.20 he puts the two side by side when he states that 'they [children of Israel] shall not be able to observe the Passover in their cities or in any district except before the Tabernacle of the Lord or before his house in which his name dwells'.[25]

The author is distinguishing between the presence of God in the tabernacle versus the presence of the 'name of the Lord' in the house or temple. The distinction is probably dependent on the word 'tabernacle', which is the traditional language of incarnation in Jewish texts.[26] As Martin McNamara notes, the tabernacle is God's 'dwelling-place par excellence' and is in Hebrew called just that – מֹשׁכָּן.[27] This seems to be in line with the attitude that Chronicles has for the temple which is where the Lord causes his name to dwell, but it is a building which cannot contain God. The tabernacle was the dwelling of God among his people (49.19).

The end of all things will take place when God builds his temple and establishes his throne on Mt. Zion – the navel of the earth and the location of the new creation (4.26; 7.19) – out of which he will rule all the nations (1.17, 26-28). This will happen because the present earthly temple has been defiled (23.21) and must be replaced by a new one.[28] According to *Jubilees* this eschatological temple is in heaven awaiting to be revealed in the Last Days (24.32).

3.3.4. *Qumran and Dead Sea Scrolls: Community as Temple*
Relocating away from the temple, it was impossible for the Qumran community to offer sacrifices and as a result they justified their religious

25. Note in 7.36 there is reference to the 'house of the Lord' in which his servants served. It is unclear though whether the reference is to the temple or the tabernacle. The reference is in light of the servants of the Lord who serve before the altar.

26. As a reference to incarnation it is largely used of Wisdom. But see *Prayer of Joseph* (Frag. A) 4-5, where the angel of the Lord speaks on behalf of Jacob as one who had descended to the earth and had 'tabernacled among men'. The well known Christian reference that uses similar terminology is John 1.14.

27. Martin McNamara, ed., *Targum Neofiti 1: Genesis* (The Aramaic Bible, 1A; Collegeville, Minn.: Liturgical Press, 1992) 36. Cf. Exod. 25.8; 29.46; Num. 5.3; Ezek. 43.9, etc., where the verb שׁכַן is used in the sense of 'settle down', 'abide', 'dwell'.

28. R. G. Hamerton-Kelly, 'The Temple and the Origins of Jewish Apocalyptic', *VT* 20 (1970) 1–15, 1.

separation by viewing their community as a 'functional substitute for the Temple'.[29] The Qumran community, therefore, has a tendency to replace the animal sacrifices with sacrifices of 'praise and thanksgiving', of a 'humble spirit' and of 'an obedient life which is acceptable to God' (1QS 9.3-6, 26).[30] Schwartz offers three historical reasons he believes made it possible for some of the Jewish communities of the Second Temple period to move the locus of sanctity from the temple to elsewhere: a) the spread of the Hasmonean kingdom to include non-Jews and so the need to explain how they could rule the Gentiles, b) criticism of the legitimacy and morality of the Jerusalem priesthood during the same period, and c) spread of Hellenism in Palestine where the maxim – 'If the temple is the house of God then it is where God is, so wherever God is, is a temple' – became standardized.

The difficulty of relating Hellenistic influence on the Qumran community based on their literature, which was mostly in Hebrew, is explained by the premise that contextually the covenanters must have 'breathed the air of the time'. While the reformulation of the *cultus* that emerged from this framework of thinking helped highlight some of the developments made by the covenanters in the realm of worship, it nevertheless created some complications in determining the nature of temple references in the DSS.

The term used for sanctuary/temple in Qumran is מקדש, and it has both literal and figurative usages.[31] Just as it is clear that there is more than one theology in the Qumran material, so it is difficult to find major consistency in the variegated and large volume of materials that comprise the DSS concerning the temple. It is quite uncertain if there existed a unified view of the temple among the DSS where several views prevailed.

First, the community viewed itself as a replacement of the Jerusalem temple, referring to themselves as the מקדש אדם – 'sanctuary/temple of Men' (4QFlor 1.6).[32] Whether this was the historical temple, either the first

---

29.   1QS 9.5-6; 8.4-11; 11.8; CD 3.19–4.4. Cf. Gärtner, *Temple*, 78; Klinzing, *Umdeutung*, 11–20; Lichtenberger, 'Atonement', 159–71; Daniel R. Schwartz, 'Temple and Desert: On Religion and State in Second Temple Period Judaea', in *Studies in the Jewish Background of Christianity* (Tubingen: J. C. B Mohr, 1992) 38.

30.   Schwartz, *Studies*, 38–41.

31.   There are about seven heavens acknowledged by the Qumran material, each with its own מקדש (4Q201 4.7; Cf. also *3 Enoch* 18) while the term, in the literal sense, is consistently used in the DSS to refer to the temple in Jerusalem.

32.   Devorah Dimant, '4QFlorilegium and the Idea of the Community as Temple', in A. Caquot *et al.*, eds., *Hellenica et Judaica: Hommage B V. Nikiprowetzky* (Leuven and Paris: Peters, 1986) 165-89, who holds that the term was coined by the covenanters to distinguish it from the other two temple concepts that share the term with it, namely, the 'Temple of Yahweh' (1.3) and the 'Temple of Israel' (1.6) resulting in its having an 'analogical function to the Solomonic Temple' (177–8). The idea that the phrase מקדש אדם refers to the eschatological temple made up of the community of covenanters ('a Temple consisting of men') latent with the idea of community as temple – later to be taken over by Christians – has been argued by Gärtner, *Temple*, 30-42, and partly built upon by Klinzing, *Umdeutung*, 80–7.

temple[33] or the second temple,[34] or both,[35] or the future 'eschatological temple',[36] remains pretty much a matter in dispute. The publication of the Temple Scroll (11QTemp) put some serious questions on the previous confidence of the spiritual interpretation of the phrase מקדש אדם.[37] The Temple Scroll anticipates a physical eschatological temple but it is not always clear whether the references are to one or two temples.[38] A suggestion has been put forward that perhaps there are references to three temples – Solomon's temple, second temple and the future eschatological temple interspersed in the Temple Scroll.[39] An alternative suggestion is that there would be an 'interim' temple, between the contemporary Jerusalem temple and the future eschatological temple yet to be built.[40] Be that as it may, the scrolls seem to describe the expectation of what the idealized present reality should be which is in contrast with the contemporary Herodian temple.[41]

33.   M. Ben-Yashar, 'Noch zum Miqdaš ĀDĀM in 4QFlorilegium', RevQ 10 (1981) 586–7.

34.   D. Flusser, 'Two Notes on the Midrash on 2 Sam vii', IEJ (1959) 99–109 (102), adopted and modified by Dimant, '4QFlorilegium', 175, n. 21.

35.   Dimant, '4QFlorilegium', 175. 'If this interpretation is correct, what the pesher is actually saying is that God ordered a Temple of Men to be built for him because the Temple of Israel was desolated and the eschatological Temple was yet to be built. In other words the Temple of Men represents an interim stage between the Temple of Israel past (and present) and the eschatological Temple of the future.' The result would be a three-level gradation with ascending levels of purity parallel to the 'land/city/temple' gradation.

36.   Ben Zion Wacholder, The Dawn of Qumran: The Sectarian Torah and the Teacher of Righteousness (Monographs of the Hebrew Union College 8; New York: Ktav, 1983), 21–4, 46–7; Barbara Thiering, 'Mebaqqer and Episkopos in the Light of the Temple Scroll', JBL 100 (1981) 58–74 [60–1]. Gärtner, Temple, 30–42, argues primarily for an eschatological temple in 4QFlor. But this is challenged by J. M. Baumgarten, 'Sacrifice and Worship among the Jewish Sectarians of the Dead Sea (Qumran) Scrolls', HTR 45 (1953) 141–59. A. Jaubert, 'La notion d'Alliance dans les judaïsme aux abords de l'ère chrétienne' in Patristica Sorbonensia (Paris: Éditions du Seuil, 1963) 152–63, seems to find a compromise by interpreting the temple in 4QFlor 1.1-7 as a material temple to be built in the eschatological age, but still remaining a material temple.

37.   The translation remains ambiguous as to whether it should be translated as 'temple made by men', 'a temple made up of men', or 'a temple among men'.

38.   Cf. Y. Yadin, The Temple Scroll, vol. 1 (Jerusalem: Israel Exploration Society, 1977) 143–4.

39.   Daniel R. Schwartz, 'The Three Temples of 4QFlorilegium', RevQ 10 (1979) 83–91.

40.   Dimant, '4QFlorigelium', 179 n. 35, credits Schwartz with the identification of the three temples, but questions the identification of the 'temple of men' with the Solomonic temple. Further distinctions highlighted by Jacob Milgrom, 'New Temple Festivals in the Temple Scroll', in The Temple in Antiquity (ed. T. G. Madsen; Provo, Ut.: Brigham Young University Press, 1984), 132, is that while the second temple was considered by the covenanters as polluted, the temple outlined in the Temple Scroll was to be built by men as its replacement, but it would not itself be the messianic temple which would be built at the end of time, 'not by humans', but by God.

41.   Florentino García Martínez, 'The Temple Scrolls', NEA 66/3 (2000) 172–4, feels that the Temple Scroll in particular does not describe a future eschatological temple but a present temple because of the clear reference in 11QTemp 19.9-10 that the same magnificent temple will be replaced by another one built by God.

Second, in the *Rule of the Congregation* (1QS 9.5-6), the reference seems to be to a future rather than present state; 'At that time, the men of the community will constitute a true and distinctive temple – a veritable holy of holies – wherein the priesthood may fitly foregather, and a true and distinctive synagogue made up of laymen who walk in integrity'.[42] At the same time, the *Damascus Document* (CD) seems to preserve an anticipation for the restoration of the *cultus* and the purification of the Jerusalem temple (CD 6.1-11). Davies concludes his study by stating,

> In brief, the ideology of the temple in CD is that it is no longer the seat of the law. The temple itself is not rejected, nor has it been defiled in some specific act. Indeed, it may be suggested that the temple as such is not really an issue in CD at all, but merely one practical problem which is dealt with in terms of the overriding concern of CD: V,12, the observance of the law.[43]

But it is hard not to see the temple as polluted even though the focus is on the law since constant warnings are to do with those that did defile the temple in the past (e.g. CD 5.1-11). This is exactly what Ellen Christiansen argues for, and concludes that '... CD ties the motivation for law obedience to the command to separate clean and unclean, holy and profane, by means of which covenant is interpreted narrowly as *priestly* covenant (CD 6.17; 7.3)'.[44] Similarly, 11QTemp seems to presuppose a later restoration of the present Jerusalem temple following its present defilement by those who have entered into it unclean by laying out a master plan of the building (or rebuilding) of the temple.

Adjoined to these building directions are instructions on how not to defile the temple once it has been restored (11QTemp 46.2-18; cf. also CD 4.17-18; 6.3-10). This they will be able to do partly because they will keep the law which includes the avoidance of plundering widows, temple wealth, or murder of orphans, and building latrines outside of the holy city. These, not surprisingly, also constituted the accusations covenanters leveled against those they

---

42.   Yadin, *Scroll*, 143.

43.   Philip R. Davies, 'The Ideology of the Temple in the Damascus Document', *JJS* 33 (1982) 287–301. This is exactly what Ellen Christiansen argues for in her article 'The Consciousness of Belonging To Gods Covenant and What it Entails According to the Damascus Document and the Community Rule', in Frederick H. Cryer and Thomas L. Thompson, eds., *Between the Old and the New*, 69–97, 76–77 (emphasis original).

44.   Temple defilement is constantly referred to in the Qumran documents. In CD 4.17-18 temple defilement is equated to the other 'two' nets of Belial, namely, fornication and wealth. The defilement is blamed on sleeping with wives during the women's menstrual periods, marrying of one's nieces (or uncles), blasphemy, and disobedience against God's statutes (CD 5.6-11).

accused of defiling the temple in Jerusalem. The whole community's participation in the washing rites and the ritual cleansing, in the fashion of the OT
priests, supports the idea of the community's self-perception as a priesthood,
with *only* the covenanters presented as able to enter the temple without
defiling it (CD 6.11).[45]

Therefore, interested in maintaining the cultic ceremonies, the covenanters
oscillated between interest in the concrete temple and the anticipated eschatological temple (11QTemp 19.9-10).[46] Curiously, in spite of being extremely
critical of the concrete temple, the covenanters sometimes seemed to coalesce
the two with the anticipated purification and restoration of the existing
temple constantly mixed with the condemnations of the same temple in light
of its present desecration and pollution, as doomed for destruction.

Such tension may have led to the covenanters' self-perception as the 'temple-
like community' which, while it functionally could not replace the Jerusalem
temple, remained essentially the reconfiguration and re-appropriation of the
temple's role by the community so as to retain what it envisioned as a legitimate claim to being the true locus of God's presence.[47] As such, the
community's worship became analogous to (or even complementary to), and
contemporary of the actual temple's services.[48]

Therefore, as Carol Newsom insists, the purpose of the *Songs of the Sabbath
Sacrifice* (4QShirShabb) – with its angelic priesthood[49] – was not to replace the
polluted temple cult but acted as a 'praxis' that connected the worshipers to the
heavenly temple in a way that the futuristic 'eschatological temple' was experienced in the present.[50] A. T. Lincoln, in essential agreement, points out that:

45.   At the same time, the community maintained a gradation of status with some like the
'Teacher of Righteousness' assuming a more significant role in the community life and on cultic
matters, since it is a temple made of the house of Aaron (priests) and Israel (laity). Purity not only
marks out the different levels within the community, it also distinguishes between the members
of the community, and the outsiders. It is for the sake of maintaining purity that separation of
the outside world must occur for the Qumran covenanters. Cf. Raymond Brown, J. A. Fitzmyer
and J. Murphy-O'Connor, *The Jerome Biblical Commentary* (Englewood Cliffs, NJ: Prentice-
Hall, 1968) 2.554.

46.   García Martínez, 'Scrolls', 172.

47.   Dimant, '4QFlorilegium', 187. Note also the *Hodayot* and *Songs of Sabbath Sacrifice*
where the community understands itself as being in the heavenly realms evidenced by the
presence of angels in their midst. Cf. 4Q400 2, 2-3, and 1QM 12.1-3.

48.   Dimant, '4QFlorilegium',187. If the interest was to recreate not the temple but rather
the 'congregation of priests', as Dimant suggests, then this has obvious affinities to 1 Peter 2.6-
8, where the body of believers is identified as 'a holy priesthood'.

49.   The key lies in the translation of the word אל והי‍ם. García Martínez, *Dead Sea Scrolls*,
translates it as 'gods' while Carol Newsom, 'Merkabah Exegesis in the Qumran Sabbath Shirot',
JJS 38 (1987) 11–30, 13, understands it to refer to angels. Cf. also C. Newsom, *Songs of the
Sabbath Sacrifice* (Harvard Semitic Studies 27; Atlanta: Scholars Press, 1985) 18-19.

50.   C. Newsom, 'He has Established for Himself Priests: Human and Angelic Priesthood
in the Qumran Sabbath Shirot', in L. H. Schiffman, ed., *Archeology and History in the Dead Sea
Scrolls* (Sheffield: JSOT Press, 1990) 116. Margaret Barker, *The Gate of Heaven: The History*

At Qumran the place of future fellowship with the angels was thought of not only as heaven or the heavenly sanctuary but also as the eschatological Temple (cf. 4QF/ I, 4; 1QSb IV, 25) and since the community understood itself as the eschatological Temple (cf. 1QS VIII, 4ff; XI, 3ff) it could hold that participation with the angels in worship was already taking place.[51]

The covenanters still anticipated the rebuilding of the eschatological temple (following the destruction?/purification? of the present one) as evidenced by their structural outline of the heavenly temple in the pattern of Ezek. 40–48.[52] But what were the hymns for if there was no temple? Were they to be sung in the future temple? Or were they sung proleptically given that the community was the temple?

Given that no temple was actually found in Qumran, it is reasonable to assume that the temple in view in the scrolls was the physical historical temple of Jerusalem. Yet covenanters expected a God-made sanctuary to appear only at the end time.[53] Since Qumran eschatology maintained the perception that the end time was the period in which they were living, it really does little to clarify which temple is in focus.[54] Self-identification of the covenanters with the temple explains their rigorous observation of matters of purity given that the temple has to be kept perpetually pure (4Q400 1.14-16; 4QMMT).[55] While partially explaining the reason for the polemical references to the temple and priesthood in Jerusalem, there remains the expectation that the Qumran covenanters would inherit the Jerusalem temple in the future (1QM 2.3; 7.11).[56]

In conclusion, the stipulations in the Dead Sea Scrolls concerning the temple, priesthood and eschatology are variegated and multivalent with some of the writings equivocating about the present Herodian temple as *the* temple of God

of the Temple in Jerusalem (London: SPCK, 1991) 61, '... in the Song of the Sabbath Sacrifices the angel figures on the Temple walls are alive because the songs describe the heavenly Temple'.

51.   A. T. Lincoln, *Paradise Now and Not Yet: Studies in the Role of the Heavenly Dimension in Paul's Thought With Special Reference to his Eschatology* (SNTSMS 43; Cambridge: Cambridge University Press, 1981) 149.

52.   Pilchan Lee, *The New Jerusalem in the Book of Revelation: A Study of Revelation in Light of its Background in Jewish Tradition* (WUNT 2 Reihe 129; Tübingen: Mohr Siebeck, 2001) 110.

53.   Y. Yadin, 'Discussion', in Avram Biran, ed., *Temples and High Places in Biblical Times: Proceedings of the Colloquium in Honor of the Centennial Hebrew Union College – Jewish Institute of Religion, Jerusalem, 14–16 March 1977* (Jerusalem: Nelson Glueck School of Biblical Archeology of Hebrew Union College – Jewish Institute of Religion, 1981) 29.

54.   The community was living in the last days, but it also had the provision that God would prolong these last days in His own mysterious plan (1QpHab 7.1-8).

55.   See Richard Bauckham, 'Josephus' Account of the Temple in *Contra Apionem* 2:102-109', in Louis H. Freedman and John R. Levison, eds., *Josephus' Contra Apionem* (Leiden: Brill, 1996) 327–47. Gradations of temple, Jerusalem, Israel, cf. Josephus, *Contra Apionem.*, 2.102-104; *m.Kelim* 1.6-9, which expands the different levels of holiness to between 10 and 11.

56.   Shemaryahu Talmon, 'Waiting for the Messiah: The Spiritual Universe of the Qumran Covenanters', in Neusner *et al.*, eds., *Judaisms*, 97–137.

while for others it is simply *a* temple structure that stands on the Holy mount that would eventually be replaced by *the* eschatological temple of God. In this regard, the Temple Scroll presents the ideal temple which Solomon should have built when he built the first temple, but did not, and which still remains a utopian dream yet to be achieved (anticipated to find fulfillment in the end times). In essence, then, the realistic and the utopian are interwoven such that the ideal is the real.[57] One is not always sure which one of the two is being referred to in the Qumran texts. And so, rather than understanding Qumran to possess a three-temple perspective, *á la* Daniel Schwartz, they actually have just two – the Jerusalem temple, and the eschatological or ideal temple.[58] The latter is variously presented and interpreted by the community documents. The complexity is such that the ideal was only partly realized in the first and second temples and, therefore, the inadequacies highlighted by the covenanters are accompanied by the anticipation of a yet more perfect structure.

3.3.5. *Philosophical Judaism: The Ambulatory Temple*
Like the DSS, Philosophical Judaism does not seem to have had one general opinion concerning the temple. Two contrasting views of the temple, negative and positive, emerge from these writings held together in uneasy tension. We will first examine how this situation looked before examining each of the writings in its own developments.

3.3.5.1. *Positive and Negative views of the Temple in Philo, Josephus and Jubilees*
Towards the end of the first century BCE – following the expansion of the temple by Herod – a more or less positivist view of the temple was developed as seen in Philo of Alexandria, Josephus and *Jubilees*.[59] Philo spiritualizes and *de*historicizes the coming messianic age with the result that 'it is God alone who moves the people by the collective and unseen vision to give up their places and nations in the Diaspora'.[60] Philo had something of a 'realized eschatology' where specific elements that could be nationalized and identified with certain historical figures in Jewish thinking were made allegorical designators for the Logos.[61]

For Philo, the two seemingly contradictory elements could be held together side by side because the Jews of the Dispersion could find fulfillment in exile (as

---

57. *Contra* Dimant, '4Florilegium', 177, who states that this is 'an interim stage between the Temple of Israel of the past (and present) and the eschatological Temple of the future'. Cf. Maier, *Scroll*, 59, who notes that in Ezek. 40ff, there is the image of the large gulf that had developed between the real and the ideal ritual conceptions in the First Temple.

58. Maier, *Scroll*, 59.

59. The Babylonian Talmud also gives glowing tribute to the Herodian structure (*Baba Bathra* 4a): 'He who has not seen the Herodian building, has never seen a beautiful thing.'

60. Richard D. Hecht, 'Philo and Messiah', in Neusner *et al.*, eds., *Judaisms*, 139–68, 162.

61. Ibid.

Philo himself did), yet honor and desire for the homeland remained the 'prime legacy of all'.[62] In *De Praemiis et Poenis*, 29.94-97 the return of Israelite captives from the Dispersion is only after instruction by chastisement, repentance, and turning to virtue. Restoration of cities that once lay in ruins would be followed by abundant prosperity.[63]

Josephus echoes much of what Philo says by seeing no reason to be ashamed by the state of exile, even as it remains a reality whose end has to be desired to with hopeful anticipation.[64] The exile can be described as worse than death because, while death ends troubles, 'banishment (φυγή) is not the end but the beginning of other new misfortunes and entails in place of the one death which puts an end to pains a thousand deaths in which we do not lose sensation' (Philo, *De Abrahamo*, 14.64) While it has been observed that Josephus never uses the term φυγή to describe the exile of Israel, it is clear that the idea is not missing in this passage.[65] On other occasions, when Josephus does refer to the Israelite exile he usually turns to the typical LXX vocabulary of μετοικίζω and αἰχμαλωσία (e.g. *Ant.* 11.1, 91; 20.231; *C. Ap.* 1.132; 2.38) – usually a reference to a colony (ἀποικία) with self-governing councils (Philo, *De Vita Mosis*, 2.232).

As such, and perhaps not surprisingly, both Philo and Josephus have a glowing perspective of the temple based on its later modification and enlargement (or rebuilding) by Herod.[66] Josephus intones;

> The exterior of the building wanted nothing that could astound either mind or eye. For, being covered on all sides with massive plates of gold, the sun was no sooner up than it radiated so fiery a flash that persons straining to look at it were compelled to avert their eyes, as from the solar rays. To approaching strangers it appeared from a distance like a snow-clad mountain; for all that was not overlaid with gold was of purest white. (*War* 5:222-224)[67]

---

62.   Philo, *In Flaccum*, 7.45-47: 'So populous are the Jews that no one country can hold them, and therefore they settle in very many of the most prosperous countries in Europe and Asia both in the islands and on the mainland, and while they hold the Holy City where stands the sacred Temple of the Most High God to be their mother city, yet those which are theirs by inheritance from their fathers, grandfathers, and ancestors even farther back, are in the each case accounted by them to be their fatherland.' Cf. also Gruen, *Diaspora*, 252.

63.   Sanders, *Jesus*, 86. While the temple is not explicitly mentioned, according to Sanders, the rebuilding of the cities assumes its restoration.

64.   Josephus, *Ant.* 10.100. Josephus perceives it wiser to give up oneself to an invading power than let the temple and land be destroyed. Given Josephus' apologetic agenda – presenting Jewish history and faith to the Hellenistic world – his advice and opinions must be understood in terms of an effort to ingratiate his religion to Greco-Romans.

65.   Louis H. Feldman, 'The Concept of Exile in Josephus', in Scott, ed., *Exile*, 145–72, 147. The word φυγή occurs in Josephus no less than 147 times but does not even once refer to Israelite exile.

66.   The *Letter of Aristeas* (2nd c. BCE), in line with the Chronicler, presents the temple in positive light, perhaps a reflection of the idealization of the temple by the Jews in Dispersion.

67.   Josephus, *The Jewish War* (Loeb Classical Library; Cambridge, Mass.: Harvard University Press, 1976), cf. 3.269.

He also expresses strong emotion following its destruction: 'Deeply one must mourn for the most marvelous edifice which we have ever seen or heard of, whether we consider its structure, its magnitude, the richness of its every detail, or the reputation of its Holy Places' (*War* 6.267). However, Josephus' apologetic impulse calls for the treatment of such expressions with caution since they must be assumed to be uttered with a tinge of exaggeration for the sake of presenting to Romans the Israelite religion in positive light.

Concurrently, Josephus conveys a positive view of the exile, encouraging his country folk to surrender, arguing that by so doing they would win the war (*War* 5.389-390; cf. *C. Ap.* 1.32).[68] While Josephus' only use of the verb διασπείρω (*Ant.* 8.271) is negative – making reference to it as punishment much in the same way it is used in 1 Kgs 14.15 – he, nevertheless, still felt the need to cater to a Jewish readership (*Ant.* 1.4; 4.197) necessitating his attempt to explain his apparent contradictions.[69] Philo, on the other hand, defends life at a distance from Jerusalem (ἀποικία) as the result of over-population of the homeland and not of transgression (*Vit. Mos.* 2.232; *Leg. All.* 281-82; *Conf. Ling.* 78). In contrast to Philo, who anticipates the ingathering of the Jewish people from exile (*Praem.* 29.165), Josephus perceives the Jewish exile as a permanent state with no anticipated end.[70]

Jubilees spiritualizes both the return from exile, and the land, by presupposing that Israel's failure to keep the covenant with God is inevitable until the dawn of eschatological salvation (1.7-14; cf. Deut. 31.14-21).[71] The election of the descendant of Jacob, and not the return to the land, is the primary focus with God assuring Moses of a post-exilic restoration and eschatological spiritual transformation of Israel. Whether this has occurred by the time of the author is not possible to tell from the text (1.12-26; cf. 23.26, 27-31).

While Eden is in the land, a return to the land is not a return to Eden. That has to wait for a new time 'when the heaven and all earth shall be renewed …', 'When Zion and Jerusalem shall be holy' and 'the sanctuary of the Lord is created in Jerusalem upon Mount Zion' (1.28-29).[72] This is further confirmation of *Jubilees'* view of its present state as one still in anticipation of restoration – a state of bondage without the necessary purity in the temple but anticipating the *eschaton* to establish this missing purity, once and for all.

The end of all things will happen when God builds his temple and establishes his throne on Mt. Zion – the navel of the earth and the location of the

---

68. The appeal, however, is earnest since the Babylonian exile is referenced as a negative example of that which is undesirable.

69. Gruen, *Diaspora*, 252, feels that the Diaspora Jews did not see the need to reconcile the seeming contradiction.

70. Feldman, 'Concept of Exile', in Scott, ed., *Exile*, 164ff.

71. Betsy Helpern-Amaru, 'Exile and Return in Jubilees', in Scott, ed., *Exile*, 127–44.

72. Ibid., 143; John Sietze Bergsma, 'The Jubilee: A Post-Exilic Priestly Attempt to Reclaim Land?', *Biblica* 84/2 (2003) 225–46, answers the question he raises in the negative.

new creation (4.26; 7.19) – out of which he will rule all the nations (1.17, 26-28). This would happen because the present earthly temple had been defiled (23.21) and must be replaced by a new eschatological temple in heaven awaiting revelation in the 'last days' (23.22).[73]

3.3.5.2. *Tabernacle/Temple in Philo*

Philo, who was primarily an exegete, chose to focus his apologetic writings on Moses 'the blessed Law giver', meaning he seldom invokes other parts of the Scriptures, and then only as they relate to the Mosaic text. For this reason, Philo does not quite deal with the Jerusalem temple except as a projection backwards to the symbolism in the tabernacle (cf. also Josephus, *Ant.* 3.115-133). In language reminiscent of 1 Peter 2.4-10, Philo makes reference of the Βασίλειον and ἱεράτευμα (*De Sobrietate* 66.1). However, in Philo, Βασίλειος is the adjective 'royal' used substantively to mean 'royal place' or 'royal house' (palace). This is perhaps the only text in Philo where interpretation of the sanctuary is in relation to the collective rather than the individual. Concerning Jacob, the symbolic referent to the nation Israel, Philo notes:

> Jacob is the source of the twelve tribes, of whom the oracles say that they are 'the palace (Βασίλειον) and the priesthood of God (ἱεράτευμα θεοῦ)' (Ex XIX: 6), thus following in due sequence the thought originated in Shem, in whose houses it was prayed that God might dwell (<ἐν>οικῆσαι). For surely by 'palace' is meant the King's house, which is holy indeed and the only inviolable sanctuary (ἱερός).[74]

While the rest of his references focus primarily on the individual, the statement above shows that the conceptualization of the sanctuary in light of a collective was not foreign, at least, to Hellenistic Judaism.[75] And so while the ultimate referent for Philo remains the individual, here we find an exception that clearly shows the awareness of collective understanding in theological interpretation in Hellenistic Judaism.[76] However, apart from that difference with 1 Peter, Philo's other conceptions of the temple are significant in relation to our epistle. In answering the question 'What is the tabernacle?' (*QE* 1.2.49-106; cf. Exod. 26.1a; *Vit. Mos.* 2.73), Philo makes certain observations.

---

73. Hamerton-Kelly, 'Temple', 1.
74. It is significant to note that the verb ἐνίκεω is known to Philo since as Gärtner, *Temple*, 52–3, indicates, it is missing in the LXX.
75. Philo's was an apologetic endeavor of presenting Judaism in Greek utilizing not only the Greek language but also Greek philosophical frameworks and paradigms. As a result of this it has been argued that Philo represents a distinctly different stream of Judaism from that of the Rabbis.
76. Coppens, 'Spiritual', 63, feels that the sequence of this reference 'seems to restrict the vision to the individual soul' and so it might not be quite the exception one may consider it to be. See also Philo, *Vit. Mos.* ii: 73.

First, 'the tabernacle is a portable temple (φορητόν ἱερόν) of God and not a stationary or fixed one' (*QE* 2.83).[77] The tabernacle has both a 'corporeal' (intelligible side), and 'sense-perceptible world' (τοῦ αἰσθήματος) side. The temple and the tabernacle are thus equated by Philo. The one is the replica of the other with the only difference being that one is permanent and stationary while the other is ambulatory. It is the character of mobility that is of importance for Philo since it designates, just as was experienced by the Israelites in the wilderness, a visible presence of God that has no geographical limitations.[78]

Subsequently for Philo, '... every house became an altar and a temple of God for the contemplative...' during the Passover and that is why they were painted with blood on the door frames (*QE* 1.12). In so doing, Philo decentralizes the place of the temple in the life of the Jews by designating the presence of God as spread abroad in the houses of the Israelites. It would seem that this is one of the reasons that led Baudouin Decharneux to conclude that for Philo, the temple and the holy land of Israel were places where the spirit blows, but were not strictly necessary for the practice of the Jewish religion.[79] Yet while it is true that Philo is interested in presenting a more universally applicable Judaism, the concrete elements of the temple and the land of Israel maintain great significance.

Second, the tabernacle and temple are given a cosmic interpretation. For Philo, the tabernacle has an allegorical function as the bodily representation of the presence of God in the world. In Platonic fashion, he talks of 'the divine temple of the Creator' woven of 'such things as the world is made of' since it is the 'universal temple' (τό πανίερός) that was in existence before the 'holy temple' (*QE* 2.85).[80] The presumption here is that the earthly temple is a replica of the universal one and that indeed the universe becomes the temple of God (Cf. *Vit. Mos.*2.88). In *Spec.* 1.12, 66, he argues that 'the highest, and in the truest sense the holy, temple of God is, as we must believe, the whole universe, having for its sanctuary the most sacred part of all existence, even heaven, for its votive ornaments the stars, for its priests the angels'.

Third, Philo regards the rational soul (σόφος) as the sanctuary of God. *QE* 1.2.52: 'For the beginning and the end of happiness is to be able to see God. But this cannot happen to him who has not made his soul, as I said before, a sanctuary and altogether a shrine of God.' He refers to Lev. 26.12 as incul-

---

77. D. T. Runia, 'How to Read Philo', *Nederlands Theologisch Tijdschrift* 40/3 (1986), 185–98.

78. Baudouin Decharneux, 'De Israel Historique au Judaisme Universal: Histoire religieuse de l'annexation territoriale de l'univers', in Jeanne-Françoise Vincent, Raymond Verdier, and Daniel Dory, eds., *La Construction Religieuse de Territoire* (Paris: Ed. l'Harmattan, 1995) 55–65.

79. For Philo, both the physical object and the allegorical interpretation are of equal significance since the allegorical interpretation does not negate the corporeal temple.

80. Robert G. Zimmer, 'The Temple of God', *JETS* 18 (1975) 41–6, 43. Plato's concept of the *idea* as found in his *Republic* seems to form the background for Philo's parallel of the heavenly temple.

cating the presence of God in the soul of the 'wise man'/'rational soul' and goes on to talk of the human being as 'an animate/spiritual (πνευματικόν or ἔμψυχον) shrine of the Father', better than or of more value than the stone structure in Jerusalem.

In this respect Philo sounds very much like the Roman Stoics of the first century such as Seneca, the Stoic philosopher/statesman who states – concerning man as God's dwelling – that, 'God is near you, he is with you, he is within you...a holy spirit (*sacer spiritus*) indwells within us, one who marks our good and bad deeds and is our guardian (*custos*). As we treat this spirit, so are we treated.'[81] The anticipated end result of this Stoic teaching is some form of human deification as the seeker identifies with the divine via philosophy, 'For that is what philosophy promises to me, that I shall be made equal with God.'[82]

Unlike the Qumran community with the view of itself as a collective temple, Philo's (and the Stoics') views of the body as temple remained very individualistic concepts.[83] However, Philo does not abandon the physical temple building. In fact, he denounces those who with 'easy-going neglect' would disregard the physical requirements of the Torah concerning sacrifices in the temple (*Migr. Abr.* 16.89; 91-93).[84] For this reason he maintains, together with his countrymen, that he values the physical temple more than his own life (*Leg. Gai.* 29.192; 32.230, 233-236; 39.308). So, while he admits that there is need for the physical temple 'made by hands', he maintains that there has to be 'only one temple'.[85]

3.3.5.3. Josephus and the Mobile Temple

Josephus, in his intent to ground the tabernacle in historical permanency, retrojects the conception of the existing temple back onto the tabernacle: 'For of these materials did Moses build the tabernacle, which indeed was no other than a portable and itinerant temple' (*Ant.* 3.102-4). It might have been Josephus' apologetic impulse to show that the Jewish faith always had a temple, i.e. the tabernacle, even if it did not have a permanent *topos* like a temple usually does. The temple is thus equated to the tabernacle in so far as they share commonalities.

---

81. Seneca, *Epistulae Morales* (LCL) 41.1.

82. Seneca, *Epistulae Morales*, 48.11. Cf. also Epictetus, *Discourses* I (LCL) 14.13f, 'God is within you, and your own genius is within you'.

83. Notice that even Paul, while also understanding the individual body as the temple of the Holy Spirit, still expresses it in light of a corporate reality (1 Cor. 6.16-19; 2 Cor. 6.16).

84. Yet, for Philo, it is the mind that is purifying itself (a *noumenal* experience) and not some moral or practical holiness. In his neo-Platonic interpretation, it is the mind (νους) beholding the 'divine light' (τον νοητον ἥλιον). The literal understanding is a reference to the tent, but the deeper/allegorical meaning (το προς διάνοιαν) is an apprehension of the mind (*QE* 2.51).

85. Harry Austyn Wolfson, *Philo: Foundations of Religious Philosophy in Judaism, Christianity, and Islam* (Cambridge, Mass.: Harvard University Press, 1947) 2.247.

The entreaty of God to send a 'portion' of his Spirit (*Ant.* 8.114) seems to be reflective of Josephus' struggle to reconcile both immanence and the transcendence of God, as we have seen to be true of other Jewish writers.[86] Writing after the destruction of the temple, he was less eager to defend it as the residence of God and rather apportions the interpretation of immanence to others as a '... *token* of God's presence, and, *as men thought*, of his habitation in this newly built and consecrated place'.[87] For, according to Josephus, God's abode is in heaven and therefore only a portion of his being, i.e. his Spirit, can dwell among the people in the temple (Cf. *Ant.* 3.100, 202, 290; 8.102, 106, 117, 131). He thus speaks of the cloud that covered the temple as the Lord 'pitching his tabernacle' in the temple (*Ant.* 8.4.2).

Congruently, Josephus could also talk of the temple as the meeting point between God, whose abode is the 'vaults of heaven', and the people who live on earth.[88] The whole tabernacle then represents the universe: 'In fact, every one of these objects is intended to recall and represent the universe' (*Ant.* 3.183; cf. *War* 5.212-13).[89]

And so when he talks of the destruction of the temple in the form of prophecy *ex eventu*, he puts the blame on the sinful disobedience of Israel resulting in an act of God delivering the temple to Israel's enemies (*Ant.* 8.4.5). For this reason, the veil symbolically separates the heavenly tent of the Creator and the earthly dwelling of the creation. The temple is the sacred space where the people of God can get a glimpse of the eternal God; a place, though poor in comparison with the majestic Creator, where the mortal can connect with the immortal.[90]

Josephus ultimately interprets the destruction of the temple as a sign of the fulfillment of God's prophetic judgment which had already been passed on the second temple years earlier(*War* 6.249-50), controversially noting that the destruction of the first temple occurred on the exact same date as that of the second (10th of the fifth month) did under the Babylonians (some five hundred years earlier) intoning simply that the fateful and inevitable time had arrived.[91]

---

86.   John R. Levison 'The Debut of the Divine Spirit in Josephus's *Antiquities*', *HTR* 87 (1994) 123-38, argues for identification of a Stoic portrait of the Spirit in this section of Josephus. But Mehdad Fatehi, *The Spirit's Relation to the Risen Lord in Paul: An Examination of its Christological Implications* (WUNT 2 Reihe 128; Tübingen: Mohr Siebeck 2000), 125–6, persuasively argues against Stoic influence and would rather see the identification of the Spirit with God in Jewish terms rather than Stoic.

87.   *Ant.* 8.4.1 (emphasis added)

88.   Barker, *Gate*, 61.

89.   Similar cosmological interpretation of the temple is evidenced in Philo (*Vit. Mos.* 2.101-104; *Plant.*126).

90.   In *Antiquities* 1.13.2 Josephus notes that the mountain upon which Abraham was to sacrifice Isaac was the same one on which David built the temple.

91.   Josephus talks of 10th *Lous* which is equated to *Ab* in the Syrian calendar. But in 2 Kgs 25.8 the date of the destruction of the first temple is given as 7th *Ab*. (Thanks to Prof. Joel Marcus, Duke University, for pointing out this reference to me!)

In essence, Josephus implies that none who would have been conversant with the Scriptures should have been surprised by the destruction of the second temple since it was already announced. Rather than allow for Roman victory in destruction of the temple, Josephus formulates instead what he perceives was a foreordained plan of YHWH that only used Romans as divine instruments. This is the hermeneutical balancing act that Josephus exercised throughout his work in an attempt to offend neither Jew nor Roman, resulting in questionable historical readings.

3.3.6. *The* Targumim

In the *targumim*, the general impulse is the expectation that the Messiah would rebuild the temple.[92] Though the *targumim* are the products of early Judaism (that is, before rabbinic Judaism took root) and while they are said to reflect traditions that are much older than their late dating, they form the background for what was to develop later as rabbinic Judaism.[93] *Tg. Isa.*'s interpretation of Isa. 53 replaces the Messiah's body with the temple in what seems to be a reversal of the NT's application of the passage to Christ.[94] On the basis of the restoration of the temple, the inhabitants of the earth will then be able to partake of the joy that proceeds from the rebuilt sanctuary (24.16; 38.11). Having both a physical and spiritual dimension to this rebuilding, the Messiah is to restore not only the physical structure but the spiritual function of the temple as a light to all the nations of the world.[95] Only then would the peoples of the earth be drawn to the temple (2.1-3).

   Tg. Neb. renders v. 3, which in the MT reads, 'to speak to the priests who (belong) to the house', as 'priests who *were serving in the Sanctuary*'. As such since he understood the house in v. 3 as referring to the Sanctuary then it made sense for him that בית אל in v. 2 should be referring to the same thing, i.e. the temple of God. Subsequently the house is equated to the sanctuary, and Bethel in turn is interpreted as the 'house of God', even though the use of אל for God in the *targumim* is unusual.[96]

---

92.   *The Targum of the Minor Prophets* (translated with critical introduction, apparatus, and notes by Kevin J. Cathcart and Robert P. Gordon; Wilmington, Del.: Michael Glazier, 1989) 198 n. 13. Cf. *Tg. Isa.* 53.5, *Tg. Zech.* 6.12-13. In comparison, *Sib. Or.* 5.414-33, is ambiguous as to who the builder of the new temple is (either God or the 'blessed man'). It is possible that the better reading indicates that the messianic figure, called the 'blessed man', is to build the new or heavenly temple. In the Talmud (*Pesachim* 4.4), the Jerusalem temple, God's throne and the Law existed before the foundation of the world.

93.   *The Isaiah Targum* (The Aramaic Bible 1; translated with introduction, apparatus and notes by Bruce Chilton; Wilmington, Del.: Michael Galzier, 1987) xxvii–xxviii.

94.   It is not clear whether this is a polemic against Christianity's interpretation of the passage from a christological point of view, but it is a possibility.

95.   This very aspect of pollution in Israel's relation to other nations is what prompts the exile according to *Tg. Neb.*, Zech. 5.5-10.

96.   *Targum Minor Prophets*, 199 n. 2–4.

The Holy Spirit and the *Šekinah* are closely related in rabbinic Judaism and are interchangeably used.[97] Both are closely related to the temple in reference to the dwelling presence of God in the temple, even as *Šekinah* shares the same root (שׁכן) with the tabernacle (משׁכן). Together with avoiding anthropomorphism, these terms also perpetuated the internal dynamic of tension between the omnipresence and immanence of God that existed in Judaism.[98] The difference lies primarily with function. Concerning this Fatehi clarifies that '[Š]ekinah and the Holy Spirit *refer to the same thing when seen or experienced in slightly different ways*. The former denotes the immediate presence of God with and among his people as such, the latter the inspiring activity of the same God.'[99] This is not some 'kind of hypostasis distinct from God' but rather it is 'the *immediate inspiring activity* (i.e. prophetic inspiration) of the same God whose *immediate presence* is referred to by the term [Š]ekinah'.[100]

In *Tg. Ps-J.*, on Gen. 44.27, the *Šekinah* is identified with the building of the temple in the land of Benjamin: 'In his land the *Šekinah* of the ruler of the world will dwell, and in his possession will be built the house of the sanctuary.' Making reference to the same passage the *Fragmentary Targum* states that: 'In his borders the house of the sanctuary will be built and in his possession the glory of the *Šekinah* of the Lord will dwell.'[101] Given that the *Šekinah* is

97.   In this section I am indebted largely to Fatehi, *Spirit's Relation* 154–7. Note that Koester, *Dwelling*, 71, following A. M. Goldberg, *Untersuchungen über die Vorstellung von der Schekhinah in der frühen rabbinischen Literatur* (SJ 6; Berlin: de Gruyter, 1969) 1–12, is of the opinion that the *targumim* that mention the Šekinah are from second century CE or later, with the exception of the term 'the camp of the Šekinah' which may have originated earlier. I think a case for an earlier provenance for substantial parts of the *targumim* can be made.

98.   The general understanding has been that the concepts of 'Glory' (*Yeqara*, *'Iqar*), 'Presence' (*Šekinah*) and 'Word' (*Memra*) were used by the *targumim* to remove any anthropomorphism in the biblical texts. They substituted the sections of scripture where God is described as 'going forth', 'coming', 'revealing himself', etc. Cf. Martin McNamara, *Targum and Testament: Aramaic Paraphrases of the Hebrew Bible, A Light on the NT* (Grand Rapids: Eerdmans, 1972) 98ff. But see Michael Klein, 'Anthropomorphisms and Anthropopathisms in the Targumim' in *Congress Volume, Vienna 1980* Leiden: Brill, 1981) 162–77, who argues that there is not much consistency in the *targumim* on the matter.

99.   Fatehi, *Spirit*, 156–7 (emphasis original).

100.   Fatehi, *Spirit*, 157 (emphasis original).

101.   Similar views are echoed in *Num. Rab.* 15.10 and *Lam. Rab.* 3.49, while highlighting the five things that are missing in the second temple. With the destruction of the first temple the presence of God (*Šekinah*/Holy Spirit) was withdrawn from Israel, and would only return with the building of the eschatological temple. However, see G. I. Davies, 'The Presence of God in the Second Temple and Rabbinic Doctrine', in William Horbury, ed., *Templum Amicitiae: Essays on the Second Temple Presented to Ernst Bammel* (Sheffield: Sheffield University Press, 1991) 32–6, who identifies at least five references in rabbinic writings to suggest a belief in God's presence in the second temple.

not said to reside in the second temple it fails to amount to the true eschatological temple (*Yoma* 9b).[102]

3.4. *Summary and Conclusion*

Disappointment with the standing Jerusalem temple or with the pollution attributed to it (*Jub.* 49; *T. Levi* 17.8-10; *1 Enoch* 89.73-77) seems to have been a widespread view in Second Temple Judaism and it led to the desire for a cleansing or even an outright replacement of the Jerusalem temple and, in some cases like Qumran, the priesthood also. As a result, there arose the expectation of the more glorious eschatological temple and 'a future high priest who would cleanse the earth' (11QTemp; 1QS 8.4ff; 11.3ff; 4QMMT; 4Q174; *Jub.* 23.20-23; *1 Enoch* 89.50).[103] While the collection of literature identified with the community in Qumran is rather complex and it is difficult to find a unified expression, it seems that one of the projections of the Qumran community was a view of themselves as a replacement of the Jerusalem temple.[104]

Moreover, in Qumran, the matter becomes even more complicated. There was the possibility of a third temple – the ideal eschatological temple reminiscent of the visionary temple of Ezekiel.[105] While this remains a viable possibility of understanding the temple imagery in Qumran, it is our contention, following Johann Maier and John J. Collins, that it is more likely that in the Qumran documents the ideal and the real are constantly interwoven, creating a certain tension between the present temple in Jerusalem and the expected ideal yet to be achieved.[106] One is not always sure which one of

---

102. Peter Schäfer, *Die Vorstellung vom Heiligen Geist in der rabbinischen Literatur* (SANT 28; Munich: Kösel, 1972) 137–9. That is partly why Schäfer argues that the commonly used phrase in Rabbinic literature – רוח הקדש – should be translated as 'Spirit of the Sanctuary' rather than the 'Spirit of Holiness'.

103. George W. E. Nickelsburg, *Ancient Judaism and Christian Origins: Diversity, Continuity, and Transformation* (Minneapolis: Fortress, 2003) 116: 'Although the priesthood continued to function in a postexilic temple and was accepted by many as efficacious, some considered the priesthood to be polluted and the temple cult defunct. Some solved this problem by positing a future high priest or an angelic high priest who would cleanse the earth.'

104. The primary proponent of the above view is Gärtner, *Temple*, 30–42, later bolstered by Klinzing, *Umdeutung*, 80–7. It continues to hold sway even with lingering concerns of the paucity of the evidence (cf. Coppens, 'Spiritual', 53–66).

105. Schwartz, 'Temples', 83–91.

106. Johann Maier, *The Temple Scroll: An Introduction, Translation and Commentary* (JSOTSup 34; Sheffield: JSOT Press, 1985), 59. After examining some of the material in the Jewish Apocalyptic literature concerning the temple, John J. Collins, 'Jerusalem and the Temple in Jewish Apocalyptic Literature of the Second Temple Period', *International Rennert Guest Lecture Series* 1 (1998) 28–9, expresses doubt about an 'interim temple' and simply wants to see the heavenly temple and its earthly replica as the two structures referred to in these documents.

the two is being referred to in the Qumran texts, they actually have just two – the Jerusalem temple, and the eschatological temple. The latter is variously presented and interpreted in light of the community.

In fact, Oscar Cullmann conceived of a complete split within Judaism so that there developed two distinct and opposing groups in regard to the temple – an anti-temple group (e.g. Qumran) and a pro-temple group (e.g. 'Jews' in the Fourth Gospel).[107] But Cullmann also recognized the complexity of the situation when he pointed out that some Jews still regarded the Jerusalem temple as the definitive center of Judaism while others looked elsewhere (e.g. Torah, community, circumcision, food laws, etc.).[108]

Overall, the Jews were so influenced by the cosmology of the temple and tabernacle that they 'carried a mental image of a neat closed world order, an architectural complex in which they were God's only people. That shared image enabled them to survive by separating them from others.'[109] The images were a response to mental or psychological insecurities that faced the Jewish people, and in particular those involving the Flood (Noah's Ark), escape from Egypt (Moses' tabernacle), permanent presence of God beside the Davidic palace (Solomon's temple), and hope during the exile (Ezekiel's temple vision).

Without the physical structure, the mental structure kept up the hope in exile. However, this mental image takes strikingly different forms between Christianity and later Judaism, and even within Christianity itself.[110] This notwithstanding, there is still a certain level of harmony that characterizes these Christian documents; that is, they all understand that the temple has to be interpreted in light of the life, death and resurrection of Jesus Christ. 1 Peter takes it one more step by incorporating, in line with the Second Temple Jewish literature reviewed, the community's identity within the temple imagery (priesthood, purity and exile).

---

107. Oscar Cullmann, 'L'opposition contre le Temple de Jerusalem, motif commun de la theologie johannique et du monde ambiant', *NTS* 5 (1958–9) 157–73. Cf. also *idem*, *The Johannine Circle: Its Place in Judaism, Among the Disciples of Jesus and in Early Christianity* (London: SCM Press, 1975) 39–56.

108. Cullmann, 'L'opposition', 72.

109. John Onians, 'Tabernacle and Temple and cosmos of the Jews', in Emily Lyle, ed., *Sacred Structure in the Traditions of India, China, Judaism and Islam* (Edinburgh: Edinburgh University Press, 1992), 147–8, 'Arguably too, unfortunately, the psychology of it induced an unspoken sense of the valuelessness of all outside the Tabernacle or Temple court, also contributed to provoking the cycle of persecutions. At the same time the power of the image of the building which, whatever happens reappears, and while all around is changing, is repeatedly rebuilt in better and better forms, only gives those who survived a greater confidence.'

110. One can speak of a Pauline, a Petrine, a Johannine or even a Lukan conception and interpretation of the temple.

Chapter 4

EXEGETICAL ANALYSIS OF TEMPLE IMAGERY IN 1 PETER

4.1. *Introductory Comments*

Temple imagery reverberates throughout 1 Peter and it is our contention that the idea and imagery of the temple is more pervasive and intentional than is usually acknowledged.[1] Such imagery is reflected in the vocabulary of 1 Peter and is central in elucidating the message of the epistle.[2] We have so far maintained that, overall, the second temple 'enjoyed a status which in paradoxical fashion was both substantially higher and substantially lower than the first'.[3] The result of this is that, in mainstream Judaism, there was increased dissatisfaction with (or perhaps a dilemma concerning) the Jerusalem temple's ability to function as the abode of God.[4] It is into this general morass that the temple ideas in 1 Peter present to the Christian believers a means of resolving this conundrum.

The temple imagery in 1 Peter is closely related to the eschatological passages of the epistle in which the understanding is entwined with an exodus/exile motif (παρεπιδήμοις διασπορᾶς – 'exiles of the Dispersion' 1.1), establishing a mental framework that incorporates a progression of thought that very loosely resembles the larger history of Israel.[5] In essence, passages

---

1.   Even when acknowledged, such as in McKnight's *1 Peter*, 30, its ramifications for interpretation of 1 Peter in light of the exile background are not usually taken into consideration.

2.   It is the assumption of this study that the temple reference in 1 Peter is to the Jerusalem Temple given the heavy reliance on OT imagery in the epistle. The imagery does not, however, preclude the possible connection to Gentile temples (cf. analysis of λύτρόω in 1 Pet. 1.18 below).

3.   Shaye J. D. Cohen, *From Maccabees to the Mishnah* (Philadelphia: Westminster Press, 1987) 131.

4.   Alan Cole, *The New Temple: A Study in the Origins of the Catechetical 'Form' of the Church in the New Testament* (London: Tyndale, 1950) 11–13, elaborates on the words of Jesus in Mt. 12.6 τοῦ ἱεροῦ μεῖζόν ἐστιν ὧδε – 'something greater than the Temple is here', showing that it is in Christ that the fullness of God dwells and not in the temple. We shall see that 1 Peter builds his argument primarily on this understanding of Jesus' words, but extends it further to the church. In fact Cole thinks that the neuter 'some*thing* greater' could be an undertone reference to the collective embryonic church (11–12).

5.   Deterding, 'Motifs', 58–65. Cf. also Davids, *1 Peter*, 15; Gärtner, *Temple*, 72ff; E. G. Selwyn, 'Eschatology in Peter', in W. D. Davies and David Daube, eds., *The Background of the New Testament and Its Eschatology* (Cambridge: Cambridge University Press, 1964), 374–401; Russell, 'Eschatology', 78–84; Michaels, 'Eschatology', 394–401; Joseph William Dalton, '"So

that echo or allude to temple imagery are directly related to the eschatological concerns of the epistle, which in turn are centered around the person of Jesus Christ.[6] These include 1.3 (ῥαντισμὸς αἵματος – 'sprinkling of blood', animal sacrifices); 3.18-20 – Noah's κιβωτός as the prototypical sanctuary; 2.4-10 – the construction of the temple (οἶκος πνευματικὸς) and offering of πνευματικαι θυσίαι; 4.14 – the descent of the *Šekinah* into the temple; 4.17 – judgment that starts within the temple; 5.10 – the temple's subsequent restoration.[7] It is our contention that, while the most explicit use of temple imagery occurs in 2.4-10, temple imagery undergirds the entire letter of 1 Peter.[8]

4.2. *Temple/Tabernacle Imagery in 1 Peter*

4.2.1. *'Tabernacle' Imagery and Sprinkling of Blood (1 Pet. 1.2b)* ῥαντισμὸν αἵματος Ἰησοῦ Χριστοῦ

Sprinkling in the OT was in order to purify the people, the tabernacle and the vessels for service to God (Exod. 12, 24; Num 19; Lev. 8, 16). However, sprinkling of people with blood was rare, being mentioned only in Exod. 24.8 and Leviticus 8, while the sprinkling of the altar and the sanctuary with blood was more common (Exod. 12, 24; Lev.16).[9] The language of purification that runs through the first chapter of 1 Peter, and that of ῥαντισμὸς αἵματος ('sprinkling of blood' – 1.2) in particular, is a call to a cleansing that is reminiscent of the purification undertaken before approaching the presence of God, with the aid of pure sacrificial animals whose blood was sprinkled on recipients.[10] As such, 1 Peter's use of the phrase ῥαντισμὸς αἵματος carries with it a cultic imagery that reflects not only on sacrificial victims, but also on the people and on the sanctuary.

that Your Faith May Also Be Your Hope in God" (1 Peter 1.21)', in Robert Banks, ed., Reconciliation and Hope: New Testament Essays on Atonement and Eschatology presented to L. Morris on his 60th Birthday (Exeter: Paternoster Press, 1974), 262–74; Parker, 'Eschatology', 27–32; Reiser, 'Eschatologie', 164–81.

6. So Gärtner, *Temple*, 72; Schutter, *Hermeneutic*, 168, for whom it is not simply a Jewish milieu but a 'peculiar Jewish hermeneutic'.

7. See proposed structure of 1 Peter below: Appendix.

8. Schutter, *Hermeneutic*, 169–70, argues that the main point of 1 Peter is the self-identification of the church as the Temple-Community (2.9-10; 2.4-8; 3.15-16; 4.12-17) built on OT testimonies, texts and allusions. The words of John R. Lanci, *A New Temple* 128, coined in respect to 1 Corinthians, hold true too for 1 Peter: '… [it] contains numerous instances of imagery associated with both Jewish and Gentile temple cults, which follow upon the temple like a wake behind a great ship. This explains the presence of so much cultic terminology unique to this letter: it keeps the image of the temple, and cult, in the mind's eye.'

9. Walton *et al.*, *Background*, 104.

10. Selwyn, *First Peter*, 120; Goppelt, *1 Peter*, 75 n. 1. Irrespective of whether the sprinkling is connected to the washing of baptism (3.19-21) as it is in Heb. 1.22, the typological connection to the sanctuary is not obscured.

The metaphor of blood sprinkling introduces the epistle's utilization of language that relates to temple/tabernacle imagery. Appropriately, Perdelwitz's attempt to explain 1 Peter 1.2b in terms of dipping of the initiate in the blood of the bull in the Mithraic *taurobolium* (mystery religions) has found little following.[11] Ample evidence in the OT (Exod. 12, 24; Num 19) has been shown sufficiently to account for references to blood sprinkling in 1 Peter without recourse to the *taurobolium*, with the strong emphasis on eschatology in the epistle militating against Perdelwitz's theory.[12] It is our contention also that reference to ῥαντισμὸς αἵματος would more aptly evoke the images of sacrifice in both the tabernacle and the temple of Israel. Instituted in the tabernacle (Exod. 24–25; Num 19; Lev. 16; etc.), the practice of sprinkling with blood (and water) remained significant in the temple, though questionable in the second temple given that the *kapporet* might not have figured as part of the temple furniture in the second temple.[13] Sprinkling was particularly significant in the annual *kapporet* ritual of *Yom Kippur* described in Lev. 16.11-19, in which blood was sprinkled before the 'mercy seat'/ 'atonement cover' of the ark of the covenant.[14]

Exodus motifs, especially in the first chapter of 1 Peter, enhance the likelihood of tabernacle background. 1 Pet. 1.2 and 1.19 form an *inclusio* with the phrase ῥαντισμὸς αἵματος in 1.2 echoed in 1.19, where the Paschal lamb imagery is clearly applied to Jesus (τιμίῳ αἵματι ὡς ἀμνοῦ ἀμώμου καὶ ἀσπίλου Χριστοῦ). Christ's blood is like that of the Passover lamb, which was 'without blemish or spot', and which brought life to the Israelites in the midst of death.[15] Similarly, for 1 Peter's audience, the blood of Jesus brings life in the midst of suffering, persecution, and even possible death.

11.   E. Richard Perdelwitz, *Die Mysterienreligion und das Problem des 1. Petrusbriefes* (Religionsversuche und Vorarbeiten 11/3; Giessen: Töpelmann, 1911) 42–4. See also Selwyn, *First Peter*, 305-11, a generally negative evaluation of Perdelwitz's proposals.

12.   Lapham, *Peter*, 134: given the eschatological predisposition of the epistle, and in light of such a grave concern, 'it is hardly likely that the liturgical structure of the Christian initiation ceremony would represent a major concern'. A number of indicators of how deeply eschatological this epistle is include use of the language of ἀποκάλυψις (1.5, 7, 13; 4.13; 5.1) to describe the ever nearing end, the focus on κρίμα (1.17; 4.14-17) and the reference to the heavenly κληρονομία that awaits the faithful (1.4, 16-18; 4.17-18).

13.   Michael Newton, *The Concept of Purity at Qumran and in the Letters of Paul* (Cambridge: Cambridge University Press, 1985) 9 n. 81, 75–7.

14.   See, however, Joseph Gutmann, 'The Strange History of the Kapporet Ritual', *ZAW* 112 (2000) 624–6, who argues that the annual *Kapporet* ritual in Lev. 16.11-19 was initially established in the tabernacle and seemed to have faded out of the Israelite *cultus* until its revival in the festival of *Yom Kippur* in the second temple. Not only are the people to be atoned for but also the altar and the sanctuary, which is also sprinkled with blood to make it clean from the uncleanness of the people. See Paul's reference to Jesus as the *kapporet*, the mercy seat/cover of the ark, in Rom. 3.25 (ἱλαστήριον). Cf. also J. Herrmann, 'ἱλαστήριον', *TDNT* 3.318, and W. Eichrodt, *The Theology of the Old Testament* (Philadelphia: Westminster Press, 1961) 1.130, who notes that this ceremony was the epitome of the sacrificial law.

15.   This essentially was the Christian understanding of Jesus' death as is reflected in the use of ἀμώμος in Acts 20.28; Eph. 1.7; Rev. 1.5, 9; 15.1-5.

All three OT passages suggested as possible background for ῥαντισμὸς αἵματος (Exod. 12, 14; Num 19) seem to have a certain claim to legitimacy. As a result, interpreters typically try to defend the suitability of one passage over the other two. However, there is a good possibility that 1 Peter might not have had *a* particular OT passage in mind. Rather, he would have had in mind the OT *motif* of 'sprinkling', a *collage* of all the above (and possibly other) OT passages, especially as they relate to the blood of Christ.[16] Such a conception of the OT background of 1 Peter becomes even more likely given the fact that the complete phrase ῥαντισμὸς αἵματος, which is unique to 1 Peter, was probably coined by the author to express his own peculiar interpretation of the OT passages he had in mind.

Could 1 Peter be fusing the ideas of covenant and atonement by locating them both in the redeeming work of Jesus Christ? For example, the words of Jesus recorded in Mark 14.24 combine Exod. 24 with Isa. 53, thus bridging the covenant theme with that of atonement. If, as we claim, these two OT motifs are playing a significant role in the concept of ῥαντισμὸς αἵματος in 1 Peter, then it is likely that these words of Jesus might be influencing the thought of 1 Peter. This perspective would then provide the most likely scenario for understanding 1 Peter's use of the phrase. This would be in line with 1 Peter's characteristic use of the OT which is to amalgamate several different passages (e.g. 2.4-9 and 4.14-17).[17]

The point to keep in mind concerning 1 Peter 1.2 is that the work of the Spirit is to sanctify (ἐν ἁγιασμῷ πνεύματος). Moreover, the same God at work in the Jewish nation of Israel is now working among the Petrine believers, through Jesus Christ and his Spirit.[18] By applying the 'trinitarian formula' in this verse ('chosen and destined by God the Father and sanctified by the spirit

16   Such a perspective would find more support especially if one accepts the proposition by Goppelt, *Typos*, 156, that the context of 1 Pet. 1.18 is more dependant on Isa. 52.3, 4, than on any of the passages above. See also 1 Pet. 2.9 which amalgamates Exod. 19.5-6 and Isa. 43.20-21.

17.   While making a comment on another aspect of the letter, the words of Elliott (*Elect*, 213) would seem to concur here – 'As is obvious throughout 1 P[eter], the author in composing his messages made up of various wells in various regions. The resultant mixture cannot be attributed to a single spring or solely one source' – the 'spring' and 'well' representing the textual sources of 1 Peter.

18.   In spite of Levison, 'Did the Spirit Withdraw', 35–57, and Davies, 'Presence of God in Horbury, ed., *Templum*. Howard Kee, *Understanding the New Testament* (5th edn; Englewood Cliffs, NJ: Prentice-Hall, 1983) 358 n. 18, surprisingly states that, '[a]part from the mention of the Spirit in the trinitarian formula at the opening of the letter ("God the Father ... Spirit ... Jesus Christ", 1:2), the Spirit plays no role in 1 Peter'. This is simply not the case. Understood from the point of view of the temple imagery and its connection to the eschatological expectation of the author, the Holy Spirit is fairly significant in 1 Peter. This is especially so if understood within the framework of the fulfillment of the Jewish eschatological expectation of the return of the Šekinah presence of God to the Jerusalem temple and the resumption of the spirit of prophecy in Israel. The Holy Spirit sanctifies the believers (1.2), is the spirit of prophecy among the

for obedience to Jesus Christ and for sprinkling with his blood' – RSV), 1 Peter is not only applying to Christ the OT imagery of sacrifice, but also affirming the connection to the tabernacle. In this way it incorporates the tabernacle into the new 'spiritual house' in which sacrifices are to be performed by the new 'priesthood' (2.5, 9).

In the same way that the blood of the animals established the purification necessary for the connection with God, so now the blood of Jesus purifies the believers, enabling them to establish the new connection to God. And while the OT sacrifices and sprinkling took place on the altar at the sanctuary, the sacrifice of Jesus is on the cross (1.18-19) and the 'sprinkling' is on those that make up the new 'spiritual house' (2.5), the eschatological dwelling of God.

4.2.2. Temple Rites: Purity, Holiness and Identity in 1 Peter (1 Peter 1.15-16)

Apart from their cultic significance alluded to above, purity laws and regulations also govern a community's boundaries between insiders and outsiders.[19] The concern is to maintain the wholeness of the social unit, usually a minority, from the danger of being assimilated by the strong forces of the larger society.[20] Therefore, both individual and corporate elements of purity are

---

prophets who pointed to Christ (1.11), empowers the preachers of the Good News (1.12), and is the same Spirit that resurrected Christ from the dead (3.18). The dead souls were preached to by Christ in his death so that 'though they had been judged in the flesh as everyone is judged, they might live in the spirit as God does' (4.6), and finally, the 'Spirit of God and of Glory' rests on the believers (4.14). At least two of these references are of significance: the mention that Jesus was raised by the Holy Spirit stands out against Lukan and Pauline references to the resurrection where God is the agent of the resurrection (Acts 3.14; 4.10; Rom. 6.4, 9; 7.4; 1 Thess. 1.10. Cf. 1 Cor. 15.12, 20; 2 Tim. 2.8 where no agent is identified), and also against the Gospels where no agent is mentioned even though the clear assumption is God (Mt. 17.9; 27.64; 28.7; Jn 2.22; 21.14). Second the Spirit of God rests on the believers in a manner reminiscent of the Spirit of God resting on the tabernacle and the first temple in the OT. The use of the term πνευματικὸς to describe the nature of the new temple and the sacrifices to be offered leaves little doubt concerning the connection of the Spirit with the temple and the *cultus*. Cf. also Furnish, 'Sojourners', 5, who argues that the appearance of the Spirit in 1.2 is programmatic for the entire epistle. Cothenet, 'Orientations', 35, also point to a distinctive Petrine conceptualization of the Holy Spirit, whose function is primarily prophetic (1.10–12; 4.14): 'The Spirit does not retain the same significance to doctrine in 1 Peter as it does in Paul. From the general allusion in 1 P 1,2, the one and only function of the Spirit is prophecy.'

19. 'Purity' and 'Holiness' are terms that have been understood differently by different scholars. Jacob Neusner, *The Idea of Purity in Ancient Judaism* (Leiden: Brill, 1973) 18–22, for example, sees the terms as interchangeable and virtually synonymous. On the other hand, David P. Wright, 'Holiness (OT)' in *ABD*, separates the two terms arguing that they belong to two distinct pairs of concepts – 'holy/profane' versus 'pure/impure' – which interact in the OT in culturally significant ways. While the distinctions do not have a significant effect on our discussion, we find Wright's distinctions helpful.

20.   Philip Peter Jenson, *Graded Holiness: A Key to the Priestly Conception of the World* (JSOT 106; Sheffield: Sheffield Academic Press, 1992) 47, identifies the sanctuary as the sphere within which the divine and profane (human) meet. 'The holy-profane pair represents (positively and negatively) the divine sphere, and this may be distinguished from the human sphere (which

closely related, maintaining the special identity of the group (2.5, 9).[21] All these concerns are real for 1 Peter (1.14-16; 2.5, 9, 11-12, 22), closely tying his emphasis on matters of purity and holiness to the identity of the Petrine community as the 'new Israel'. This identification, in turn, is couched in cultic language and imagery, with purity premised not only on God (1.16), but also on the Lord Jesus (2.21-22), who committed no sin, becoming the model (ὑπογραμμὸν) for believers.

4.2.2.1. γέγραπται ὅτι ῞Αγιοι ἔσεσθε, ὅτι ἐγὼ ἅγιος εἰμιω *(1 Pet. 1.16)*
The Pentateuchal refrain 'be holy for I the Lord am holy' referenced in 1 Peter 1.16 originates in the reference to the Israelites' privileged elect status in relation to YHWH (Exod. 22.30; Lev. 11.44, 45; 19.2; 20.7, 26; Num 16.3). Their holiness is predicated upon the holiness of God, who makes them holy by virtue of the relationship he has established with them, climaxing with the establishment of divine residence in their midst. There are three distinct occasions in the book of Leviticus where the complete phrase is used (Lev. 11.45; 19.2; 20.7, 26), and if it is true that 1 Peter's tendency in quoting the OT involves citing a passage while having the entire context in mind,[22] then it behooves us to try and establish the context of the quote.

Arguably, perhaps with the exception of Hebrews, no document in the NT includes a more involved interpretation of purity in relation to the temple than 1 Peter.[23] The injunctions to holiness based on Leviticus have to be understood in light of the cultic framework in the OT and 1 Peter's appropriation of it in his epistle. Kelly is only partially right in asserting that 'Holiness [in 1 Peter] does not stand for mere ritual purity, as a certain strata of the OT (e.g. Ex xxviii. 2; xl. 9; Lev. xxii. 3ff; Ezr. ix. 2) might at first seem to indicate; rather it connotes the freedom from sin and absolute moral integrity which fellowship with God makes imperative.'[24] This point of view, however, would seem to

is marked by the opposition between clean and unclean). The presence of a holy God and a holy sanctuary in the midst of Israel ensures that these two points of view overlap in a complex way.'

21. Ekkehard W. Stegemann and Wolfgang Stegemann, *The Jesus Movement: A Social History of Its First Century* (trans. O. C. Dean, Jr.; Minneapolis: Fortress Press, 1999) 142–3; Daniel L. Smith-Christopher, *A Biblical Theology of Exile* (Minneapolis: Fortress Press, 2002) 137–8, concurs when he observes that the Hebrew Dispersion was characterized by two cardinal concerns in regard to holiness: '(1) a strong sense of identity that is separated from those traditions and cultures that surround them, and (2) the necessity to "maintain the social boundaries", that is, to protect this unique identity through a strong emphasis on internal solidarity'.

22. Selwyn, *First Peter*, 334.

23. We shall also pay close attention to areas of comparison with the Qumran literature drawing on perceived similarities, and differences, while trying to determine whatever relation may exist between the two, if any. Our study assumes less of a linear connection between Qumran and 1 Peter than was postulated by Klinzing and Best. Rather we perceive the likelihood of a Jewish milieu or matrix which would account for any similarity that may exist between 1 Peter and the DSS.

24. Kelly, *Peter*, 69.

obscure the only viable OT background for understanding 1 Peter's application of these concepts of cultic purity. If holiness simply stands for
freedom from sin, how then is it understood in light of the role of sacrifices
in the OT? Does it retain any vestiges of its OT use? Would a better understanding of the OT cultic practices facilitate a fuller appreciation of 1
Peter's use of the terminology?

In all the Levitical instructions, it is the entire community of Israel, rather
than a subsection, that is in view.[25] The Levitical injunction to holiness first
appears in Lev. 11.44, 45 following instructions concerning clean and unclean
animals. The whole chapter is immediately preceded by instructions to the
priests concerning their conduct while offering sacrifices in the sanctuary area
(9.1-24; 10.8-20) and is followed by instructions for restoring purity after
contamination (Lev. 12ff). The injunction recurs in Lev. 19.2, where it stands
at the head of instructions on holiness in personal conduct and, lastly, in Lev.
20.7, 26, where instructions concerning punishment for disobedience are
given. Significantly, these last instructions are not given to the Israelites alone
(unlike the first two), but to both the Israelites and 'the foreigners among
you'.[26]

That is why, in spite of Selwyn's view, there is no need to speak of a 'neo-
Levitical community' in relation to this Levitical injunction quoted by Peter.[27]
The greatest support for such an argument comes from Selwyn's understanding of 1 Pet. 2.4-10 as an early Christian hymn premised on the so-called
'Holiness Code' (Lev. 17–26).[28] He came up with what he thought to be an
equivalent 'Christian Holiness Code' underlying 1–2 Thessalonians and 1
Peter. However, it is quite unlikely that the first-century Christians would have
understood themselves as 'neo-Levitical', for this would have implied that they
were descendants of Levi. Furthermore, such an understanding would also be
incongruent with the predicate ἱεράτευμα.[29] This terminology that 1 Peter

---

25.   The exception is Lev. 21.6 where the reference is to the priests. Even here, the need for
purity is premised on the need for the priests' continued representation of the people before God,
the very task for which they were chosen by God in the first place (Num. 3.8, 11-13). In Lev.
15.15b the phrase 'because I, the Lord, have made him holy', is used not as an injunction to
holiness, but as the reason for the high priest not to dishonor his clan. It is used again in the same
way in Lev. 21.23.

26.   In both Leviticus 11 and 19 the instructions are to the 'entire community of Israel'. In
Leviticus 18 where instructions concerning forbidden sexual relations are given, there is also the
mention of the fact that these are to apply to both Israelites and foreigners (v. 26b).

27.   Selwyn, *First Peter*, 369–74, 404–6, 459–60. However, see Elliott, *Elect*, 208–13, for a
decisive argument against Selwyn's terminology. Even when addressed to Aaron and his sons, the
instructions are to the entire community, while the 'neo-Levitical' term would only be identifiable
with the lineage of Levi.

28.   Selwyn, *First Peter*, 268–98, 388ff.

29.   See Elliott, *Elect*, 208–9, for arguments against Selwyn.

adopts from Exod. 19.6 is more accurately used to describe the whole nation of Israel rather than a select group within it.[30] Torrey Seland decries what he considers a regular pattern in which most works that deal with 1 Pet. 2.5, 9 make reference to Exod. 19.6 (the primary text in question) but fail to take into consideration the author's view of Israel at large as a priesthood.[31] It therefore would not make sense if, indeed, 1 Peter wanted to make his readers 'neo-Levites', since, as far as he is concerned, they make up the entirety of the 'new Israel'. Furthermore, this 'new Israel', while made up of both Jews and Gentiles, also incorporates all the elements that were unique to the priesthood.[32]

If 1 Peter is not establishing a 'neo-Levitical' community, then what is he trying to achieve? For Israel, purity affected all spheres of life but was epitomized in the priesthood and in the Jerusalem temple (and in the wilderness tabernacle before it). How, then, could a community removed from the temple (as 1 Peter's was) maintain the rites of purity? How could they retain the presence of God or his Spirit in their midst without the visible sanctuary?

There were at least two groups that separated themselves from the temple in Jerusalem: the Christians and the covenanters of Qumran. While the early Christians were eventually forced out by increased persecution in Jerusalem (Acts 12.1ff), the Qumran covenanters deliberately chose to move out to the desert in reaction to their fellow priests, whom they felt had defiled the Jerusalem temple. For both groups, there was a transformation in the understanding of the temple. These two communities began to understand themselves as the true temple of God – 'Temple-Community'.[33] They maintained that as a community they harbored the presence of God in their midst, effectively constituting the precincts within which the Spirit of God dwelt. This was made possible by the community's extension to themselves of cultic ideals that had previously been used to describe the sanctuary, priests, and sacrificial animal victims (1QM 3.5; 12.7; 16.1; 1QSb 1.5; 1 Pet. 2.4-10).[34]

---

30. J. Blinzler, 'IERATEYMA: Zur Exegese von 1 Petr 2.5 u 9', in *EPISKOPUS: Festschrift für Kardinal Michael von Faulhaber* (Regensburg: F. Pustet, 1949) 49–65, 59, argues that 1 Peter may have taken some of his interpretations of Exod. 19.6 from Hellenistic Jewish interpretations. Cf. Torrey Seland, 'The "Common Priesthood" of Philo and 1 Peter: A Philonic Reading of 1 Peter 2:5, 9', *JSNT* 57 (1995) 90.

31. Seland, '1 Peter 2:5, 9', 90.

32. While 1 Peter exhorts the believers to conduct themselves honourably among the 'Gentiles' (ἔθνος– 2.12), he is simply assuming language categories from the OT. The new reality that is the Church, irrespective of the origin of its membership, is now the 'new Israel' and all those outside are Gentiles.

33. Gärtner, *Temple*, 73ff.

34. This point is made by Neusner, *Purity*, 117ff, while discussing the issues of purity in relation to the rabbis following the destruction of the temple in 70 CE. It has been shown that those referred to as the *haverim* had been teaching before 70 CE that one could keep the purity rules outside the temple, thus providing the seed for the Qumran community to develop its

The question is not whether the temple was still standing in Jerusalem or not, but whether it had ostensibly ceased to be the focus of worship for these two groups. For the Qumran community, its separation was prompted by possible fallout with the priestly group that remained in the temple. For the Christians, separation was initially gradual given that believers initially continued attending the temple for prayer during hours for '*Tamid*-offering' (cf. Lk. 1.22; Acts 2.46; 3.1).[35] Soon, a fallout with the Jewish religious establishment would ensue, triggered off by John and Peter's healing of a lame man by the temple gate (Acts 3–4). The result was the beginning of persecution against the Christians forcing some like the apostle Peter (Acts 12) to flee from Jerusalem. With this began the dispersion of the church, divorced from the Jerusalem *cultus*.

As a result, whatever mark of purity one needed to gain entrance into the physical structure now becomes symbolic of the requirement for entering the community for both Qumran and 1 Peter, albeit in some restructured form.[36] The cultic rites and functions that characterized the temple (e.g. sacrifice) are transferred to the community, only now the sacrifices are not physical but 'spiritual' (πνευματικὰι θυσίαι in 1 Peter and 'Sacrifices of Praise and Thanksgiving' – שפתים ותרומת in DSS, e.g. 1QS 9.3-6, 26). Therefore, Jacob Neusner's remark that the temple provides the context in which the role of purity in early Christianity should be understood and interpreted holds true for 1 Peter.[37] The cultic elements are transferred to the community of believers, both allowing for their reinterpretation within the Christian faith and connecting the community of believers to the Lord Jesus Christ, the perfect sacrifice (1.18-22).

A general schema has been suggested for the section of 1 Pet. 1.13–2.3 in connection with certain rites practiced in the Qumran community.[38] These include conversion (1.14-17) followed by separation from evil (2.1), resulting in unity among the believers (2.5). 1 Peter also includes images of birth (1.2, 23-25; 2.2) and growth (2.2).[39] However, while it is plausible for one to

---

concepts (see Gedalia Alon, 'The Bounds of Levitical Cleanness', in Jacob Neusner, ed., *Jews, Judaism and the Classical World: Studies in Jewish History in the Times of the Second Temple and Talmud* [Jerusalem: Magnes Press, 1977] 211). This notwithstanding, the conditions that necessitated the rabbinic formulations were distinctly different from those of the Christians and the Qumran community – (destruction, spiritualization) and (alienation), respectively.

35. Werner Foerster, *From the Exile to Christ: A Historical Introduction to Palestinian Judaism* (trans. Gordon Harris: Philadelphia: Fortress, 1964) 153–4.

36. Jacob Neusner, 'History and Structure: The Case of Mishnah', *JAAR* 45 (1977) 161–92.

37. Neusner, *Purity*, 59. Look at Jesus' defense of the disciples' right to break the Sabbath ritual of cleanness in Cole, *Temple*, 6–12.

38. F. Nötscher, 'Heiligkeit in den Qumranschriften', *RevQ* 6 (1960) 161–81, who enumerates the affinities between the NT and the Qumran community on the matters of holiness.

39. Elliott, *Elect*, 214. See also D. Barthélemy, 'La sainteté selon la communuaté de Qumrân et selon l'Évangile', in J. van der Ploeg, ed., *La secte de Qumrân et les origines du christianisme:*

envision a Qumran influence on 1 Peter at the level of patterns of thought, especially as relates to the supposed 'Holiness Code' (Lev. 17–26), any direct dependence on Qumran literature cannot be upheld.[40]

More importantly, most scholars recognize the uniqueness of the arrangement of the material in 1 Pet. 2.4-10 and the focus on the relationship between Jesus and the believers.[41] It is this focus that gives 1 Peter's use of the schema its originality. It is through the relationship to Jesus that the community becomes 'the elect and the holy eschatological community of God'. They are reminded, 'He to whom you come in faith is the Messiah, the raised, the elect Stone of God through whom you too receive life and election and the spirit of holiness.'[42]

The concept of purity in 1 Peter pervades all aspects of the believers' lives – in their relation to Christ, family life, results of sinful acts, baptism, identity, sexual matters[43] – much in the same way that Israelite life was centered around the temple and its *cultus*.[44] This, as Cole argues, is partly based upon the claims of Jesus both to be greater than the temple (Mt. 12.1-7) and to be the replacement of the physical temple (Jn 3.20).[45] And as we have seen, 1 Peter is also motivated by concerns that find correspondence in some other Jewish communities, especially the Qumran community.

The pervasive vocabulary of ἅγιος in 1 Peter thus fits well within the heightened concern for purity in first-century Judaism, a concern motivated by the apocalyptic outlook in Jewish thinking.[46] The view generated by this apocalyptic outlook was the conviction that priestly purity would characterize eschatological Israel. Therefore, any pollution of the land or defilement of the sanctuary would be understood to have had immediate and long-term adverse effects.[47] 1 Peter is therefore applying the doctrinal principle of the 'new temple' which originates from the 'abolition of the material temple and inclusion of the Gentiles' by Jesus, to a situation that is concerned with purity and holiness as boundary markers and definers of the Petrine community's identity.[48]

communication aus IXes journées bibliques Louvain, Sept. 1957 (Paris: Desclée De Brouwer, 1959) 203–16.

40. So Goppelt, *1 Peter*, 70.
41. Elliott, *Elect*, 214ff.
42. Elliott, *Elect*, 218.
43. See E. Best, *1 Peter* (NCB; London: Oliphants, 1971), 286, who argues that the early church had already fused the various Levitical and neo-Levitical cultic ideas enough to form a useful backdrop for 1 Peter.
44. Elliott's contention that the idea of Christ's priesthood, being developed according to the Levitical pattern as opposed to the concept of ἱεράτευμα which relates to Exod. 19.6, cannot deny the connection of the two. His distinction between the priesthood and holiness is also puzzling given that the two are usually integrally intertwined (cf. Elliot, *Elect*, 220).
45. Cole, *Temple*, 31.
46. Bryan, *Judgement*, 156.
47. Bryan, *Judgement*, 146: 'pollution of the Land was thought to accumulate inexorably until a threshold was reached which demanded the punishment of exile'.
48. Cole, *Temple*, 31.

While the injunctions remain the same as in the OT, their function is markedly different in 1 Peter since, unlike the OT, the 'elect' now include Gentiles, and the premise of determining the insider is no longer obedience to the *Torah* (including the cultic life), but faith and baptism in Jesus Christ (covenant identification) who, significantly, is also the perfect or holy sacrifice (1.18-20; 2.24).

The *nomen actionis* ἀγιασμῷ ('sanctification'/ 'consecration'/ 'holiness' – 1.2) occurs in reference to the process of sanctification that is being worked out by the Holy Spirit of God in the body of believers.[49] This is the process of setting aside as *sacred* – much in the same way that holy objects dedicated to God were sprinkled with the blood of animals in the OT – the believers who are sprinkled with the blood of Jesus Christ (the perfect sacrifice without blemish – 1.19).

4.2.3. *Some Petrine Vocabulary on Holiness and Purity*

4.2.3.1. ἅγιος *(1.2; 1.15-16; 2.5, 9; 3.5-7)*

The original use of the term ἅγιος simply meant 'sacred' and referred specifically to sanctuaries, not people.[50] However, in the LXX ἅγιος was used to translate the Hebrew root קדשׁ, which referred to anything related to the *cultus*, including people. In 1 Peter, ἅγιος and its cognates are used to refer to sanctification (1.2), to the call to exercise holiness in all spheres of life (1.15), to model holiness after (or in relation to) God's holiness (1.16), and to its premise on Jesus, the sacrifice without blemish (1.18-20). The ἅγιος vocabulary becomes the means by which 1 Peter designates the believers as the 'spiritual house' that is being built (2.5) and must be kept holy, identifies the believers with the elect and holy nation of Israel (2.5, 9), and uses OT characters as examples to be emulated (3.5-7).[51]

Based on the cultic understanding of the believers' relationship to God – through Christ the perfect Lamb of God (ὡς ἀμνοῦ ἀμώμου καὶ ἀσπίλου Χριστοῦ) – 1 Peter is able to encourage his audience to assume, without apology, their role as the 'new Israel'. This they must do by keeping the command initially given to the nation of Israel (Lev. 11.44, 45; 19.2; 20.7, 26), but which now defines their status. The standard, just like in the OT, is the perfect character of the God who is ἅγιος. This same God of the OT is the Father of the Lord Jesus Christ (1.2-3) whose Spirit was prophesying in the prophets of old (1.10-12).

---

49.   Procksch, 'ἁγιασμός', *TDNT* 1.113. There is no clear equivalent in LXX.
50.   Procksch, 'ἁγιασμός', *TDNT* 1.88ff.
51.   Dan McCartney, 'The Use of the Old Testament in the First Epistle of Peter' (Ph.D. diss., Westminster Theological Seminary, 1989) 89.

This call to holiness has implications not only for sanctification, but also for all aspects of life (1.15 – πάσῃ ἀναστροφῇ). The aorist imperative γίνομαι indicates that there is to be no exception to this call to holy living; holiness is to characterize the believers' conduct in every life situation. However, the call to holiness is not a call to physical separateness from the rest of the world *contra* Qumran covenanters (CD 10.14–11.18; 1QS 9.20). Rather, it is a call to exhibit holiness through acts of godliness, especially in the midst of a hostile world (2.16-25; 3.5-12). As Cerfaux points out, this element is consistent with that of the Diaspora Jews who, even as the term ἱεράτευμα brought into relief a religious dimension, did not want to perceive themselves simply as foreign colonies in Hellenistic cities. They rather understood themselves as a priesthood charged with the worship of YHWH.[52] By applying the command 'Be holy because I am holy' in 1.19-20, 1 Peter anticipates 2.5 where he refers to the believers as the ἱεράτευμα ἅγιος leaving no doubt about this identification of the believers as the 'true Israel' of God. The adjective ἅγιος in 1.15 reflects the character of God whose attributes of perfection distinguish him from his creation while, in v. 16, where the adjective appears as part of the OT quotation, it is the standard set for the character of the believers.

For 1 Peter, uniqueness based on relationship to Christ, and a concern for the people to live out their faith among the non-believing populace – for the sake of the gospel – characterizes the dual emphases of identity and social boundaries.[53] On the one hand, a certain level of acculturation must be entertained for the sake of the Gospel (2.17-20), accentuating the constant threat they must watch out for concerning assimilation (4.3-4, 15). On the other hand, the Christian believers are addressed in terms and language reminiscent of the OT priests, sacrifices, and sanctuaries reminding them of their true identity that 'marks them out' as specially elect by God.[54]

As Hort explains, the separateness found in the Hebrew word קדש which forms the background for the Greek adjective ἅγιος is not one of aloofness or remoteness but 'rather of eminence or perfection'.[55] It indicates a certain immunity from defilement or disease, an understanding of the term that is distinctly different from the way it was interpreted and applied in the Qumran community. The call to be קדש in Qumran meant literal physical separation, not just from Gentiles (CD 10.14–11.18; 1QS 9.20), but especially from other Israelites who did not keep the Qumran brand of the Law (1QS 5.1, 10, 18; 8.13).[56]

52. Cerfaux, 'Sacerdotium', 11–13.
53. Smith-Christopher, *Theology*, 137–8.
54. Cerfaux, 'Sacerdotium', 25ff. Elliott, *Elect*, 221.
55. Hort, *St. Peter*, 70.
56. See also 11QTemp and CD 6.11-17, where the common verb used to denote separateness from the unclean world is בדל. The verb בדל has more polemic overtones – less the sense of separation due to specialness – in comparison with קדש and is significant in the covenanters' self-understanding of priesthood especially in light of Lev. 10.10.

Based on Hort's understanding, Michaels maintains that the adjective ἅγιος denotes a 'religious, almost numinous, quality characteristic of God (or the gods) and of the priests, Temples, and all kinds of cult objects [which] is boldly translated here into positive ethical virtues'.[57] Michaels postulates that this understanding of ἅγιος provides the genesis of 1 Peter's 'ethical implications of the ἁγιασμῷ πνεύματος mentioned [earlier] in v.2'.[58] In this regard, the command to be holy anticipates the emphatic beginning of the next major section in 2.11: 'Beloved, I urge you as πάροικος καὶ παρεπιδήμος to abstain from the desires of the flesh that wage war against the soul.' In this exhortation, the ethical virtues are related to the believers' pilgrim status as perceived through the lens of exile (1.17).

Similarly, Dalton notes that, 'while God's holiness is eternal, the holiness to which he calls his people must be worked out in the struggle of a pilgrim and exile existence'.[59] It is a holiness that is grounded in their involvement in this world which must find its outworking in the midst of all the challenges of pilgrim life – the life of exile. Not only are holiness and exile inextricably bound, they form the premise on which eschatological hope is built (1.20). Subsequently, this restoration hope anticipates its fulfillment based on God's act of raising Jesus from the dead (1.21).

Elliott identifies the motifs of holiness and election as the two central elements in 1 Peter's reformulation of the Christian experience.[60] For Elliott, it was as the 'elect eschatological people of God' that the believers of 1 Peter were being urged to maintain a life of holiness befitting the eschatological calling brought about by their election. Elliott is able to conclude that the 'explication of the two thoughts which figure so determinatively in 1P[eter], the election and holiness of the believing community, make it [1 Peter 2.4-10, the climaxing indicative statement to the paraenetic segment 1.3-2.10] ultimately the fundamental indicative of the entire epistle'.[61]

In sum then, we can conclude that this section on holiness is related to at least three things. First, it is related to the moral character of the believers (1.13-15). Second, it is related to the *cultus*, especially as it relates to sacrifice of Jesus (1.18-20). Third, it is related to obedience (1.22). This call to holiness is both a privilege (2.5, 9) and a preparation for the coming judgment.[62] The believers are called upon to display characteristics that are in keeping with the salvation and purification that they have been granted through the shed blood of Jesus Christ (1.18-19), which has made pure their souls and given them a new life

---

57. Michaels, *1 Peter*, 59.
58. Michaels, *1 Peter*, 59.
59. Dalton, 'So that', 271.
60. Elliott, *Elect*, 146ff.
61. Elliott, *Elect*, 219ff.
62. Davids, *1 Peter*, 17.

through the imperishable word (λογος) of God. Thus, 1 Peter has taken that which in Israelite religious traditions was epitomized in the cultic ceremonial sphere and re-appropriated and expanded it to apply to *all* spheres of life.[63]

4.2.3.2. ἡγνικότες / καθαρᾶς (1.22)

Building on the above discussion about the close proximity between purity and obedience in 1 Peter, we now turn to 1.22 where these two concepts are explicitly combined: 'Now that you have purified (ἡγνικότες) your souls by your obedience to the truth (ἀληθείας) so that you have genuine mutual love, love one another deeply from the heart.' The word ἀγνίζω usually carries a ceremonial referent both in the LXX (Isa. 66.17; 2 Chron. 29.16, 17) and in the NT (John 11.55; Acts 21.24, 26; 26.18; Jas 4.8; 1 Jn 3.3) and is probably doing the same here, while the use of αληθείας is probably in contrast to ἀγνοία in v. 14 which defines the falsehood of unbelief.

This section of 1 Peter echoes Jer. 6.16, in which the Lord calls the Israelites to purify themselves through obedience but they reject the offer: 'Thus says the LORD: Stand at the crossroads, and look, and ask for the ancient paths, where the good way lies; and walk in it, and find rest (ἀγνισμὸν) for your souls. But they said, "We will not walk in it".' This disobedience is soon followed by judgment on the temple, after Jeremiah's oracle that condemns the false security the people have derived from the presence of the temple in their midst (7.4-11). Consequently, due to their disobedience, the symbol of God's presence among them – the temple – would be removed. The Lord pronounces the destruction of the temple to the disbelieving hearers who had thought that the presence of the temple meant security, safety, salvation, and assurance of God's favor. Greater shock and astonishment follows the fact that it is God himself would destroy the place where his name dwells (7.12-15).

Jeremiah's judgment theme is echoed in the words of 1 Peter (1.17), who reminds his audience that all human acts will be subject to God's impartial judgment. As in the time of Jeremiah, it is a judgment that would begin in οἴκου τοῦ θεοῦ – the 'house of God' (4.14-17).[64] This then becomes the basis of 1 Peter's exhortation to his audience to maintain conduct that is pleasing to God (2.12), for the Lord's ear is inclined towards the righteous (3.12). Since they have purified their souls through ὑπακοῇ τῆς ἀληθείας ('obedience of truth'), their conduct should be dictated by their καθαρᾶς ('purified') hearts (1.22).[65]

---

63. Gerhard Sevenster, 'Het-Koning- en Priesterschap de Gelovigen in Het Nieuwe Testament', *NThT* 13 (1958) 301–17. Sevenster recognizes priesthood of believers as connoting worship with one's life reflecting the splendor of God and allowing for a voluntary approach to God.

64. Lohmeyer, *Temple*, 69. 'Kingdom of God and the church are ... linked together in the "House of God" metaphor, and become one with it over against the present and in anticipation of the future "other temple".'

65. A textual variant exists in 1 Peter 1.22, where the adjective καθαρᾶς is omitted by very few mss (A B 1852 it vg) and included by most (P⁷² ℵ* C Ψ K L P 33. 1739 *Byz Lect* vg syr cop). ℵ² and vg ᵐˢˢ read ἐκ καρδίας ἀληθινῆς almost certainly a misreading of ἀλλήλους, – the reason it is included in square brackets in the text.

For 1 Peter, obedience is an act of faith and not a prerequisite to faith meaning he is not calling for works righteousness but rather the expression of faith that demonstrates the believers' purification.

4.2.3.3. ὡς ἀμνοῦ ἀμώμου καὶ ἀσπίλου *(1.19)*

The phrase ἀμνοῦ ἀμώμου is in line with the characteristics specified for OT sacrificial animals (Lev. 14.13, 21, 24-25; Num 7.14, 15, 21, 27, 33, 39), but arguably here it recalls the Passover lamb of Exod. 12.5.[66] This connection is strengthened by the use of the rather uncommon classical word ἀσπίλος ('without spot or stain').[67] While ἀσπίλος does not occur in the LXX, it is added here to emphasize the holiness and purity of Christ's sacrifice,[68] given 1 Peter's melding the ideas of a faultless sacrificial lamb (Lev. 2.19-20) with the Isaianic silent lamb – the suffering servant (Isa. 53).[69]

The metaphor of the sacrificial lamb that describes Jesus Christ's blood as precious is drawn from Isa. 53.7, which invokes the deliverance from Egypt. As van Unnik observes, 'Isa. [53] is closely connected to the sacrificial service and consequently to the Paschal lamb: the yearly Paschal lamb was a memorial of the single Paschal lamb of the Exodus.'[70] Of the three annual events that brought Jewish pilgrims to Jerusalem *en masse* (Passover, Pentecost/ 'Feast of Weeks', 'Feast of Tabernacles' – five days after *Yom Kippur*), none was more significant to the Jewish psyche than the Passover ceremony. It commemorates the paradigmatic events of God's deliverance of the people of Israel from Egypt which, in essence, became *the* definitive divine act on Israel's behalf in Jewish lore according to which God's subsequent acts of Israelite redemption are interpreted. With time, the Deuteronomic code restricted the celebration of the Paschal sacrifices to the Jerusalem temple while integrating the lamb image into the deliverance theme.[71] The celebration in Jerusalem culminated with a sacrifice of a lamb at the temple altar as a re-enactment of the events of the redemption of Israel from Egypt.[72]

---

66. Kelly, *Peter and Jude*, 75 and Goppelt, *1 Peter*, 116; *Odes of Solomon* 14.17, commenting on Isa. 52.13, talks of the suffering servant as the ὁ ἀμνὸς τοῦ θεοῦ. See also Melito of Sardis, *On Pascha*, §§ 71, 103.

67. Hort, *St. Peter*, 77. Even though it was not necessarily always a lamb, it usually was. Its function was also not one of removal of sin, but an 'apotropaic to the angel of Death' (Exod. 12.13).

68. Achtemeier, *1 Peter*, 128-9; Kelly, *Peter and Jude*, 75.

69. Dubis, *Woes*, 51.

70. Van Unnik, 'Redemption', 19.

71. Melito of Sardis, *On Paschal*, §§ 288-91 (text and translations by Stuart George Hall, 1979, n. 11), notes, 'References to the Temple and Jerusalem allude to the celebration of the paschal sacrifice, restricted in the Deuteronomic code to Jerusalem. They gain particular point from the cessation of sacrifice when the Temple was destroyed.'

72. Philo elaborates on the priestly character of the Passover festival as the priestly duty of the whole community: 'The victims are not brought to the altar by the laity (οἱ ἰδιῶται) and sacri-

The difficulty for this view, as Hort notes, is that the Passover lamb was not represented in Exodus as a ransom paid for the deliverance of the Israelites from Egypt, since only the first born of Israel was saved by it and not the whole nation.[73] However, as Mark Dubis explains, 'the sprinkling of the blood of the paschal lamb conjures up images of atonement, especially when such sprinkling averts destruction of those within (Exod. 12:13)'.[74] Furthermore, 'the exodus allusions in the pericope suggest an allusion to the paschal lamb specifically, not just the OT sacrificial system in general'.[75]

This is also exactly how the early church understood the Paschal sacrifice. Melito of Sardis in his sermon *On Pascha*, §103, classifies Christ in language reminiscent of 1 Peter as the sacrifice lamb (ἀμνός), ransom (λυτρόω) and king (Βασιλεύς).[76] For Melito, both the Paschal lamb and the temple are replaced by the 'spotless Son' and 'Christ', respectively: τίμιος ἄφωνος ἀμνός νῦν δὲ ἄτιμος διὰ τὸν ἄμωμον υἱόν τίμιος ὁ κάτω ναός νῦν δὲ ἄτιμος διὰ τὸν ἄνω Χριστόν ('Precious was the lamb, but now it is precious no more because of the spotless Son. Precious was the Temple, but now it is precious no more because of the Christ above').[77]

In conclusion, the concepts of purity and holiness in 1 Peter not only recall OT cultic purity rites, they expand them to incorporate all spheres of life. It becomes definitive not only for a select group among the larger community, but for the entire community of believers imposing certain ethical and moral responsibilities that were previously restricted to a select group, the priests. Cultic elements of the OT such as sanctuaries and sacrifices are reinterpreted and applied to the community of believers, who make up the 'new Israel' and the new sanctuary, the 'spiritual house'.

---

ficed by the priests, but as commanded in the Law, the *whole nation acts as priests*, each individual bringing what he offers on his own behalf and dealing with his own hand' (*Vit. Mos.* 2.224 – emphasis added). In the same manner, *Spec. Leg.* 2.145ff also interprets the Paschal offering in light of the whole community: 'But on this occasion *the whole nation performs the sacred rites and acts as priest* with pure hands – ἀγναῖς χερσὶν ἱερουργεῖ καὶ ἱεράται (emphasis added). However, Philo's language is distinctly different from that of 1 Peter and he also does not treat the theme of priesthood in Israel. Nonetheless, see Seland Torrey, *Strangers in the Light: Philonic Perspectives on Christian Identity in 1 Peter* (BIS 76; Leiden: Brill, 2005) 114–15 for a more positive reading of Philonic connection to 1 Peter.

73. Hort, *St. Peter*, 77.
74. Dubis, *Woes*, 50 n. 8.
75. Dubis, *Woes*, 50 n. 8. *Contra* Achtemeier, *1 Peter*, 129.
76. For Melito, λαός refers to Israel who are essentially replaced by the ἐκκλησία (§ 43). However, when he attributes the death of Christ to Israel he mentions Israel by name (e.g., §§ 72–99). This, then, is the reason why the mystery of the Pascha has been fulfilled in the body of the Lord (§ 56).
77. See also Melito, *Pascha*, § 68, where clearly modifying 1 Peter 2.9, instead of βασίλειον ἱεράτευμα, he talks of βασίλειον αἰώνιον ('*eternal* kingship/royalty') and ἱεράτευμα καινόν ('a *new* priesthood'). He also alters ἔθνος ἅγιον, λαὸς εἰς περιποίησιν to simply λαὸν περιούσιον αἰώνων ('an eternal people special to him'). Cf. Mishnah *Pesahim* 10.5 and *Exod. Rab.* 12.2.

4.2.4. λυτρόω *and Temple Sacral Manumission* (1 Pet. 1.18-19)

The idea of Paschal sacrifice and ransom are also connected by the use of the verb λυτρόω.[78] In the LXX λυτρόω usually means 'ransom', while of the words it usually translates in the Hebrew (פדה and גאל) neither contains the idea of 'purchase' – both rather have the sense of 'deliver' or 'liberate'.[79] The verbal form of the word (ἐλυτρώθητε) occurs only here in the entire NT where it clearly carries the idea of 'purchase'.[80] However, since Chrysostom, this connection to freedom from slavery has been understood as the primary point of reference for these passages. Van Unnik points out that in both Hebrew (Aramaic) and Greek, these distinctions between 'ransom' and 'redeem' are not attested in the manner in which they function in modern Euro-American languages, and that both meanings are to be simultaneously found in the word λυτρόω.[81]

Like Paul's, 1 Peter's understanding of λυτρόω most likely derives from Jesus' Greek saying in Mt. 20.28 and Mk 10.45 that describes his own death as the λύτρον ἀντὶ πολλῶν ('ransom for many').[82] While some have tried to explain away the element of 'cost' attached to Jesus' metaphorical use of the term λυτρόω, such an interpretation would only obscure the substitutionary significance of Jesus' death. The idea of a substitutionary death only makes sense if there is a 'cost' or 'debt' to be paid.[83]

---

78.   Dubis, *Woes*, 51. 'In the midst of 1 Pet. 1.13-22's strong allusions to the *exodus*, however, 1 Pet. 1.18 alludes to Isa. 52.3, a text that is concerned with Israel's *exile*. As other exodus-oriented OT texts, Isa. 52.3, also speaks of God's "redemption" of Israel.' While it is true that in Exodus 'It is a redemption "without money" because God sovereignly determines when he will act – he is vassal to no kingdom', this does not seem to be implied for 1 Peter for whom a price, 'though not silver or gold', is nevertheless paid (1 Pet. 1.18). See also Spicq, *Saint Pierre*, 66; Goppelt, *1 Peter*, 115 n. 52; Michaels, *1 Peter*, 63.

79.   Van Unnik, 'Redemption', 12. A. Ritschl, *Die christliche Lehre der Rechtfertigung und Versöhnung* (Adolf Marcus, Bonn: 1899), 178–9, 222–3, 225, 239. Lev. 25.26-27 discusses the redemption of property from mortgage using λυτρόω.

80.   The verbal form occurs only two other times in the NT (Lk. 24.21; Tit. 2.14), always in the middle passive. Hans Windisch, *Die Katholischen Briefe* (Tübingen: Mohr, 1930) 49, considered the passages as pieces of a baptismal paraenesis, 1.13–2.10.

81.   Van Unnik, 'Redemption', 49. *Contra* Beare, *First Peter*, 77, who argues that the NT use has a 'weakened' force conveying the idea of '*deliverance*, not necessarily the paying of a ransom'.

82.   Deissmann, *Light*, 314ff. For Paul, adoption of Hellenistic terms and embellishing them with Judeo-Christian meaning, or vice-versa, is common. For example, the term Lord (Aramaic *Marana*) was a local Aramaic 'cult-title' that was adopted by Paul and applied to Jesus the Messiah. Paul utilized the metaphor of 'sacral manumission' especially in adapting the slave concept to the Hellenistic world. Selwyn, *1 Peter*,144–45 compares use of λυτρόω with Paul (1 Cor. 6.20; 7.23) and concludes that they are not quite identical. Also Mk 10.45 and Mt. 20.28.

83.   Sydney Page, 'Ransom Saying', in *DJG*, 660–2. Support for this understanding comes from the background OT text in Isaiah 53 (cf. 52.3) where the servant is depicted as suffering vicariously, and the use of the preposition ἀντι which suggests equivalence or exchange. Cf. C. K. Barrett, 'The Background of Mark 10.45', in *New Testament Essays for T. W. Manson* (ed.

Windisch adduces references from 1 *Clement* (7.4 and 12.7) in defense of understanding λυτρόω as ransom.[84] However, these passages would have to have been independent of 1 Peter to play that role, a proposition difficult to prove. The generally accepted view is that the word λυτρόω here implies freedom from slavery.[85] Van Unnik cites examples of Israel's deliverance from bondage in Egypt (Deut. 7.8; 15.15; 24.18; Ps. 77.42; 105.10; 135.24), from Babylonian exile (Ps. 106.2; Isa. 44.23; 63.9; Jer. 38.11; Sir. 48.20), and of the individual's deliverance from harm or danger (2 Sam 4.9; 1 Kgs 1.29; Dan. 3.88; 6.28).

This connection of sacrifice with manumission, together with Jesus' self-identification with the OT ransom and his subsequent sacrificial death, must have provided the point of contact for the early church in formulating this imagery. For example, it is the hope for the eschatological restoration of Israel that is expressed in the use of the verb λυτροῦσθαι in Luke 24.12. From the point of view of the imagery created by such language, it is difficult to refute the possibility of a 'temple sacral manumission' falling within the scope of 1 Peter 1.18.[86] Such an image of the substitutionary death of Jesus as described in 1 Peter 1.18-19 was probably connected to the sacral manumission of slaves in Greco-Roman temples, a practice inextricably bound with sacrifice as Deissmann aptly notes:

> It is clear from 1 Peter i.18, 19 that at a very early period the price was understood to be the Blood of Christ. The union of the idea of manumission with the idea of sacrifice was made easier for the ancient Christians by the fact that sacral manumission, *e.g.* at Cos, was not complete without sacrifice.[87]

A. J. B. Higgins; Manchester: Manchester University Press, 1959) 1–18, who calls to question the special connection that people have put between Jesus' concept of ransom and Isaiah 53. However, David Hill, *Greek Words and Hebrew Meaning* (SNTSMS 5; Cambridge: Cambridge University Press, 1967) 79, fittingly concludes on the matter that while Barrett's linguistic analysis is convincing, nevertheless, 'the *ideas* expressed in the Suffering Servant passages are echoed in the Markan verse' (emphasis original). R. Watts, 'Jesus' Death', in Bellinger and Farmer, eds., *Suffering Servant*, 140–1, further points out that it is strange that Barrett should argue against Isaiah 53 on the basis of absence of clear linguistic connection only to postulate an Exodus background whose only linguistic parallel is the root כבר. Far less obvious is Moses offering himself as a substitute for Israel, for he identifies with them and seeks to share their fate (Exod. 32.30ff).

84. Windisch, *Briefe*, 57: '... probes the precious blood of Christ (1 Clem 74,127) that people in antiquity very well had designated as a price, since money is within sacred actions often only replacement for original demand for blood'. Cf. Van Unnik, 'Redemption', 11 n. 16.

85. Van Unnik, 'Redemption', 12.

86. So Beare, *First Peter*, 79.

87. Deissmann, *Light*, 330. Romans had a fairly utilitarian conception of gods and temples with the edifices being as much part of the political and governmental life as they were religious (cultic). In this regard Cicero complains that a Roman gave thanks to gods, 'because he was rich, because he was honored, because he was safe and sound. They call Jupiter Best and Greatest because of these things, not because he makes us just, temperate and wise, but safe, secure, opulent, and well supplied'. *Cicero XIX* (LCL 268; trans. and ed. H. Rackham; Cambridge, Mass.: Harvard University Press, 1951) 372–3.

However, this is more than simply the transference of a Hellenistic concept into Judeo-Christian thought. While we recognize the Greco-Roman origin of the concept of temple sacral manumission, we also note the new meanings imported into it with the Judeo-Christian adoption of the λυτρόω vocabulary.[88]

By virtue of this sacrifice, the freedom thereby wrought was irreversible, so that the freed slave was completely loosed from any obligations to the former master and could not again be enslaved by his/her former master. For this reason, there were witnesses to the manumission in addition to a stone (*stele* or wall of the temple) engraved as evidence of the pious obligations imposed on the old master.[89] 1 Peter's reference to the price which is 'not silver or gold', but the 'precious blood' of Jesus Christ, leaves little doubt as to the fact that a transaction is taking place.[90] While it is not the case that a ransom payment is being made to another to 'purchase' the believers, the redemption nevertheless has a high cost – the precious blood of Jesus.

The verb λυτρόω also carries with it an exodus/exile motif, pointing to the deliverance of Israel from Egypt in relation to the paschal lamb (Exod. 6.6).[91] With its allusion to Isa. 52.3 in 1.18 (cf. 35.9; 41.14; 43.1, 14; 44.22-24; 62.12; 63.9), this passage also echoes the Babylonian exile incorporated in the Isaianic 'Second Exodus'.[92] Note, however, the difference between Isa. 52.3, where the people 'were *sold for nothing*', and would be 'redeemed *without money*', and 1 Pet. 1.18, where the people are ransomed with a price more precious than gold or silver, i.e. money. Zion is summoned to depart Babylon in language reminiscent of the exodus in Isa. 52 with the redemption's purpose

88. The noun λυτρωτής ('redeemer') is only found in biblical writings, including LXX Ps. 18.15 and 77.35 in reference to God, and in Acts 7.53 to Moses. Cf. also Lk. 24.21 compared to Isa. 44.22; Acts 28.19; Tit. 2.14; 2 *Esd.* 11.10.

89. The extremely numerous documents of this nature that have been found in Greek, Jewish, Judeo-pagan and even Christian records is ample evidence that it was common practice. Cf. Deissmann, *Light*, 321–7. *Contra* Beare, *First Peter*, 77.

90. So Elliott, *1 Peter*, 369; Van Unnik, 'Redemption', 12, elaborates that, 'the God of the Christians is not to be bought in any way that the judges were bought by money and the deities by sacrifices in Antiquity: The Christian is ransomed by precious blood'. Cf. 'λύτρον', in BAGD, 482b–483a.

91. U. Holzmeister, *Commentarius in epistulas SS. Petri et Judea, I Epistula Prima S. Petri* in *Cursus Scripturae Sacrae* III 13 (Parisiis, 1937), as referenced in Van Unnik, 'Redemption', 8. Cf. Charles Bigg, *Epistles of St. Peter and St. Jude* (ICC. New York: Charles Scribner's Sons, 1922) 118.

92. Hans M. Barstad, *A Way in the Wilderness: The 'Second Exodus' in the Message of Second Isaiah* (JSTS 12; Manchester: University of Manchester, 1989) 88. Barstad opposes the idea of distinct 'second exodus' texts in Isaiah and rather sees a collage of different ancient Israelite traditions used by Isaiah available to him, including exodus tradition. This is owing to the heavily metaphorical language of Isa. 40–55 whose primary literary expression is poetry. It is, however, unlikely that even in poetic writing the imagery of so significant an event in the life of the Israelite nation would not resonate with Isaiah's message of exile and restoration.

(Isa. 53 – λυτρόω) being a glorious reconciliation of Zion (Isa. 54) and a rejoicing over the miraculous increase of her offspring.[93] Both the exodus and the Babylonian exile represent a pattern of subjugation followed by liberation that has repeated itself in the history of Israel, and is here being incorporated by 1 Peter to describe his audience's state – spiritual and otherwise – and to point to the subsequent hope such imagery stimulates.

The author seems to have deliberately chosen these images, since these are two central motifs in his message (1.1-3, 18-20; 2.21-24; 3.17-18; 4.12-14, 16, 19; 5.10). For this reason, Selwyn says the image portrayed in 1.19 is that of the 'Egypt' out of which the audience of 1 Peter was redeemed.[94] The two images of exodus and manumission are inextricably entwined so that with the single word λυτρόω, the author manages to capture both. This understanding helps to elucidate the manner in which the sacrificial death of Jesus would have been comprehended as a vicarious ransom (Mk 10.45).

Furthermore, it might be inaccurate to describe the imagery drawn from λυτρόω as split between a Jewish understanding based on the exodus motif versus a Hellenistic understanding associating λυτρόω with sacral manumission.[95] Both the Gentile and the Jewish audience of 1 Peter would have correctly appropriated the imagery adduced by λυτρόω, whether interpreted in light of Israel's corporate redemption from Egyptian slavery or that of the emancipation of an individual slave *via* temple sacral manumission.

In sum, we have thus far sought to establish that the exodus/exile restoration motif provides a useful backdrop for understanding 1 Peter's use of the concept λυτρόω. As pilgrims or sojourners, 1 Peter's audience is not at home in their present situation, allowing the author to draw parallels between his audience and the wilderness/exile experiences of the nascent nation of Israel. Their pilgrimage, then, is to culminate in a restoration which had already begun with Jesus, but which is continuing as they are built up into the new 'spiritual house of God' where 'spiritual sacrifices' are offered. Jesus, their example, was offered up as a ransom for their redemption. They, in response, have to offer up spiritual sacrifices to God (2.11).

---

93. Elliott, *1 Peter*, 369.
94. Selwyn, *First Peter*, 145a.
95. Cleon L. Rogers, Jr. and Cleon L. Rogers III, *The New Linguistic Exegetical Key to the Greek New Testament* (Grand Rapids: Eerdmans, 1998) 569a. So Selwyn, *First Peter*, 144b. This is not to deny that these imageries are probably more pronounced in the respective groups (exodus motif for the Jews and temple sacral manumission for Hellenists) but that the latter was not as strange to the Jew as would be assumed.

4.2.5. *Living Temple: 'Living Stones' Built into a 'Spiritual House'*
(1 Peter 2.4-5, 9-10)

λίθον ζῶντα, θεῷ ἐκλεκτὸς ἔντιμος, λίθοι ζῶντες , οἶκος πνευματικὸς εἰς ἱεράτευμα ἅγιον
ἀνενέγκαι πνευματικὰς θυσίας (4-5) [Ps. 118:22; Isa. 28:16; Isa. 8:14]
βασίλειον ἱεράτευμα, ἔθνος ἅγιον, λαὸς εἰς περιποίησιν (9-10) [Isa. 43:20, 21; Exod. 19:6;
23:22; Hos. 1:6, 9]

This section of 1 Peter (2.4-10) relates most plainly the temple imagery in the epistle.[96] As we have been arguing through the previous sections, this imagery did not simply emerge out of nowhere but is rather anticipated in the first chapter with references to blood sprinkling, injunctions to holiness, precepts of incorruptibility, and the concepts of manumission. We have argued that all these concepts draw to themselves the image of the tabernacle/temple and really only make sense within the thought frame of the epistle if seen to relate to the tabernacle/temple image.

4.2.5.1. οἶκος πνευματικὸς: *Spirit and Temple in 1 Peter*
The traditional understanding of this section, as represented by Selwyn, is that in using the language of a 'spiritual house' (οἶκος πνευματικός), 1 Peter refers to the temple.[97] Elliott, on the other hand, has argued that the term is not used to describe the community in cultic terms, but rather is simply a metaphor used 'to *affirm* the elect and the holy identity, solidarity and status of the eschatological people of God'.[98] It thus should not be connected to the temple, since if that was 1 Peter's intention the word ναός would have been more appropriate.[99] Elliott has forcefully argued that οἶκος in this case should be understood simply as 'household' rather than a temple in accordance with its use in 1 Pet. 4.17.[100] Elliott's argument, however, is rather difficult to maintain (and confusing), given that it is precisely in the use of οἶκος in cultic form that the OT was able to designate the Israelites' identity as the elect and holy people of God.

Furthermore, as Albert Vanhoye points out, the term οἶκος conserves the double sense of the Hebrew word בית as a reference to physical structures, e.g. house of God, and to family units, e.g. house of David.[101] In addition, a

---

96. Jacques Schlosser, 'Ancien Testament et christologie dans la *Prima Petri*', in Charles Perrot et al., eds., *Étude de la Première Lettre de Pierre* (Lectio Divina 102; Paris: Éditions du Cerf, 1980) n. 1; however, see Elliott, *Home*, 165–266.
97. Selwyn, *First Peter*, 285–91.
98. Elliott, *Home*, 168. (emphasis added)
99. Elliott, *Home*, 158–59.
100. Elliott, *Home*, 39–48; *idem*, *1 Peter*, 414ff. See Achtmeier, 'Excursus', in *1 Peter*, 158-9, for a response to Elliott.
101. Albert Vanhoye, 'L'Epître (1 P 2,1-10): La maison spirituelle', *AsSeign* 43 (1964) 16–29, 16.

third aspect in the LXX for the οἶκος metaphor was reference to the nation of Israel.[102] And for Joseph Coppens, it is only in 1 Pet. 2.4-11 that the temple image is logically construed on the basis of a building. Only here, in the entire NT, are the three elements of temple, priesthood and sacrifices mentioned together, making the cultic context and intention unquestionable.[103] Unlike Eph 2.21, which identifies the structure explicitly as the ναὸς ἅγιος, 1 Peter prefers to use the more elusive οἶκος πνευματικός.[104] However, there is no denying that the main imagery presupposed by the Petrine passage is the temple (cf. 1 Pet. 4.17 and Ezek. 9.7).

In this regard, Paul Achtemeier is right on target when he concludes that '... one can only with great difficulty fail to find references to the temple in these passages'.[105] Nonetheless, Elliott's point about the importance of 1 Peter's interest in the household needs to be upheld maintaining the spiritual nature of the household in 1 Peter in contrast to the racial or bloodline brotherhood that characterized Israel.[106]

It is in this section of 1 Peter (2.4-10) that the contrast is sharpest between the conception of the 'new Israel' – the new 'Temple-Community' – and the Israel of old with its physical temple. The Christians are now the 'elect and holy nation' (1.2), and in contrast to the letter to the Hebrews where Christ is the High Priest, here there is a corporate priesthood which is both 'holy' (2.5) and 'royal' (2.9) '... inasmuch as the context is concerned with the people of God as one nation (ἔθνος ἅγιον, 2:9) among others (ἐν τοῖς ἔθνεσιν, 2:11f.)'.[107] It is difficult not to see a hint of a polemic with first-century Judaism, especially the Jerusalem temple and its priesthood.[108] As Cohen notes, in 'ancient

---

102. Lohmeyer, *Temple*, 65: 'In the OT the Temple has a threefold function; it is the house where God rules, where He judges, and where one worships Him.'

103. Joseph Coppens, 'The Spiritual Temple in the Pauline Letters and its Background', *Studia Evangelica* 6 (1973) 53–66, 50. So also Achtemeier, *1 Peter*, 158–9. Selwyn, *First Peter*, 296, gives a warning: 'Temple – priesthood – sacrifices: we are not entitled to regard these terms as purely metaphorical.' See also how it echoes OT references to the Temple like ὁ οἶκος τὸ ἅγιον of Isaiah 64.11 (64.10 – LXX).

104. Bigg, *St. Peter*, compares Petrine and Pauline writings and concludes the following: In areas of dogma Paul and Peter are substantially in accord (cf. Gal. 2.6, 15, 16) while in the practical sphere they differ widely from one another. The difference is not as one (Peter) who misunderstands a teacher (Paul). If there is dependency between Peter and Paul, it is Paul that borrows from Peter since, whenever they differ, Peter stands nearer to the evangelists and Acts (34–35). Prophetism sums up in one word the difference between Paul the mystic and Peter the disciplinarian.

105. Achtemeier, *1 Peter*, 159. See Elliott, *Elect*, 50–108; *idem., Home*, 168ff.

106. Beare, *First Peter*, 96. The exile resulted in certain significant alterations in the social structures of the community. Determination of the 'true Israelite' (or the 'purified sons of Exile') shifted from a family unit base to 'social adaptation to the conditions of the group'. See Norman K. Gottwalt, *The Tribes of Yahweh* (New York: Maryknoll, 1979) 285ff; Smith, *Landless*, 93–126; Weinberg, *Citizen-Temple*, 135.

107. Schutter, *Hermeneutic*, 171.

108. C. F. D. Moule, 'Sanctuary and Sacrifice in the Church of the New Testament', *JTS* 1 (1950) 29–41. *Contra* Goppelt, *1 Peter*, 140, who argues that οἶκος πνευματικός is used 'neither

Judaism sectarian alienation, whatever its origin, generally expressed itself in polemics against the central institutions of society (notably the temple), its authority figures (notably the priests), and its religious practices (notably purity, Sabbath and marriage law)'.[109]

The call for a reasonable *apologia* to any who seek a reason for what the Petrine community believes (1 Pet. 3.15) increases the plausibility of such an assumption. On the other hand, it might be the result of a general outrage against Christians' lack of a sacrificial system.[110] Either way, it is difficult to rule out polemical overtones against the Jerusalem temple and its priesthood in the Petrine declaration of the community as the new dwelling place of God.[111]

The interpretation of the community as an 'edifice' was preceded by the Qumran community's interpretation of itself as a temple (1QS 5.6; 8.5), a house (CD 7.11ff; 20.10, 13), and a city (1QH 6.25-29).[112] 1 Peter, reminiscent of the Qumran community, had to formulate a new religious expression that was not premised on a physical temple.[113] Both groups display characteristics of sectarian tendencies that suggest a polemic against the Jerusalem temple, its priesthood and religious practices.[114] With the 'idea of exile' as a controlling metaphor, and 1 Peter's identity of the community as the new temple and the new priesthood, there is present here what N.T. Wright calls a 'counter temple' ideology.[115] This ideology characterized both 1 Peter and the Qumran community, albeit with significant differences.

Qumran represents a more decisive break within the Jewish priesthood in the Jerusalem temple, which led to the withdrawal of some of the priests into the desert at Khirbet Qumran. Their self-removal from the temple and its

polemically over against Judaism, nor apologetically in relation to Gentile temples, nor 'salvation-historically' in relation to the temple of the Old covenant'. However, see Goppelt, *1 Peter*, 141.

109. Cohen, *Maccabees*,168. Cf. also Wright, 'Dialogue', 254.

110. Moule, 'Sanctuary', 29.

111. Jonsen, 'Moral', 99: 'The life builds up the holy community: holy because it is the place where the Lord dwells. The venerated name of the Temple, residence of the Glory of Yahweh, may aptly be applied to this community.'

112. Similarities between the Qumran material and 1 Peter have been used to argue for dependence of the latter on the former (see Ernest Best, 'I Peter II. 4-10: A Reconsideration', *NovT* 11 (1969) 270–93, 285). Schutter, *Hermeneutic*, 138, points out that use of the *pesher*-like hermeneutics in 1 Peter bears strong resemblance to the midrashic exegesis at Qumran. However, any direct dependence is highly unlikely and, if at all, very secondary (Achtemeier, *1 Peter*, 151–2).

113. Cohen, *Maccabees*, 131–2, finds the distinguishing element between Qumran and New Testament conceptualization of the temple as primarily one between the view of a temporary replacement in the former, and a permanent replacement in the latter. Otherwise, both groups identified themselves as the new spiritual temple that was a replacement of the physical structure due to the latter's weakened ideological significance for both communities. See also ch. 2 above.

114. Cohen, *Maccabees*, 168; Wright, 'Dialogue', 254.

115. Wright, 'Dialogue', 254.

cultus meant that they had to reinterpret their self-understanding without access to a temple. The result was the community's self-understanding as the embodiment of the temple (1QS 8.4-6; 4QpIsa[d], frag. i). In CD 3.18–4.10 the idea of a בית נאמן בישראל ('sure house in Israel') built by God, and connected to the community as the 'true' priesthood is developed (1QpHab 12.2ff).[116] While it is not clear in CD that the 'sure house' is a reference to the temple, its equivalent use in *1 Enoch* 53.6 ('house of this congregation') and in 4QFlor, leaves no doubt about that reference.[117] Likewise we can conclude that the use of the term in CD is also in reference to a temple, in which the council of the community is understood to be identified with 'Lebanon', a term that Geza Vermes has argued is best understood as a reference to the temple.[118]

Consequently, we see that the Qumran covenanters identified themselves as the 'true or genuine Temple of God'.[119] Based on this understanding, Ernest Best has argued that the community of Qumran was 'the cradle from which the NT conception of the temple and priesthood of the church is derived'.[120] However, based on arguments that have been levied against a direct influence of Qumran on the NT writers,[121] we have to disagree with Best and argue that, for 1 Peter in particular, a milieu of Jewish thought in the Second Temple period provided the framework of temple imagery that was independently arrived at both in Qumran and in 1 Peter. Both are distinct products of a common Jewish mindset that had lost confidence in the physical temple as the abode of God and had sought an alternative (Cf. *Jub.* 23.21; *1 Enoch* 89.72-75; Bar. 4.2-6).[122]

Furthermore, there are at least three significant points of difference between the NT understanding of the temple and Qumran. First, unlike the NT which generally prefers the complete replacement of the temple in Jerusalem, Qumran covenanters did not stop believing in the physical temple.[123] In fact, they anticipated a time when they would return to take charge of the Jerusalem temple and offer righteous sacrifices (War Scroll; 11QTemple). It is for this reason that the rules of purity were so stringently applied in the community so that they would be ever prepared to suddenly take over the temple to cleanse it and restore the purity perceived to be lacking.

---

116. Achtemeier, *1 Peter*, 151. 1QH 6.25ff the subject 'I' could be representative of either the collective community or the Teacher of Righteousness.

117. Donald Juel, *Messiah and Temple: The Trial of Jesus in the Gospel of Mark* (Missoula, Mont.: Scholars Press, 1977) 163ff.

118. Geza Vermes, *Scripture and Tradition in Judaism* (SPB 4; Leiden: Brill, 1961) 26–39.

119. Klinzing, *Umdeutung*, 210ff, maintains that the Qumran community's self-understanding as a 'temple of believers' may have had formative influence on the Christian understanding of the church as the 'new temple'. Yet any notion of a direct influence has to be ruled out. Cf. Lichtenberger, 'Atonement', 159–71.

120. Best, 'Reconsideration', 284.

121. See, for example, Michaels, *1 Peter*, 96 and Gärtner, *Temple*, 78.

122. See Chapter 3 above.

123. Cohen, *Maccabees*, 168.

Second, the NT understanding of the temple as spiritual seems to stem more from the words of Jesus as recorded in Mark 14.58 ('We heard him say, "I will destroy this Temple that is made with hands, and in three days I will build another, not made with hands"') and interpreted in John in light of the body of Jesus (Jn 2.18-22 'But he was speaking of the Temple of his body'). This is precisely the reason that 1 Peter first talks of the believers coming to the λίθος ζῶντα ('living stone') – a post-resurrection designation of Jesus – who was rejected by the people (ὑπὸ ἀνθρώπων μὲν ἀποδεδοκιμασμένον).[124]

1 Peter perceived the spiritual house as the eschatological temple where God's presence rests permanently. Gärtner, following Selwyn, explains that 'spiritual' refers to its belonging to a 'new sphere', which is itself a product of the outpouring of the Holy Spirit. In that case the term 'spiritual' would also suggest the meaning '*true* temple of God' versus a '*false* temple'.[125] However, such a distinction (true/false) may be too radical. Instead, it might be more appropriate to conceive of the 'new temple' as a typological fulfillment of the 'old temple'. In this regard, the 'old temple' foreshadowed the new, the former prefiguring the latter.[126] This way the comparison is not on the basis of true versus false, since both are 'true', but rather the physical temple was pointing to the new eschatological reality, the church.[127]

Evidence from the early church also indicates that this interpretation is to be preferred. For example, Melito of Sardis uses the language of typological supersession.[128] Melito understood the physical temple to have been precious but incomplete, and only a type of that which had been revealed in the latter days in the person of Jesus Christ by the power of his Holy Spirit. This would suit better Gärtner's description when he states that the use of the word does not relegate this structure to the realm of the 'less real' but rather it indicates the elevation of the new temple and *cultus* through Jesus Christ: 'The Holy Spirit is the new sphere of reality to which the Church and the company of Christians belong.'[129] The primary difference is that the 'former' temple is

---

124. Eduoard Cothenet, 'Le réalisme de l'espérance chrétienne selon 1 Pierre', *NTS* 27 (1981) 564–72, 565. Rejection is also important in Mark 12 where the parable of the vineyard is an implicit reference to temple imagery, i.e. tower =temple. And in Mark 13.1-2, Jesus 'rejects' the physical temple.

125. Gärtner, *Temple*, 73. While I think Gärtner's sense is correct, it might be reading too much into what is not a property of the word itself.

126. Koester, *Dwelling*, 156 n. 12. The use of ἀντίτυπος in 1 Pet. 3.21 is compared to its use in Heb. 9.24 and for the former it compares the past versus the present while in the latter the comparison is between the earthly and the true heavenly sanctuary.

127. Selwyn, *First Peter*, 291. While Selwyn quotes *Barn.* 4.11: 'Let us become spiritual. Let us become a temple perfect unto God' in support of his interpretation of the 'true temple', the imagery is perhaps better understood in terms of our proposed paradigm of 'imperfect' and 'perfect'. Cf. *Barn.* 16.10, where the 'spiritual temple' is used as an analogy of Christian community.

128. Melito, *On Pascha*, §§ 280–300.

129. Gärtner, *Temple*, 73 n. 1.

only a type of the latter, a shadow of the 'real' temple composed of the believers. The 'imperfect' looking forward to the 'perfect' of the latter's revelation, yet both remaining 'true'.

Selwyn also points out that the word πνευματικός is not found in the LXX (nor apparently in Hellenistic literature before 100 CE) while in classical Greek it is solely connected to 'wind' and 'air'. He thus argues for a Christian coinage of the term describing the new state in which Christians now live through the Spirit.[130] Paul in Rom. 7.14 describes the law as πνευματικός, in contrast to his carnal and sinful self (cf. Gal. 6.1; 1 Cor. 3.1). The πνευματικός person is able to discern the things of God (1 Cor. 2.13-15; 14.37) while the gifts of the Holy Spirit are designated πνευματικός (Rom. 1.11; 1 Cor. 12.1).

Through Christ, Gentiles become partakers of the πνευματικός blessings (Rom. 15.27; Eph 1.3), while the resurrected bodies are described as πνευματικός (1 Cor. 15.46). The rock which followed the Israelites in the desert wanderings is referred to as πνευματικός (1 Cor. 10.4), while the manna was πνευματικός food (1 Cor. 10.3). Eph 5.19 speaks of πνευματικός songs of worship (cf. Col 3.16), while in Eph 6.12 the evil spirits are called πνευματικός. Rev 11.8 uses the adverb πνευματικῶς metaphorically to describe Jerusalem as 'Sodom and Egypt'. And so, 1 Peter's combination of the term πνευματικός with οἶκος (cf. 4.17) implies that he intends this structure to be understood as the realm within which the Spirit of God dwells. This is the 'new temple', formed by the Spirit and indwelt by the Spirit – a significant component regarded as missing in the second temple.[131]

The phrase οἶκος πνευματικός combines the two themes that are significant for 1 Peter in relation to the presence of God – the temple and the Spirit.[132] In comparing 1 Peter's terminology with the *targumim* the word *Šekinah* provides a helpful corollary to the reference to the Spirit in 1 Peter. As a cognate of the verb שׁכן ('to dwell'), *Šekinah* is also used to describe the numinous immanence which is commonly associated with the glory of God in the *targumim*.[133] For example, *Tg. Neofiti* Exod. 24.17 explains that 'the appearance of the glory of the *Šekinah* of the Lord (was) like a devouring fire, a devouring fire on the top of the mountain, in the eyes of the children of Israel'[134]

---

130. Selwyn, *First Peter*, 160, 281–4.

131. The lack of the cloud of glory (the *Šekinah*) in the second temple was a clear sign that the presence of God was suspect, at least in comparison to the tabernacle and the first temple (Psalm 74.9; *Prayer of Azariah* 15 [Theodotian Daniel 3.38]; 1 Macc. 4.46; 9.27; 14.41; Josephus, *C. Ap.*1.37-41; *2 Apoc. Bar.* 85.3; *b.Yoma* 9b; *b. Sanh.* 11a; *b. Sot.* 48b; *j. Sot.* 9.17). Cf. Adolf von Schlatter, *Petrus und Paulus nach dem Ersten Petrusbrief* (Stuttgart: Calwer Vereinsbuchhandlung, 1937) 94.

132. Dubis, *Woes*, 125ff.

133. This is distinct from the OT use of the term כבוד (LXX: δόξα) which refers to the weightiness, and usually refers to the invisible essence, of God. Even when used in the cloud of the storm in the desert it is necessarily a cloud that veils the presence of God. See G. Von Rad and G. Kittel, 'δόξα', *TDNT* 2.238-46.

4.2.5.2.. λίθος: *Temple Building Blocks*

An ABCB́Á pattern emerges based on λίθος and its use in the stone word link in 1 Peter 2.4-9. At the center is the quote from Isaiah that identifies Jesus as the precious cornerstone laid by God for the construction of the temple.

A – v. 4 Jesus is the λίθος ζῶντα (living stone) *rejected* by men but *precious* to God

   B – v. 5 the believers are λίθοι ζῶντες (living stones)

      C – v. 6a God lays in Zion a λίθος (stone), a precious cornerstone (ἀκρογωνιαῖος)

   B́ – v. 7 Jesus is the λίθος (stone) the builders *rejected*

A´ – Jesus, the *rejected* stone, is now the *main cornerstone* (κεφαλὴ γωνίας)[135]

According to Brox, the connections between these OT passages are simply in their Christological use and not in their execution or utilization. For this reason, 1 Peter applies the stone imagery to Christ in v. 4, anticipating his unique contribution of designating the Christians as 'living stones' in v. 5.[136] As such, 1 Peter is an example of the loose-fitting biblical Jewish stone tradition, which could be sculpted differently depending on the purposes of individual authors. Achtemeier concludes as much when he states that, 'the most probable solution is to see here elements of an early Jewish-Christian tradition subsequently taken over by the Hellenistic Christian community as its use by Paul and the authors of the Gospels indicates'.[137]

The catchword concatenation of OT texts is produced via the *Stichwort* λίθος in a manner reminiscent of the Jewish *gezera shewa* method of linking key words.[138] This Jewish practice of interpretation of Scripture was adopted by the NT writers,[139] as evidenced by the fact that the three passages 1 Peter alludes to (Ps. 118.22-23; Isa. 8.14; and Isa. 28.16) are also cited in various combination forms in other the NT writings reflecting, perhaps, an early Christian tradition.[140] McCartney points out that the *Stichwort* is not the only

---

134. Mary Coloe, *God Dwells with Us: Temple Symbolism in the Fourth Gospel* (Collegeville, Minn.: Litrugical Press, 2001) 59. As Coloe notes, the term preserves the sense of the holy transcendence of God 'while acknowledging the god's presence within Israel's midst' and that '[it is also] associated with the fiery light'.

135. Manns, 'La maison', 209–10. Only after developing this chiasm independently did I come across the two developed by Manns who divides up the passage between 2.1-5 and 2.6-10.

136. Brox, *Petrusbrief*, 100.

137. Achtemeier, *1 Peter*, 152.

138. Manns, 'La maison', 209 n. 9; Craig Keener, *A Commentary on the Gospel of Matthew* (Grand Rapids: Eerdmans, 1999) 515–16. The λίθος *Stichwort* did not have a pre-Christian origin and may even have originated with Jesus himself according to J. Rendall Harris, *Testimonies* (Cambridge: Cambridge University Press, 1916) 2.96.

139. Cf. *Florilegium* and *Testimonies* from Cave 4. See also Schutter, *Hermeneutic*, 87, who finds similarities between 1 Pet. 3.10, 4QTestimonia, 4QFlorilegium and 11QMelchizedek.

140. Karen H. Jobes and Moisés Silva, *Invitation to the Septuagint* (Grand Rapids and Carlisle: Eerdmans and Paternoster, 2000) 198. So Kelly, *Peter and Jude*, 95; Elliott, *Elect*, 32.

relationship in these verses since all three OT passages evidence a metaphorical reference to God's action in establishing the covenant, while the stone can be understood as God's personal agent who executes divine intent (cf. also Dan 2.34, 45).[141] Ps. 118.22-23 is quoted in Mk 12.10-11 (cf. Mt. 21.42-43; Lk. 20.17) and in Acts 4.11; Isa. 8.14 is cited in Rom. 9.33; Isa. 28.16 is cited in Rom. 9.33 and in Eph 2.20; Isa. 28 is found in Rom. 9.32-33; 10.11, and an allusion in Eph 2.20. Ultimately, all the NT quotations seem to have fairly common variations from the LXX indicating a common source or a common Christian tradition.[142]

Elliott subdivides 1 Peter 2.4-10 into three sections (vv. 4-5. 6-8, 9-10) with the last two sections consisting of a conflation of OT themes around a pre-Christian tradition of the λίθος.[143] If this is true, it was not a consistent tradition. While 1 Peter uses a text very similar to the LXX, significant differences emerge, e.g. the LXX reads λίθον πολυτελῆ ἐκλεκτὸν while 1 Peter omits πολυτελῆ. At least three suggestions have been advanced to explain this omission: First, that πολυτελῆ and ἐκλεκτὸν are two adjectives used to translate the same Hebrew word (חֵן). However, πολυτελῆ is never used to translate חֵן in the OT. A second possible solution is that the original translation of חֵן was ἐκλεκτὸν, with πολυτελῆ added later by a scribe. A third possibility is that a translator confused בֵּחַן and חֵן, and included both in the translations of the text. In this case, 1 Peter would have used a text with the word πολυτελῆ and deliberately left it out. Ultimately, it seems more plausible that 1 Peter simply had a text that did not have πολυτελῆ in it.

The psalm is about David, and thus also inferentially about the Messiah (Midrash on Psalms) and it is also a Passover psalm (and thus a tabernacle psalm) displaying a strong sense of redemption.[144] The importance of this is that Ps. 118 (117) had been linked to the temple in its use in the liturgical procession to the temple and already had been associated with the feast of tabernacles, one of the three pilgrim festivals.[145] Congar, who argues that the psalm reflects 'a reconstruction of Sion and the temple after a period of trial

141. McCartney, 'OT in First Peter', 83. The reference to the 'stone not cut with human hands' (λίθος ἐξ ὄρους ἄνευ χειρῶν) in Dan. 2.34-35, 45, was interpreted in messianic terms within Jewish literature. Cf. J. Jeremias, 'λίθος', *TDNT* 4.272–83.

142. Pierre Prigent, *Les testimonia dans le christianisme primitif. L'Épître de Barnabé I – XVI et ses sources* (Paris: Études Biblique, 1961) 16–28, 22, proposed the existence of a 'testimony book' that was used in the early church for catechism. 'This *Testimonia* hypothesis, at once both a flexible and firmly documented form, appears to have acquired true maturity ... in productions of patristic works, finding support in an indisputable manner and not as an hypotheses of occasional utilization by the authors of the Christian scriptures.' However, it is more likely that the source was oral rather than written. Cf. also Snodgrass, 'Affinities', 99.

143. Elliott, *Elect*, 16–49,

144. J. Duncan M. Derrett, 'The Stone that the Builders Rejected' in *Studia Evangelica* 4 (1968) 180–6, 181.

145. A. Cohen, *Psalms* (Soncino Books of the Bible; London: Soncino, 1945) 389–93.

equivalent to death and from which Yahweh has delivered his people', also points to at least two possible situations that Ps. 118(117) could have been alluding to: a) destruction of Jerusalem in 587/6 BCE (or 538 BCE) and b) desecration and purification of the temple in 168–65 BCE.[146] The establishment of this psalm's connection to the temple happened before its combination with the Isaianic passages as commentary on the 'temple-community' while its connection to commencement of exile situates it within the framework of the anticipation of a restoration from exile true also of the Isaianic passage.

The common element is that the catena of OT passages was applied in the NT to Jesus as the λίθος – the living foundation for the Church (Mt. 21.42; Mk 12.10-11; Lk. 20.17; Acts 4.11; Rom. 9.25-33; Eph 2.20).[147] Jesus uses Ps. 118(117).22-23 eschatologically to prophesy about his death and resurrection[148] and 1 Peter applies the 'stone *testimonia*' to his readers in a manner that also goes beyond Paul's by directly connecting the λίθος to the new temple.[149] The mystery of the passion-resurrection is evoked by the image of the rejected stone[150] with 1 Peter totally ignoring the significant Pauline Jew/Gentile distinction.[151]

The use of these texts would have been encouraged by their accessibility, made possible by the LXX's inclusion of the phrase καὶ ἐὰν ἐπ' αὐτῷ πεποιθὼς ᾖς ('and if you put your confidence in him'), which has no corresponding text in the MT. It is likely that the LXX translator was influenced by Isa. 8.17 (καὶ πεποιθὼς ἔσομαι ἐπ' αὐτῷ) – which in the MT is a warning about God being a trap and a stumbling-stone (i.e. a stone that causes stumbling – וְקִוֵּיתִי־לוֹ) – and changed it into an assurance that God would not be a cause of stumbling.[152]

Dodd argued that Rom. 9.30-33 recorded the older tradition of this OT catena, but Elliott's argument is that 1 Peter might have the older tradition which Paul abbreviated and revised for his purpose.[153] Alternatively (and

---

146. Congar, *Mystery*, 139–40.

147. Thomas Lea, 'How Peter Learned', 96–102, 100.

148. Joel Marcus, *The Way of the Lord: Christological Exegesis of the Old Testament in the Gospel of Mark* (Louisville, Ky.: Westminster/John Knox, 1992) 114–21.

149. McCartney, 'OT in First Peter', 84. However, the claim by C. H. Dodd, *According to Scriptures: The Sub-structure of New Testament Theology* (London: Nisbet, 1952) 41ff, of an independent *testimonium* commonly utilized by the NT authors, remains simply a hypothesis. Cf. Elliott, *Elect*, 130ff.

150. Manns, 'La maison', 211; Marcus, *Way*, 111–29.

151. Cothenet, 'Orientations', 34: 'the resemblances are balanced by the differences, since Paul's dialectic between Jew and Gentile is ignored by Peter'.

152. Jobes, *Invitation*, 198. ἐπ' αὐτῷ is added in the LXX Isa. 8.17 connecting it to Isa. 8.14, since the MT וְקִוֵּיתִי־לוֹ has no referent.

153. Dodd, *According to Scripture*, 43; Elliott, *Elect*, 30 n. 2.

preferably) both Paul and 1 Peter used independent traditions which each shaped according to his purpose.[154] This would be the case especially considering the similar combinations of OT passages in Qumran, Gospels, and in Acts.[155] Note that 1 Peter agrees with Rom. 9.31-33 against LXX by omitting the negation and by using qualifying genitives (προσκόμματος and σκανδάλου) instead of datives (προσκομματι and πτωματι). 1 Peter and Romans also replace the LXX ἐμβαλῶ with τίθημι and omit εἰς τὰ θεμέλια while including ἐπ᾽ αὐτῷ which occurs only in some LXX mss. Ultimately, Michaels is right to conclude that

[1] Peter stands in contrast to most other early Christian uses of such biblical texts as Ps. 118:22. The same text is cited in Matt 21:42-43 to prove that 'the kingdom of God will be taken from you [i.e., the 'Jewish high priests and Pharisees', v. 45] and given to a nation [i.e. the Gentile Christian churches] accomplishing its deeds'...[n]or does he link his two Isaiah quotations (i.e., 28:16 and 8:14) to Israel's failure to attain its own standards of righteousness as Paul did in Rom. 9:31-33.[156]

4.2.5.2.1. *Absence of* θεμέλιος *in 1 Pet. 2.4-10*

In contrast to the Qumran community, for whom the foundation terminology was fundamental – as a *descripta* of their elect status and as a link to the temple (1QH 6.25-29; 7.8-9; 1QS 5.6; 9.5; 8.5-10; 9.4-5) – 1 Peter omits θεμέλιος from the OT quotation. Gärtner expresses surprise at the absence of the emphasis in 1 Peter, while for Elliott it is exactly this absence of the term that is indicative of 1 Peter's independent and creative utilization of the OT passages to suit his purpose.[157] Snodgrass, however, maintains that this omission has little to do with 1 Peter's interpretive motive but rather that this form of quotation 'apparently resulted from the frequent use of Isa. xxxviii. 16 in the Jewish world'.[158]

An important point about 1 Peter's omission of θεμέλιος from 2.4-10 is the fact that the use of θεμέλιος in describing the work of Christ is specifically highlighted in other NT writings like Rom. 15.20 and in 1 Cor. 3.11, where it is Christ who is said to be the θεμέλιος of the Church (in contrast to Eph 2.20,

154. Snodgrass, 'Affinities', 106: 'While Isa. viii. 14 had been joined to Isa. xxviii. 16 in pre-Christian Judaism, there is no indication that Psa. cviii. 22 had. It is unlikely, however, that the writing of 1 Peter was the first occasion for the use of the three passages together.'

155. Snodgrass, 'Affinities', 103: 'Any theory of dependence that would do justice to the parallels with Rom. ix. 25-33; Eph. ii. 14-22; and 1QS viii. 4-10 would be too complex for acceptance.'

156. Michaels, *1 Peter*, xlix. Cf. Keener, *Matthew*, 515.

157. Elliott, *Elect*, 27; Gärtner, *Temple*, 133 n. 6; K. Gärtner gives two possible reasons for this scenario: 1 Peter may be polemical to the 'claims of the Qumran community' or it is a 'complete shift in focus, from the firmly based [Qumran] community to faith in Christ'.

158. Snodgrass, 'Affinities', 98 n. 2, *contra* Barnabas Lindars, *New Testament Apologetic* (London: SCM Press, 1961) 178, Lloyd Gaston, *No Stone On Another: Studies in the Significance of the Fall of Jerusalem in the Synoptic Gospels* (Leiden: E. J. Brill, 1970) 219–22 and Elliott, *Elect*, 27.

where it is the apostles and prophets that are designated as the θεμέλιος upon which the οἶκος τοῦ θεοῦ is being built).[159] 1 Peter instead chooses to put his emphasis on the 'rejected stone' (λίθος ὃν ἀπεδοκίμασαν) as the premise of the οἰκοδομήσω ('foundation') terminology. This not only distinguishes 1 Peter from Pauline literature, it also shows that the conception of the Church as an οἰκοδομή was not fixed and could be articulated in various formulations.[160] In Mt. 16.18 Jesus identifies the disciple Peter as πέτρα upon which he will lay the foundation (οἰκοδομήσω) of his Church. These words of Jesus provide the theological framework of foundation terminology, and any claim that Jesus is not the foundation for the temple in 1 Peter (because the reference to him here is only on the basis of the stone *Stichwort* and not θεμέλιος) is unfounded. As Snodgrass correctly asserts, 'τιθέναι λίθον in the context of ἀκρογωνιαῖος would point to the foundations apart from the use of θεμέλια'.[161] Note also in the chiasm above that the central element is Christ as the cornerstone (ἀκρὸ γωνιαῖος).

1 Peter's choice to emphasize the 'stone tradition' (λίθος = πέτρα; Isa. 8.14 and Isa. 28.16 are here combined in 1 Pet. 2.8) over the θεμέλιος tradition (to which is also added the concept of the 'rejected stone' – λίθος ὃν ἀπεδοκίμασαν),[162] provides a unique element in the use of the concept of the 'living stones'.[163] This 'rejected stone' concept does not seem to have a parallel outside of the references to Jesus in the Gospels (Mt. 21.42; Mk 12.10; Lk. 20.17) and stands in antithesis to that of the 'elect'.[164] In this regard, Elliot is correct to assert that the 'antithetical formulation: "by men, rejected; before God elected, precious" is … Petrine *interprementum*. In no part of the NT λίθος tradition is exactly this contrast to be found.'[165]

159. This is based on understanding τῶν ἀποστόλων καὶ προφητῶν in Eph 2.20 as epexegetical genitive. *M. Cant.* 1.5 refers to Rabbis, teachers of Judaism and their students, or the Sanhedrin who through their teaching of the Torah 'build up' the world.

160. Stig Hanson, *Unity of the Church in the New Testament: Colossians and Ephesians* (ASNU 14; Uppsala: Almquist and Wiksells, 1946) 130.

161. Snodgrass, 'Activities', 98 n. 2.

162. McKelvey, 'Upon This Rock', Appendix B in *New Temple*, 193-4. In Jeremiah 8.9 the phrase τὸν λόγον κυρίου ἀπεδοκίμασαν σοφία τίς ἐστιν ἐν αὐτοῖς ('since they have rejected the word of the LORD, what wisdom is in them?') indicates that the rejection of the Word of God is not too far removed from the Isaianic concept of rejection of the stone. The word (Law?) is occasionally defined as the foundation on which to build in the OT.

163. McCartney, 'OT in First Peter', 117.

164. Derrett, 'Builders Rejected', 181. Cf. 1 Sam 16.6-10 where 'rejection' and 'election' are contrasted in relation to God's anointed.

165. Elliott, *Elect*, 34. It is on this premise that Elliott has argued that the term cannot be interpreted as anti-Jewish since the author's choice of words (ἀνθρώπων μὲν ἀποδεδοκιμασμένον – 'rejected by mankind') rather than appropriation of the term in v. 7 (ἀπεδοκίμασαν οἱ οἰκοδομοῦντες – 'rejected by the builders') is used. Verse 7 is a quote from the LXX and 1 Peter did not alter it; however, its referent in the 1 Peter context is more akin to a universal reference to ἀνθρώποι in

In comparison,1QS 8.1-10 [8.4] references the 'chosen cornerstone'[166] on the basis of Isa. 28.16 and interprets it in accordance with the Qumran community's idea of the immovable foundation.[167] Gärtner perceives this interpretation of Isa. 28.16 in light of an immovable foundation as symbolic of the Qumran community's self-understanding as the temple-community (1QH 6.26ff; 1QS 8.4ff).[168] The λίθος image here is identified with Qumran's eschatological temple-community both in terms of *entrance* into and the *maintenance* of community purity (1QS 8.7).[169]

Such a community interpretation is distinct from some of the later Jewish traditions where the *collective* 'tested stone' (אבן בחן) in Isa. 28.16 represented the *individual* Messiah/King (*Tg. Isa.* 28.16: 'Behold I lay in Zion a king [מלך], a king mighty and strong.' See also *Tg. Ps.* 118.22ff, where the 'stone' is replaced with 'youth' and 'cornerstone' with 'king and ruler').[170] 1 Peter, more than likely aware of these different applications of Isa. 28.16, combines them by applying the λίθος motif to both the collective (temple-community – 2.5) and the individual (Jesus, the resurrected Messiah – 2.6-8) . 1 Peter does this by combining the 'λίθος complex' (6-8) with the 'λαός/ἔθνος complex' (9-10), infusing an originally Christological thrust with a soteriological pronouncement.[171] By making the phrase 'tested stones' plural, 1 Peter applies it to the community of believers, the 'new Israel' that God had redeemed through the sacrificial death of the Christ (1.18-19).

While it is possible to try and understand the concept of 'living' in relation to Jewish concepts of 'living water' and 'living bread' (e.g. John 4.10; 5.51), it is more appropriate to see 1 Peter's use of the term in relation to temple

---

place of the usual Jewish specific use of οἱ οἰκοδομοῦντες which as used in Rabbinic sources like *p. Yoma* 3.40c, 26; *b. Shab.* 114a. So the slight, but significant shift by 1 Peter, is to apply the concept of builders to the general populace rather than to a specific subgroup as was common with the Jewish application of the passage.

166. By translating τιμὴ as 'precious' instead of 'honor', the RSV/ NRSV translations miss the significance of the honor/ shame language utilized here. By virtue of their relationship with God, i.e. being chosen by God, the Petrine community can now enjoy a more honorable life that is distinctly contrasted to those that are not the 'elect nation'.

167. Gärtner, *Temple*, 134. Cf. also 1QS 5.5; 1QpIsa^d 1; 1QH 6.26; 7.8-9. However, note that 1QS 8.7-8 omits reference to the foundations in quoting Isa. 28.16, even though it understands the imagery to be referring to the foundation stone.

168. Gärtner, *Temple*, 77–8. The terms used in the DSS are 'tested wall' (חומת הבחן) for Isaiah's 'tested stone' (אבן בחן) and 'wall' and 'cornerstone' to describe the community. 1QH uses 'stones'. See also 1QH 6.25-27; 7.8-9; 1QS 9.5ff; *j. Sanhedrin* 29a; *Exod. Rab.* 15.7; *Leviticus Rabbah* 20.4.

169. Elliott, *Elect*, 27. 4QFlorilegium employs the concept of building in relation to the temple in Qumran referring to a 'temple of [among] men' (לבנות לוא מקדש אדם) being built by God (cf. 4QpPs. XXX 2.16; CD 3.9). Verb בנה is translated as οἰκοδομεῖν in the LXX.

170. Jeremias, 'λίθος', *TDNT* 4.272-83.

171. Elliott, *Elect*, 38, 129. Cf. Rom. 9.30-33. Note that we are not saying 1 Peter was the first to combine the Isa. 28.16 and 8.14, and also Ps. 118 (117).22 passages.

symbolism and in direct connection to the person of Jesus Christ.[172] Jesus died in the flesh but was made 'alive' in the spirit (3.18), a clear reference to the death and resurrection upon which this language of 'living' depends.[173] The nature of the stones as 'living' would refer to Christ, who is the fulfiller of the prophecies concerning the 'cornerstone that the builders rejected'. And so in the words of Gärtner, 'through Christ, a living person, Christians can be built up to form that "living", "spiritual" temple in which Christ is Lord'.[174]

In conclusion, it is the premise of the 'living God' who makes Jesus the λίθον ζῶντα ('living stone') that produces in the believers the special characterization of λίθοι ζῶντες ('living stones'). Even in the text that most closely resembles 1 Pet. 2.4-10; Eph 2.20, the concept of 'stones' is not applied to the believers.[175] Therefore, McCartney is right to assert that the classification of Christians as 'living' stones points to a contrast with the '*un*living' stones of the literal temple, referred to elsewhere as χειροποίητος (Mk 14.58; Acts 7.28; 17.24; Heb. 9.24).[176] Because the believers are connected to the λίθον ζῶντα who was rejected, they should not be surprised if they themselves are rejected like their Lord. Yet, theirs is not a hopeless case since they have the 'living hope' (ἐλπίδα ζῶσαν – 1.3) premised on the fact that the stone that was rejected has now become the 'chosen/precious stone' through which the believers will share in that reality of the resurrection life as they are joined to the λίθος ζῶντα and find honor before God (1.3).[177] This is 1 Peter's unique spin on the λίθος tradition.[178]

---

172. Gärtner, *Temple*, 75. Connection to the 'living water' motif would still connect the passages to Ezek. 44, which presents a picture of the water that flows from the temple as a sign of God's abundant Spirit of blessing. In Rabbinic literature the foundation-stone (אבן שתיה) is believed to be at the navel of the earth (Zion) where it seals off the waters of the mythical subterranean ocean (cf. Midrash Tanhuma, *Qedoshim* (Shelomo Buber recension); Beit ha-Miqdash 5.63.1ff).

173. This is the only use of ζωοποιεῖν to refer to Jesus' resurrection (ζωοποιηθεὶς δὲ πνεύματι). The expression 'in the spirit' could be in reference to the Holy Spirit or to the spirit of Christ. Cf. W. J. Dalton, *Christ's Proclamation to the Spirits: A Study of 1 Peter 3.18–4.6* (AnBib 23; Rome: Pontifical Biblical Institute, 1965), 138–40; Best, *First Peter*, 137ff.

174. Gärtner, *Temple*, 75. Cf. Rom. 12.1.

175. Eph 2.20-22 simply talks of the believers as being built together into a holy temple in Christ: ἐν ᾧ πᾶσα οἰκοδομὴ συναρμολογουμένη αὔξει εἰς ναὸν ἅγιον ἐν κυρίῳ. The words ξένος and πάροικος are used to describe the believers. The former describes the status and class of foreigners while the latter was used for freed persons and slaves who occupied an even lower rank in Roman society. However, movement up the scale of ranks was permissible between these two groups primarily on basis of longevity in a city. Cf. Fika J. van Regensburg, 'Christians as "Resident and Visiting Aliens": Implications of the Exhortation to the Πάροικοι and Παρεπίδημοι in 1 Peter for the Church in South Africa', *Neot* 32 (1998) 573–83.

176. McCartney, 'OT in First Peter', 117. The word ἀχειροποίητοις (Mt. 14.58; 2 Cor. 5.1; Heb. 9.11, 24) does not occur in the LXX but χειροποίητοις is found in Lev. 26.1, 30; Dan. 5.4, 23; 6.28; Jdt 8.18, Wis. 14.8; Isa. 2.18; 16.12; 10.1; 19.1; 21.9; 31.7; 46.6 and *Bel and the Dragon* (Theodotian) 1.5.

177. Jeremias, 'λίθος', *TDNT* 4.275, points out that Ps. 118.22 becomes a proof text of the death and resurrection of Christ in the early Church. Cothenet, 'l'espérance chrétienne', 565.

178. Elliott, *Elect*, 34–8.

4.2.5.2.2. ἀκρογωνιαῖον *as the Foundation Concept in 1 Peter*

At the center of the chiasm above is Christ as the 'cornerstone'/ 'foundation stone' (ἀκρογωνιαῖος) on whom the building is to be built. In the same way that Christ is the 'head' (κεφαλή) of the 'body'(σῶμα) in Eph 1.22; 4.15, so is he the ἀκρογωνιαῖος of the οἰκοδομή in 1 Peter.[179] The ἀκρογωνιαῖος in 1 Peter contrast glory and judgment (fulfillment and vengeance) much in the same way that the stone of offense and blessing does in the Gospels and Qumran.[180] In this respect, J. Jeremias introduced a significant argument for understanding the ἀκρογωνιαῖος as the 'top-stone' rather than the 'foundation stone' and argued against connection to the foundation of the temple.[181] However, McKelvey has persuasively argued that the references in 1 Pet. 2.6 (and Eph 2.20) are more appropriately understood as the 'cornerstone' (rather than a 'head-stone') in conjunction with the Hebrew of Isa. 28.16 particularly as applied in Qumran (1QS 5.6; cf. *Yoma* 54a).[182] The emphasis is not on height but rather on the extremity of the stone – its elect and honored status by God in contrast to its rejection by humans – making the contrast that much more intense if it is the temple building in view (cf. Mk 12.10; Lk. 20.18).[183]

Because the cornerstone sets the shape, size and location of the building, rejection implies a thorough human examination following which it is set aside as a discard, unfit to use in the construction[184] – a veiled reference to the crucifixion of Jesus.[185] Rejection is key to understanding the humiliation and

---

179. Hanson, *Unity*, 131.

180. Gärtner, *Temple*, 134.

181. Jeremias, 'λίθος', *TDNT* 4.274.

182. McKelvey, 'Christ the Cornerstone', *NTS* 8 (1962) 352–9. So Kelly, *Peter and Jude*, 94, and Richard Longenecker, 'The Rejected Stone-Copestone', in *The Christology of Early Jewish Christianity* (Naperville, Ill.: SCM Press, 1970) 50–3; Brox, *Petrusbrief*, 100; Norman Hillyer, 'Rock-Stone Imagery in 1 Peter', *TynBul* 22 (1971) 68–73. Cf. also Karl T. Schafer, 'Zur Deutung von ἀκρογωνιαῖος Eph 2.20', in *Neutestamentliche Aufsätze: Festschrift für Professor Josef Schmid zum 70. Geburtstag* (ed. Joseph Blinzler, O. Kuss and F. Mußner; Regensburg: Friedrich Pustet, 1963) 218–24, whose article was written independent of McKelvey's but came to the same conclusion on interpretation of ἀκρογωνιαῖος as 'cornerstone' (*Eckstein*) rather than the 'foundation stone' (*Grundstein*).

183. Kelly, *Peter*, 95; Jeremias, 'λίθος', *TDNT* 4.276. Isa. 28.16 refers to Christ's salvation of believers as the living stone, while Ps. 118.22 and Isa. 8.14 reflect on the 'perdition of the unbelievers'. The important point is the connection to the temple pointed out by Jeremias (cf. Mk 12.10; Lk. 20.18) given that the themes of judgment and redemption remain embedded in this imagery – the stone is a stone of stumbling and a rock of offense.

184. W. Grundmann, 'δόκιμος', *TDNT* 2.255-60; W. Mundle, 'πέτρα' *TDNT* 3.382; Derrett, 'Builders Rejected', 182, points out that another possible interpretation of rejection, especially as it related to the Messiah, is that in many of the instances of the OT where the junior persons, e.g. Abraham, Isaac, Jacob, Joseph, etc., are chosen as God's instruments of redemption of Israel, the Messiah would be one 'as the "specialists" might reject'. In the mean time the rejected ones ('not a people') become the elect – 'God's people' (1 Pet. 2.10).

185. Goppelt, *Typos*, 154. The metaphor of living stones has already been used by Jesus to 'announce his cross and the glory that would follow (Mk 12:10f. par = Ps. 118:22f)'.

exaltation of Jesus Christ on the cross as a model of suffering for the believers (4.1-2) who also must undergo suffering and rejection for the sake of their Lord and savior (1 Pet. 2.21-24).[186] This stands in stark contrast to the approval of Jesus by God, not only as fit to be used for the 'building', but even more so, as the 'chief cornerstone' (LXX) or 'precious, select stone' (MT) which in its blindness humanity had rejected.[187]

In that which humans despise, God finds special value. The worth of the believers is not based on human standards of judgment and valuation which are tainted in sin, but rather on God's standards which, through Jesus Christ, are able to find worth in what the world in its blindness considers of no significance.

4.3. *Royal/Holy Priesthood and Temple Imagery*

4.3.1. ἱεράτευμα ἅγιον (2.5)/ βασίλειον ἱεράτευμα (2.9)

The language of ἱεράτευμα which belongs to the LXX (Exod. 23.22; 19.6 MT) is found only in 1 Peter and in no other Greek documents outside the Bible. On this premise, Elliott suggests that ἱεράτευμα was 'manufactured' by the LXX translators as a collective noun, because the Jews of the Dispersion in Egypt did not want to perceive themselves simply as aliens in a foreign colony but as a priestly community with a God-given mission of preserving the worship of the true God even in their foreign residence.[188] And, contrary to the MT, the LXX introduces the possibility of viewing Israel as the residence of God, implying also, priestly service to society.[189] Therefore, recourse to its origins in the Masoretic Text (ממלכת כהנים) does not offer much assistance as to

---

186. Schutter, *Hermeneutic*, 108 n. 76, connects the personal and corporate suffering in 1 Peter 1.11 to the 'Messianic Woes' which were a prelude to the eschatological restoration. He explains: 'That the unthinkable had happened to God's Anointed might have compelled many to interpret it in terms of the "Woes", which was surely the category closest at hand from an eschatological perspective ... Hence it is reasonable to suppose that there was a basis to move directly from a personal frame of reference in early Christian thinking about the Messianic "Woes" to a corporate one. On this view the Crucifixion would quickly come to represent an unprecedented, concrete definition of the nature and scale of the "Woes" attending the End that would necessarily imply a collective frame of reference wherever one was not explicit.' Cf. also Dubis, *Woes*, 76, who applies the 'Messianic Woes' pattern in interpretation of suffering and eschatology in 1 Pet. 4.12-19 and stresses the need for 1 Peter's audience to identify with Jesus' suffering since '[j]ust as Jesus' suffering was necessary before his resurrection, the readers of 1 Peter likewise endure eschatological tribulation prior to their experience of resurrection'.

187. The reason the masons reject a stone for use as a cornerstone is because of the stone's perceived weakness or irregularity.

188. Elliott, *Elect*, 69–70.

189. Elliott, *Elect*, 75.

its interpretation because in different Jewish traditions it has been interpreted differently.[190] Alexandrian Judaism spiritualized the concept into a 'spiritual priesthood', Jewish apocalyptic saw visions of heavenly *cultus*, while the Rabbis, over and over, returned to the thought of the Kingdom promised to Israel.[191] *Jubilees* (33.19-20), operating with eschatological motivation, renders Exod. 19.6 in light of the prohibition against impurity for Israel as the elect people of God, without displacing the unique place of a Levitical priesthood.[192]

In almost every case in the LXX βασίλειος is used as a noun.[193] Accordingly, rather than understanding it as an adjective in this LXX passage, it should most likely be regarded as a substantive noun in apposition to the other noun ἱεράτευμα, resulting in an emphasis on the corporate nature of the priesthood. This reading is clearly supported by 1 Peter's use of the language of priesthood from Leviticus 2.5, 9 and Exod. 19.6, as reflected in the concept of ἱεράτευμα. On this point I agree with Elliott, that 'attempts to explain ἱεράτευμα on the basis of the current first century view of the Levitical priesthood are pointless. The importance of this word and of the verses in which it appears was determined rather by the import of the E[xodus] F[ormula] which was the source and import of both'.[194]

Against the traditional position, Elliott maintains that βασίλειον ἱεράτευμα in 1 Pet. 2.4-10 does not form the basis for understanding the Christian community as the 'priesthood of believers'. However, Seland's convincing critique of Elliott rightly describes 'the "common priesthood" of 1 Peter as something that was given, not something that was to be striven after (cf. οἰκοδομεῖσθε)'. Seland further argues 'that the βασίλειον ἱεράτευμα would be understood in light of the οἶκός and the sacrificial terms in its context as denoting "temple" rather than "household"; and that the role of the priesthood would be directed towards God'.[195] Specifically, the reference to the πνευματικὰς θυσίας in 2.5 leaves little doubt that the context is a temple.

---

190. Gärtner, *Temple*, 72ff. Elliott, *Elect*, 103, finds 'no spiritual' interpretation in Philo's utilization of Exod. 19.6 in *De Sobrietate* 66 and *De Abrahamo* 56.

191. Gärtner, *Temple*, 73ff. There is no citation of Exod. 19.6 in the *Mishnah* and *Tannaim*. The *targumim* (*Tg. Onkelos* and *Tg. Jer.*) read 'kings and priests'. This change is noteworthy since, unlike the MT and the LXX which imply God's kingship, the *targumim* transfer the kingship to Israel.

192. Bryan, *Judgement*, 150–1; Elliott, *Elect*, 78ff.

193. See Hort, *St. Peter*, 124. The LXX version that Hort used apparently was based on a Hebrew text that had the final ה (taw) of the construct state of the Hebrew ממלכת ('a kingdom of priests') which was later replaced by a ה (ממלכה) resulting in the current LXX use of a substantive – 'a kingdom, priests'. Cf. David Abernathy, 'Exegetical Considerations in 1 Peter 2:7-9', *Notes on Translation* 15 (2001) 24–39, 36–7.

194. Elliott, *Elect*, 221.

195. Seland, '1 Peter 2:5, 9', 87-119. Cf. also Achtemeier, *1 Peter*, 159.

The emphasis on the Christian community as a body of priests is said to be a unique development of the notion of the Christian community as a building or a body, reflecting, perhaps, a more developed understanding than Eph 2.20.[196] The tradition closest to1 Peter's utilization of these references from Exod. 19.6 is 2 Macc. 2.17-18.

> It is God who has saved all his people, and has returned the inheritance (τὴν κληρονομίαν) to all, and the kingship and the priesthood and the consecration (τὸ βασίλειον καὶ τὸ ἱεράτευμα καὶ τὸν ἁγιασμόν), as he promised through the law. We have hope in God that he will soon have mercy on us and will gather us from everywhere under heaven into his holy place, for he has rescued us from great evils and has purified the place.

This passage is found in a letter based on the feast of temple purification. Purification is referred to with the verb ὁ καθάρισμος rather than the Petrine ὁ ἁγνισμός.[197] The exile is invoked as the salvation based on God's mercy that would very soon (ταχέως) gather all (πάντα....πᾶσιν) of the Dispersion into the holy place (τὸν ἅγιον τόπον). ἅγιος τόπος could be a reference to the temple in light of the prophecy of Isa. 66.18ff, where all the people of God scattered among the nations would gather in Zion to worship YHWH. It is an expression of hope that Israel, and not its institutions, shall be God's βασίλειος, ἱεράτευμα, and ἁγιασμός.

Such a restoration would include the reestablishment of the monarchy, the priesthood and the state of holiness that should characterize the true Israel of God. While βασίλειος in LXX (Exod. 19.6) may be either an adjective or a substantive noun, in 2 Macc. 2.17 it is clearly taken as a substantive in its own right. Other places where a conjunction occurs before βασίλειος (*Jub.* 16.18; 33.20; Rev 1.6; 5.10; *Tg. Onq.* and *Tg. Ps.-J* of Exod. 19.6) 'kingdom' rather than 'kingship' is in view.[198] Nevertheless, even when applied to the totality of the nation of Israel as a collective, none of the texts eliminates a priestly class within Israel.[199] Even in Qumran, where the whole community could be assigned priestly identity, there was still a class of special priesthood (CD 3.21-44).

---

196. Horst Goldstein, *Paulinische Gemeinde im ersten Petrusbrief* (SBS 80; Stuttgart: Katholisches Bibelwerk, 1975) 271. As has been argued persuasively by Kazuhito Shimada, 'Is 1 Peter Dependent on Ephesians? A Critique of C. L. Milton', *AJBI* 17 (1991) 77–106, no literary dependence can be established between these two letters. It is more likely that they each independently used a common Christian tradition.

197. Elliott, *Elect*, 95.

198. J. A. Goldstein, *II Maccabees: A Translation With Introduction and Commentary* (AB; Garden City: Doubleday, 1983) 188; cf. Bryan, *Judgement*, 149 n. 50. Elliott, *Elect*, 90ff.

199. Philo, *De Sob.* 66, identifies the twelve tribes with the βασίλειον καὶ ἱεράτευμα τοῦ Θεοῦ – 'God's kingdom and body of priests'. For Philo, βασίλειος is understood as 'the king's house' (§ 66c) and by introducing και between βασίλειος and ἱεράτευμα he maintains the substantive force of the former.

In 1 Peter 2.5, 9, we realize that not only is the totality applied to the believers as the rest of the Jewish traditions do, but that those to whom it is applied likely also include Gentiles. For Ezekiel, the foreigner could not present offerings at the temple nor even serve as a priest.[200] 1 Peter reverses the edict and without apology regards the Gentile believers as part of the new 'holy' and 'royal' priesthood.[201] Second, we note that 1 Peter does not seem to leave room at all for any other special lineage of priests, Levitical or otherwise. The believers constitute the new priesthood. The imagery here becomes mind-boggling given that the believers also constitute the building blocks to the 'spiritual house' as we saw above.[202] The terms 'spiritual house' and the 'holy/royal priesthood' are more or less identical rather than analogous, in that they both are descriptive of the same object, the believers.[203]

This is perhaps the reason that some manuscripts leave out εἰς in v. 5.[204] The believers thus described are to offer πνευματικὰς θυσίας which Goppelt describes as the 'dedication of the entire person prompted by the Spirit'.[205] These sacrifices are acceptable to God since they are mediated through Jesus Christ, who himself is the perfect sacrifice (1.18-19), and who also is the foundation stone to which is joined the 'living stones' to construct God's 'spiritual house'.[206] Constituting both the spiritual temple and the priesthood, the believers therefore embody the essence of God's visible presence.

---

200. Ezek. 44.6-16.

201. David L. Tiede, "'Glory to Thy People, Israel": Luke-Acts and the Jews', in Jacob Neusner, Ernest S. Frerichs, Peder Borgen, Richard Horsley, eds., *The Social World of Formative Christianity and Judaism* (Philadelphia: Fortress Press, 1988) 327–41. It is perhaps that same complexity that is also reflected in 1 Peter.

202. Menahem Haran, 'Temple and Community in Ancient Israel', in Michael Fox, ed., *Temple in Society*, 17–25 [18], maintains the following concerning the OT priesthood: 'The priests, being the servants of God, are thus not regarded at all as representatives of the community. Their obligation to fulfill their role in the service of God, that is, to perform the cultic acts, is bestowed on them from birth by divine will and is taken to be their exclusive privilege. This privilege does not stem from the community's authority but is based on the notion that a special eternal covenant of priesthood was granted by God to the ancestor of priests, Phinehas son of Eleazer son of Aaron, "to him and his descendants after him" (Num. 25:13)'.

203. Goppelt, *1 Peter*, 142, rejects the concept 'priesthood of believers' as imposition by Reformation. However, see Achtemeier, *1 Peter*, 156, who finds in the use of the preposition εἰς together with the phrase ἱεράτευμα ἅγιον ('holy priesthood') the provision of the purpose of 'God's constituting Christians a spiritual house'.

204. Omission is by P, Majority Text, Vulgate and Clement.

205. Goppelt, *1 Peter*, 142. Cf. Achtemeier, *1 Peter*, 155–6; Elliott, *Elect*, 154. This idea of spiritual sacrifices was already an ideal sought after in the OT (Ps. 40.9-10; 51.16-19; Isa. 1.11-17; Jer. 6.20; 7.21-23; Hos. 6.6; Mic. 6.6-8) and in the Qumran community (1QS8.2-8; 9.3-5; 10.6; 4QFlor 1.6-7).

206. Achtemeier, *1 Peter*, 156. There are two possible ways of interpreting the phrase διὰ Ἰησοῦ Χριστοῦ. It an can either be interpreted in conjunction with ἀν putting the emphasis on the 'offering' that is only acceptable through Christ or in conjunction with εὐπροσδέκτους placing the emphasis on the 'acceptability' of the offering. In either case it is clear the Jesus Christ is the means of acceptance.

Consequently, the imagery carries a greater force than mere metaphor. The transference that 1 Peter is making of the priesthood to the believers is not simply one of expansion of the boundaries of priesthood but of a complete reconstitution. The believers are corporately priests by virtue of a covenant that is eternal, and which designates them as 'servants of the Lord' (cf. Isa. 61.6; Jer. 33.21-22; Joel 1.9, 13, etc.). It is within this understanding of the priesthood of the believers that the injunctions concerning the civil powers and imperial officials in 1 Peter (2.13-17) make sense.[207]

4.3.2. πνευματικὰς θυσίας *(2.5): Priesthood and Sacrifice*
In effect, πνευματικὰς θυσίας (2.5) designates the priesthood's primary function as service to the Lord, in his house. M.-E. Boismard, making a liturgical inter-pretation of 1 Pet. 2.5, identifies the 'sacrifice' with the eucharist, under-standing the verb ἀναφέρω ('offer') to be a technical term for 'lifting up' to God the sacrifice made to him.[208] This, however, seems to downplay the function of the language of priesthood in 1 Peter where liturgical language is used to foster the author's concern for responsible Christian living and faith.[209] This perspective emphasizes the nature of the community as the temple wherein the Spirit of God resides, it coming as no surprise that 1 Peter focuses on the spiritual *acts* of worship – not just prayer (1 Pet. 3.7) but also the equivalent of the sacrificial elements of the OT *cultus* (1 Pet. 1.18-20).[210] It is on this basis that the whole community of believers is required to maintain a lifestyle of spiritual purity (1.14-19) and even exercise the role of priesthood beyond the Christian confines (1 Pet. 2.13-17).[211]

This interpretation correlates well with 2 Macc. 2.17-18, which interprets Exod. 19.6 in light of the celebration of the purification of the temple. The inheritance is described in terms of τὸ βασίλειον καὶ τὸ ἱεράτευμα καὶ τὸν ἁγιασμόν. The predicate makes the entire people of God the object of his salvation. This inheritance has been restored to all the Jews by God. As such, the hope of the ingathering of all the scattered of the house of Israel back to the 'holy place' is highlighted. The intent is to show that the same God of the

207. Selwyn, *First Peter*, 294: 'The injunctions are less surprising in light of the priestly character of the Church.'

208. M.-E. Boismard, 'Pierre (Première épitre de)', *DBSup* 7 (1966) 1415–55, 1435. Cf. Hill, 'Spiritual Sacrifices', 61. Kelly, *Peter and Jade*, 98; Abernathy, '1 Peter 2.7-9', 37.

209. Achtemeier, *1 Peter*, 156: 'Thus Christians are made a spiritual house to the end that they be a body of priests whose purpose is to offer acceptable sacrifices to God.'

210. Haran, 'Temple', 23. This would fall in line with what Haran emphasizes, that the primary act of service by the priest was sacrifice rather than prayer, the latter being peripheral to the cult. However, it is important to highlight, even as Haran concedes, that both prayer and prostration did supplement the primary service of sacrifice and thus functioned together in some sense of a descending order of significance (24–5).

211. However, see the caution of Brox (*Petrusbrief*, 99–100), who feels that owing to the highly metaphorical language of the text, doctrinal implications should not be too readily drawn from it.

Exodus (14.30) now also saves the Jewish people, with the people's worship and pre-eminence taking prominence over the land and institutions envisaged as the heritage promised to Israel.[212]

Together with the concept of a 'spiritual house', Flusser compares the term 'a holy priesthood' with the Qumran concepts of the 'holy house of Israel' and 'a holy dwelling of Aaron', and concludes that 1 Pet. 2.5 is a modified form of 1QS 8.4-8 where the two rooms of the temple have become one house and one priesthood.[213] Subsequent studies have questioned the literary dependence of 1 Peter on the DSS making Flusser's theory somewhat untenable. Elliott warns that since Exod. 19.6 played no part in the Qumranic literature, any attempted comparison between 1 Peter and the DSS should be undertaken with great caution and, in fact, with pessimism.[214]

However, in the Jewish writing *Jubilees* (16.18) – sections of which have been found in Qumran – the Exodus passage is quoted and applied to the future Israel in language reminiscent of 1 Peter. This calls into question Elliott's claim that Exod. 19.6 'played absolutely no role in the Qumran literature'.[215] Interpretation of Exod. 19.6 in intertestamental Judaism included not only the priesthood but also the temple and its purity. *Jubilees* then applies it to the temple in terms of its restoration to purity together with the future heavenly *cultus*.[216] Theirs are 'spiritual' sacrifices that are presented to God as acts of obedience in light of their election by God.

The priesthood, then, for 1 Peter is something of an 'offshoot of the idea of God's people as a temple, or spiritual house and is rooted in Exodus 19:6 (23:22 LXX) …'.[217] This stems from Christ's priesthood over the Church (1 Pet. 3.18) both as the sacrifice and the sacrificer that offered himself for atonement of sin. This self-offering is paralleled by the obedience the believers are called upon to offer up in 'spiritual sacrifices' in 2.5. In this way, 1 Peter offers his audience a powerful temple imagery that prompts them to rethink the role of the temple in the community, the meaning of God's presence among the elect. The use of the passive 'being built', clearly indicates that the inference is to God as the master builder of this spiritual house, and not the Messiah – who in this case is a part of the building as the crucial cornerstone that holds the entire structure together. This then is presented as the anticipated Jewish eschatological temple, now fulfilled in the community of believers, based on their relation with Jesus Christ the Messiah.

212. F. M. Abel, *Les Livres des Maccabées* (Paris: Editions du Cerf, 1948) 309 n. *c*.
213. Flusser, 'Pre-Pauline Christianity', 233–6.
214. Elliott, *Elect*, 210–13.
215. Achtemeier, *1 Peter*, 151 n. 31.
216. Cerfaux, 'Sacerdotium', 5–39.
217. McCartney, 'OT in First Peter', 115.

4.4. *Worship, Prayer, and Ethics:* ἐλπίς, συγκληρονόμος, προσευχή
(1 Pet. 3.7, 9; 4.7)

In 1 Peter 3.7 husbands and wives are called συγκληρονόμοις χάριτος ζωῆς.[218] The reading συγκληρονόμοις (dative case) is found in only a few manuscripts (including א^c P^{72} P^{81} B^c [B* συνκληρονόμοις]) while the majority of manuscripts have the nominative plural συγκληρονόμοι (A C K P Ψ *Byz Lect* 33 1739 it^{ar,} ^{t} vg). The Syriac evidence is split between the two, with the *Peshitta* text supporting the former and the *Hasidic* text the latter. Adoption of the dative would mean the clause ὡς καὶ συγκληρονόμοις χάριτος ζωῆς would be in reference to the wives while adoption of the nominative would mean the reference is to the husbands. As Bruce Metzger explains, 'The transition in sense from the singular τῷ γυναικείῳ σκεύει to the plural συγκληρονόμοις may have seemed harsh to the copyists, who therefore preferred the nominative [but] the dative is more in harmony with the structure of the sentence and thought (for the presence of καὶ seems to favor taking the two clauses as coordinate)'.[219]

Συγκληρονόμοις is used in reference to the joint and equal nature of the inheritance that, in light of 1.4 and 3.9, must be thought of as heavenly and connected to salvation (1.7, 9). The implication of this is obvious from the passage. As a result, some of the later manuscripts insert the word αἰωνίου after ζωῆς.[220] Not a very common word in the NT – it appears only three other times, and all of them in relation to eschatological expectation: twice in Paul and once in the epistle to the Hebrews – it is used by Pauline literature in relation to Gentiles who previously did not belong to the kingdom of God but now are συγκληρονόμα of the kingdom because of Christ (Eph 3.6; Rom. 8.17). The letter to the Hebrews also makes it clear that the joint heritage (συγκληρονόμος) to which the patriarchs looked forward was the heavenly one not built with human hands (Heb. 11.8-10).

Συγκληρονόμος is used in 1 Peter in a section where the author had just finished admonishing the different subsets of groups in the society, including the relationship with the governing authorities (2.13-17) and relationships between husbands and wives (3.1-7). In the so-called *Haustafeln*, 1 Peter generally moves away from the focus on the earlier eschatological concerns displayed in the first chapter of the epistle. However, here he returns to it with this reference to κληρονομία. As Michaels explains, 'Peter takes up again the thread of eschatological interest that dominated 1.3–2.10 but virtually disappeared after the mention of the "day of visitation" in 2.12'.[221]

---

218. 'Co-heirs of the grace of life'; 'Joint inheritors of the grace of life'.

219. Bruce Metzger, *A Textual Commentary on the Greek New Testament* (Stuttgart: Deutsche Bibelgesellschaft, 1994) 620.

220. P72 and the Syriac *Peshitta* supply the word 'eternal'.

221. Michaels, *1 Peter*, 170.

The eschatological use of the term χάρις can be seen in 1.10, 13.[222] In these two verses the focus is on the anticipated events to which the OT prophets and the angels looked forward, but which the readers of 1 Peter have been privileged to be partakers of (v. 12). This χάρις which was expected by the prophets has now been seen in Christ Jesus by those who, though they have not seen him, have believed in him (vv. 8-9).[223] However, the fullness of this χάρις has yet to be seen, for it remains hidden until the revelation of Christ (v. 13). It remains something to look forward to, much in the same way that the OT prophets looked forward to the first coming (1.10-12). Their fervent expectation worked as the motivator, and now as an example for the readers of 1 Peter even as they await the return of Jesus Christ.

This is the context within which the instructions of 1 Pet. 3.1-7 fall. They are to be framed by the eschatological understanding of the concept of χάρις as used in 1 Pet. 1.10, 13, making them more than mere instructions for moral or godly living. They are integrally entwined with the χάρις that awaits expectation in the revelation of the Lord Jesus Christ. As such, they serve not simply as motivators for good behavior but, even more, as the basis of true worship.[224] Unlike instructions given for motivation of behavior – which tend usually to be loaded with promises of blessings and threats of curses – the primary motivator in this case is prayer (v. 7), a cultic function closely associated with the sanctuary.[225] In the early church, the prayer hours of *Tamid*-offering in the temple were still observed by the believers (Acts 2.46; 3.1), while the breaking of bread and sharing in the meals of fellowship was done at home (Acts 2.44).[226]

The only other mention of προσευχή in 1 Peter is within the context of guidelines for church life premised on an eschatological foundation (4.7). The eschatological expectation of the soon coming end is the main focus: 'The end

---

222. Dalton, 'So that', 270-1. The general sense of the use of χάρις in 1 Peter (1.2, 10, 13; 2.19; 3.7; 4.10; 5.5, 10, 12) is the common NT meaning of 'that which God gives freely'. The only possible exception is 2.19 where the term is used in the sense of 'that which pleases God'. Normally used in relation to the present Christian life, it is only in 1.13 that it has a future dimension of the final fulfillment. This same understanding of the term is expressed in the second-century sermon of Melito, *On Pascha*, especially § 58.

223. Cf. the words of Jesus in Mt. 13.17, 'Truly I tell you, many prophets and righteous people longed to see what you see, but did not see it, and to hear what you hear, but did not hear it.' See also Lk. 10.23-24.

224. So also Goppelt, *Typos*, 157.

225. Following the construction of the temple by Solomon, his prayer before the temple called on the Lord to answer prayer when directed from or toward the temple (1 Kgs 8.30-36; 2 Chron. 6).

226. Cf. Acts 10.3, 9, 30. One can also argue that it was in the context of prayer that the synagogue came into existence in the 'Dispersion'. With the Jews distanced from the temple and in need of a gathering place for prayer, the προσευχή, emerged in the 'Dispersion' and eventually found its way into Palestine.

of all things is near (τέλος ἤγγικε); therefore be serious and discipline yourselves for the sake of your prayers (προσευχάς)'. What was true for husbands and wives becomes also true of the larger church body. Their conduct is not only closely tied to their worship, but seems to be premised on it. For this reason, even when their lives are to be characterized by purity and reverence (3.2), the motivation remains witnessing to non-believers (3.1). The mission of the 'new Israel', as the light to the 'Gentiles' (Isa. 49.6), must be sustained.

A source of encouragement remains their 'living hope' (ἐλπίδα ζῶσαν – 1.3, 13, 21; 3.15) where the use of language plainly reminiscent of Exod. 12.11 (cf. Hos. 2.25) reinforces the understanding that 1 Peter's presentation of hope (ἐλπίς) is within the framework of restoration from exile.[227] The assurance concerning the antagonistic environment is such that, rather than being reflective of a negative status in relation to God, it serves to affirm the exact opposite: That it is, indeed, those who suffer – the aliens and exiles – who are the true people of God.[228] The promise of Israel's restoration from exile now belongs to the new 'temple-community', in reflection of the promise of restoration.[229]

All aspects of life are to be understood in light of the fact that, even the most basic of relationships, that of husband and wife, has serious eschatological ramifications. This relationship is that of the church in a microcosm. Attendant on it are the same expectations and regulations that pertain to the larger body of believers who constitute the 'spiritual house' (2.4-10).[230]

4.5. The Prototype Temple: Noah's κιβωτός (1 Pet. 3.20)

τοῦ θεοῦ μακροθυμία ἐν ἡμέραις Νῶε κατασκευαζομένης κιβωτοῦ εἰς ἣν ὀλίγοι, τοῦτ' ἔστιν ὀκτὼ ψυχαί, διεσώθησαν δι' ὕδατος

In this section of 1 Peter (3.18-22) we are aware of the fact that Noah's ark is incidental to the larger argument of baptism and the salvation of God. Nevertheless, it is significant that the author chooses to use this story of

227. Danker, '1 Peter 1.24-2.17', 99: 'The citations from Pss. 33 and 117, Isa. 40 and 43, Hosea 1 and 2, and Prov. 24 are all taken from OT contexts which affirm deliverance from suffering or tribulation.' 1 Pet. 2.10 quotes from Hos. 1.6-9, in a passage originally addressed to Israel but now being applied to the new community. Hos. 2.23 quoted in 1 Peter describes the exilic situation in light of the ancient Exodus experience (v. 17) coupled up with the promise of God to have pity on the 'not pitied' (v. 25).

228. John H. Elliott, 'The Rehabilitation of an Exegetical Step-Child: 1 Peter in Recent Research', in Charles H. Talbert, ed., Perspectives on 1 Peter (NABPR Special Series 9; Macon, Ga.: Mercer University Press, 1986) 3–16, 15. Achtemeier, 1 Peter, 168.

229. Beare, First Peter, 105.

230. And so the admonitions to obey the non-ecclesiastical authorities, even in the face of persecution (2.17; 3.16; 4.4), are geared towards evangelism and mission to the 'gentiles'.

Noah as the basis of teaching on baptism. While the general focus of most studies has rightly been on the issue of baptism and the *descensus ad inferos*, little attention has been paid to the role of Noah's ark in the salvation process. Therefore, little interest has been directed toward investigating the role of Noah's ark as a sanctuary in Jewish literature of the Second Temple period in connection with 1 Peter.

In some Jewish quarters (e.g. *Sib. Or.* 1.128-33; 1.279. Cf. *1 Enoch* 79.1, 36), Noah's κιβωτός was perceived as a prototypical temple. Owing to this background, a case could be made in light of the Noachic image in 1 Peter 3.19-20 that Noah's ark could be understood to function as a form of a temple. That both the ark and the temple functioned as symbols of God's redemptive act (and judgment) in the cosmological history of the nation of Israel would allow for such a connection to be inferred by the readers with limited strain. Whether such particular imagery was intended by the author cannot be ascertained, but his deliberate choice of the ark as a metaphor for salvation is rife with temple imagery connections.

In other Jewish tradition, angels/spirits were involved in the building of both the temple and Noah's ark. In *1 Enoch* 67.2, the ark is built by angels and in *Exod. Rab.* 52.4, the temple was built with help of 'spirits' (רוחות). In *T. Sol.* 2.4 the building of the temple is carried out by the servants of Solomon and δαιμόνιον (demons? fallen angels?) who, unable to move the temple corner-stone, co-opt – by force – the Arabian wind δαιμόν, Epiphas.[231] *Midrash Rabbah* seems to allude to and summarize *T. Sol.* when R. Yosi simply exclaims that 'Everyone helped [Solomon] when he built the temple of God, both human beings and spirits.' However, by leaving the spirits as unqualified, *Midrash Rabbah* might be putting a positive spin on the demon designation in *T. Sol.*[232]

Comparing 1 Peter with the Gospel tradition, where Noah's ark retains the role of refuge (or sanctuary) from God's judgment, the concern in 1 Pet. 3.17-21 is partly broadened to include the building process of the community so that the eschatological concerns about the second coming of the Messiah seem to be less emphasized. So the Gospels, unlike 1 Peter, find no need to refer to the construction of the ark and instead just focus on narrative as a warning and the ark as a source of redemption for those prepared for the Lord's return. Therefore, a connection to the 'spiritual house' in 2.9-10 could be postulated in the concept of building (κατασκευαζομένης) which is added rather curiously to the phrase ἐν ἡμέραις Νῶε in 3.20. One could argue that 1 Peter

---

231. Epiphas is said to descend (καταβαινω), leaving the impression that he too may be a fallen angel(?).

232. In 2 (Syriac) Baruch 7-8, 80 (cf. also Josephus, *War*, 6.300) the angels are said to have helped destroy the temple, while in Talmud (*Chagigah* 5b) the angels are said to weep at the destruction of the temple.

wants to make an indirect but significant connection between the idea of building (οἰκοδομεῖσθε) of the 'spiritual house' in 2.5 and the building (κατασκευαζομένης – 3.20) of the ark.

If 1 Peter 3.20 had ended with the phrase ἐν ἡμέραις Νῶε it would have sufficed, as witnessed in the Gospels' appropriation of the Noah tradition (Mt. 24.37-38; Lk. 17.26-27 – 'For as the days of Noah were, so will be the coming of the Son of Man. For as in those days before the flood they were eating and drinking, marrying and giving in marriage, until the day Noah entered the ark'). However, 1 Peter's addendum of the ark's building is crucial for his argument enabling the theme of construction to connect the two passages.

Further comparison with Hebrews where the same verb κατασκευάζω is used of the construction of a 'house' (οἶκος – 3.3), the tabernacle (σκηνὴ – 9.2) and the ark (κιβωτός – 11.7) may also lend support to our reading.[233] For Hebrews, the ark context in 11.7 is the exhibition of Noah's faith and obedience as a means of salvation from God's judgment, while for 1 Peter – even with the focus on the ark as a sanctuary and a refuge – the Noahic tradition provides opportunity to highlight the construction aspect reflective of the building of the Christian community. Of course, such correspondence is more conceptual and thematic than verbal: just as Noah was building the ark for the purpose of salvation for those who would believe his message and enter into it, so also are the believers being built into a 'spiritual house' through which those who believe would be saved.[234]

It is likely that the readers would be familiar with the Jewish legends about the ark and the temple, allowing for the connections postulated. In the same way that in 2.5 the 'temple-community' is identified with Christ, the believers are identified through Christ via the imagery of Noah's narrative.[235] Some other elements like the use of the transitive verb πορευθείς ('go', 'proceed') – which appears twice (3.19, 22) – to encapsulate the narrative of descending to the spirits in the days of Noah forming a threefold sequence of 'death-resurrection-ascension' adds to the speculation.[236] Since the community already has been identified with the temple in 2.4-9, the interpretation makes sense if the ark in 3.20 is understood to play the same redemptive and eschatological role the temple does in the earlier passage.[237]

233. Selwyn, *First Peter*, 290. This is 'a more general word covering equipment and administration as well as construction'.

234. Michaels, *1 Peter*, liii. Josephus (*Ant.* 1.90) claims that the ark came to rest on top of a mountain in Armenia with the Armenians consequently calling the spot the Landing-Place, 'for it was where the ark came safe on land and they show the relics to this day'. Cf. also *Ant.* 1.92-95 and *c. Ap.* 1.130.

235. Selwyn, *First Peter*, 334: 'makes it clear in 1 Pet. iii. 18–22 that he thinks of the Christian Church as the "antitype" or the fulfillment of the ark, and the waters of Christian baptism as prefigured by those of the Flood'.

236. Elliott, *1 Peter*, 653.

237. Kazuhito Shimada, 'The Christological Creedal Formula in 1 Peter 3:18-22 Reconsidered', *AJBI* 5 (1979) 154–76; Elliott, *1 Peter*, 653; Michaels, *1 Peter*, 197: 'the

4.6. *Temple and* Šekinah *(1 Pet. 4.14, 17)*

ὅτι τὸ τῆς δόξης καὶ τὸ τοῦ θεοῦ πνεῦμα ἐφ᾽ ὑμᾶς ἀναπαύεται

This phrase presents awkward moments for interpreters.[238] The two main proposals involve understanding πνεῦμα as a main noun to which the genitival phrases – τὸ τῆς δόξης and τὸ τοῦ θεου – are attached. The resultant phrase is either a hendiadys ('the glorious spirit of God') or epexegetical ('the spirit of glory, which is the Spirit of God'). A third option would be to reject πνεῦμα as the main noun and prefer the possibility that the two genitival phrases contain independent subjects.[239] I. Howard Marshall reasons that 1 Peter might have first simply written 'the Spirit of God' and only later added 'glory' causing the awkwardness of the phrase.[240] Admittedly, however, most scholars prefer to see πνεῦμα as the main subject modified by the two genitival phrases and we, in turn, concur with the majority by maintaining preference for the epexegetical rendering.[241]

As noted earlier – by combining πνεῦμα and δόξα in 4.14 – 1 Peter makes an allusion to the dominant theme of 'God's glory' in Ezekiel and only three verses later alludes to Ezek. 9.9 (4.17).[242] Schutter has noted that perhaps the largest portion of OT allusion is to Ezekiel 8–11, and so it comes as no surprise that the most likely reference of the judgment in 1 Pet. 4.14-17 is to be traced back to this OT section.[243] Ezekiel's vision begins with the spectacular chariot-throne (1.28; 3.23-24; 8.4; 43.3) and culminates with the image of the life-giving water rushing out of the south of the altar in the temple purifying even the Dead Sea (47.1-12). This was a symbol of the return of God's glory to Israel, which would be a source of 'life' and 'abundance' for the nations.[244]

announcement to the imprisoned disobedient spirits, the days of Noah, preparation of the ark and corresponding salvation of the baptized believers is directly linked to the event of Christ's resurrection'.

238. 'God's glorious Spirit rests on you' (Achtemeier, *1 Peter*, 303); NRSV – 'the spirit of glory, which is the Spirit of God, is resting on you'. To the phrase τὸ τῆς δόξης some mss add καὶ δυνάμεως (א* א2 A 33 811881 Byzpt syrh vg) while to the verb ἀναπαύεται other mss add κατὰ μὲν αὐτοὺς βλασφημεῖται κατὰ δὲ ὑμᾶς δοξάζεται (MT K L P [Ψ]). However, the shorter reading is to be preferred since the evidence seems to suggest that the longer readings are attempts at emendation of the shorter more difficult reading. See, Metzger, *Textual Commentary*, 625, who concludes that the evidences 'sufficiently condemn all of them as homiletic supplements to the original text'.

239. Selwyn, *First Peter*, 222–4.

240. I. Howard Marshall, *1 Peter* (Downers Grove, Ill. and Leicester: InterVarsity Press, 1991; 154.

241. So Goppelt, *1 Peter*, 323; Michaels, *1 Peter*, 264; Dubis, *Woes*, 124–5.

242. Irénée Fransen, 'Une homélie chrétienne: La première Epître de Pierre', *BVC* 31 (1960) 28–38.

243. Schutter, *Hermeneutic*, 35–43.

244. In the Gospel of John (4.10-14; 7.38-39), 'life-giving water' is associated with Jesus and with the Holy Spirit.

This is an indication that – in spite of the judgment that is to begin with the 'house of God' – the manifest presence of God would be the sign for divine favor and assurance for the community of believers.[245]

Through Christ the people have become the new temple; and, through Christ, the Spirit of God rests upon them as the *Šekinah* of God rested on the sanctuary.[246] In the words of McCartney, 'As Christ the temple was full of his tabernacling glory (John 1.14), so believers have become recipients of that glory, and as Christ was full of the Spirit, so are believers.'[247] Therefore, the spirit that rested on the Messiah, Jesus Christ, now rests on those who compose the 'new house of God'.[248]

This language of 'spirit of glory and of the Lord' is also synonymous with God's spirit resting on the tabernacle as the visible presence of God (Exod. 33.9ff) and on the first temple in the visible form of a cloud hovering on the entrance of the sanctuary (1 Kgs 8.9-11; 2 Chron. 5.13-14). Now that the believers comprise the new 'spiritual house', 1 Peter can speak of the Spirit of God as resting on them in this same fashion. For Selwyn, this interpretation is appropriate for the phrase τὸ τῆς δόξης (a *hapax* in the NT and LXX), which he understands as a reference to the *Šekinah* and so translates it as 'the Presence of the Glory, yea the Spirit of God'.[249] The preference for most scholars to treat the phrase as having two genitival phrases (τὸ τῆς δόξης and τὸ τοῦ θεοῦ) acting as adjectival modifiers for πνεῦμα, does a better job of capturing the *Šekinah* imagery.

This presence of the Spirit also extends to 1 Peter's audience the Messianic promise of Isa. 11.2 where in the LXX of Isaiah we find the use of the phrase ἀναπαύσεται ἐπ᾽ αὐτὸν πνεῦμα τοῦ θεοῦ which links to τὸ τοῦ θεοῦ πνεῦμα ἐφ᾽ ἡμᾶς ἀναπαύεται in 1 Peter 4.14.[250] Isa. 11.2 had been read messianicly by both

---

245 Schutter, *Hermeneutic*, 171. Lloyd Neve, *The Spirit of God in the Old Testament* (Tokyo: Seibunsha, 1972) 1. The רוח in the land of Palestine, just like the temple, displayed the dual roles of God's judgment and God's salvation. The Eastern רוח bringing moisture and life was a sign of God's life giving and fertility blessings. The Western רוח with its dry and harsh desert air was a reminder of God's judgment.

246. For example, in Isaiah 11.1-2, a shoot shall come out from the stump of Jesse, and a branch shall grow out of his roots. The πνεῦμα τοῦ θεοῦ shall rest on him, the spirit of wisdom and understanding, the spirit of counsel and might, the spirit of knowledge and the fear of the LORD.

247. McCartney, 'OT in First Peter', 118. Cf also Zechariah 2.10-12 where there is an eschatological promise of the Lord coming to dwell among his people.

248. Zechariah 6.12: 'Thus says the LORD of hosts: Here is a man whose name is Branch: for he shall branch out in his place, and he shall build (οἰκοδομήσει) the temple of the LORD' (MT – את-היכל; LXX – τὸν οἶκον κυρίου.).

249. Selwyn, *First Peter*, 222–4. He does not see the πνεῦμα as the main noun for both genitival phrases, arguing rather that there are two distinct subjects. Cf. also Michael E. Lodahl, *Shekinah Spirit: Divine Presence in Jewish and Christian Religion* (New York: Paulist Press, 1992).

250. Achtemeier, *1 Peter*, 308–9; Michaels, *1 Peter*, 264–5; Selwyn, *First Peter*, 250. In similar fashion, the Qumran community also actualized the elements of the Spirit (רוח) in

Jews (4QpIsaᵃ; Pss. Sol. 17.39-44) and Christians (Eph 1.17; Mt. 3.16; Jn 1.32). But 1 Peter moves beyond this conventional application to a corporate one. To 1 Peter, this Isaianic promise has been fulfilled, via Christ, in the new people of God who, like their Messiah, have been reproached and have suffered.[251] What was spoken of in regard to the Messiah (*singular*) in the OT is now actualized in the believers (*plural*) in the Petrine community. To achieve this effect, 1 Peter changes the tense of Isa. 11.2 from a future (ἀναπαύσεται) to a present (ἀναπαύεται).[252] Use of this Isaianic passage, especially the accusative ἐφ' ὑμᾶς, emphasizes not only the fullness with which the Spirit of God now rests on the believers but also the reality they now compose – the new temple of God.[253]

By pointing back to the temple imagery in 2.5, it ostensibly connects this passage to the juridical activity of God in 4.17, where God's judgment is to begin in the οἴκου τοῦ θεοῦ.[254] The *Šekinah* has returned to the new 'Israel' and

---

relation to their community. In typical dualistic mode, 1QS 3.6-26 contrasts the life of the elect with the non-elect as those who are filled with a 'spirit of holiness' – רוח הקדוש (or 'spirit of truth' – רוחות האמת) with those who are filled with a 'spirit of deception' (רוחות העול), respectively. According to 1QS 4.3-8, the elect have:

> a spirit of *meekness*, of patience, generous compassion, eternal goodness, intelligence, *understanding*, potent *wisdom* which trusts in all the deeds of God and depends on his abundant mercy; a spirit of *knowledge* in all the plans of action, of enthusiasm for the decrees of *justice*, of holy plans with firm purpose, of generous compassion with all the sons of truth, of magnificent purity which detests all unclean idols, of unpretentious behaviour with moderation in everything, of prudence in respect of the truth concerning the mysteries of knowledge. These are the *counsels/foundations* (סודי) of the spirit for the sons of truth in the world. And the visitation of those who walk in it will be for healing, plentiful peace in a long life, fruitful offspring with all everlasting blessings, eternal enjoyment with endless life, and a crown of glory (כבוד) with majestic raiment in eternal light. (emphasis added)

While the actual OT reference might not be clear in this case, there is every probability that Isa. 11.1-2 is in view in this DSS passage. In fact, it would seem from the linguistic correspondences of the adjectives that define the spirit (wisdom, understanding, counsel, justice, etc.) that this is a *midrashic* expansion of Isa. 11.1-2. Meanwhile, because of the dualistic perspective in DSS, the reference to the 'spirit of God' (רוח יהוה) is changed to an ethical reference of the 'precepts of God' – מאפטי אל (1QS 4.2-3). Applying this interpretation of the OT to itself, the Qumran community understood the promises that would have been applicable to the Messiah to also apply to itself.

251. McCartney, 'OT in First Peter', 117. In Rom. 9.4 'Glory' is the same as 'Presence'.

252. So Selwyn, *First Peter*, 224. Schutter, *Hermeneutic*, 153–4, who sees here a *pesher*-like hermeneutic.

253. Schutter, *Hermeneutic*, 153, sees the Transfiguration tradition and the martyrdom of Stephen as possible connections to 1 Peter here, especially considering the use of the term δόξα. For כבוד as an expected part of the eschatological dimension in Jewish thinking, see Isa. 9.1-9; 60.1ff; 66.1ff; Hag 2.9; Pss. Sol. 17.32ff; 1QS 4.3-8; 11QTemp 29.8-10; 4QFlor 1.5.

254. McCartney, 'OT in First Peter', 117. 'Once again the OT centers on Christ, who mediates the OT to his NT people. But it also harks back to the idea of the people of God as his Temple … Peter was certainly drawing again upon the temple imagery of 2:5, for 4:17 …'.

is in the 'spiritual temple', which is the community. This is not a sporadic or temporary presence of the Spirit, but the anticipated eschatological in-filling that confirms the restoration from exile and the assured permanent presence of God among the elect (cf. Ezek. 43.7; 4QFlor 1-3 i 5).[255] The Spirit of God that makes this new temple alive is the same spirit that raised Jesus from the dead – making him a 'living stone' (2.4) and, through him, the believers as 'living stones'[256] – confirming God's favor in the face of human disfavor. The divine judgment's final aim then is not simply punitive but, rather, purificatory.

4.7. *Temple and Judgment (1 Pet. 4.14-17 [4.5-7])*

ὅτι ὁ καιρὸς τοῦ ἄρξασθαι τὸ κρίμα ἀπὸ τοῦ οἴκου τοῦ θεοῦ

While it may be considered an exaggeration to suggest that 4.14-17 is the key to the entire epistle, its significance cannot be downplayed.[257] Clearly, from the author's point of view, the end is virtually at hand (4.7) with the Lord portrayed as exercising his juridical activities of pronouncing judgment on all sinful acts (4.17), thereby inaugurating the period of God's eschatological judgment.[258] The judgment is to be meted upon both the living and the dead (4.5-6) – death is no escape.[259] 1 Peter, even when using such Pauline themes as the cross, grace or baptism, applies them differently to suit his paraenetic interest where they lack the soteriological element so prominent in Pauline conception.[260]

A form of providing exhortation in relation to suffering, as is the case with 1 Peter's audience, is found in 2 and 4 Maccabees, where the vindicated righteous sufferer provides hope to the suffering. A passage of significance is one we looked at earlier, 2 Macc. 2.17, which closely resembles 1 Peter 2.4-10.

---

255. *Contra* F. W. Beare, *The First Epistle of Peter: The Greek Text with Introduction and Notes* (Oxford: Blackwell, 1970) 192, who views the spirit as simply sporadic and conditional.

256. Fransen, 'Homélie', 28–38, 38. Fransen points out that while Ezek. 9.6 may provide the vocabulary for 1 Peter, the imagery is derived from Mal. 3.1-5 and 4.1.

257. Lapham, *Peter*, 136–7.

258. Donald Miller, *Upon This Rock: A Commentary on 1 Peter* (Princeton Theological Monograph Series 34; Allison Park, Pa.: Pickwick, 1993).

259. The self designation of the author as συμπρεσβύτερος might have little to do with a ploy in ingratiating himself to his readers, more an acknowledgment of standing at the same risk as his fellow elders when it comes to God's judgment of his οἶκος (Cf. Schutter, *Hermeneutic*, 79).

260. Siegfried Schulz, *Neutestamentliche Ethik* (Zurich: Theologischer Verlag, 1987) 614–17. In essence, it resembles the Pauline teachings on eschatological events in the Thessalonian communications. In those letters, Paul assures the concerned Thessalonians – afraid of having 'missed' the *eschaton* – that the dead will be raised first and then the living will be joined together with them to meet the Lord (1 Thess. 4.13-18). 1 Peter, on the other hand, emphasizes the coming judgment, which will spare not even the dead (4.6).

Donald Juel points out that 1 Peter 4.13-16 is strikingly different because, even though the themes of humiliation and vindication are present, the primary source of hope is not the 'paradigmatic righteous sufferer as such but the Messiah'.[261] 'Those who suffer in the name of Christ can view God as a 'faithful creator' (1 Peter 4:19) because they are confident that the glory of Christ will be revealed (4:13) – once again, because God has already kept his word (1 Peter 1:3-12).'[262] And what is true of the Messiah is also held to be true of or applicable to the believers, by virtue of their relationship to Jesus the Messiah. 'They do not need to fight against their oppressors, since they can trust in God's righteous judgment just as Christ did (see 2.23; 3.13; 4.19).'[263] However, the messiah is the righteous sufferer and, since he suffered, those who suffer 'as Christians' should rejoice since it glorifies God (4.13, 16).

As we have maintained of the οἶκος terminology in 1 Peter, when 4.17 reckons that the judgment which already is beginning will start in the 'house of God' (οἶκου τοῦ θεοῦ) it is referring to the Petrine 'temple-community'.[264] In the latter part of the OT – especially in the eschatological strata of such writings as Amos 3.2; Jer. 7.8ff; 25.29ff; Zeph. 1–2; Zech. 13.7-9; and Mal 3.1 – there was a growing conviction that God would call *first* to account, the 'house of Israel'. A similar conviction resurfaces in Second Temple Jewish writings (*T. Benj.* 10.8-10; *2 Apoc. Bar.* 13.9) and Rabbinic sources (*Qoheleth* 45a; Mishnah *Baba Qamma* 60a; *Rosh Hashanah* 8b; *Midr. Pss.* 17a, 44b, 2121a; and *Exod. Rab.* 88d). Since in the LXX οἶκου θεοῦ typically refers to the temple (Judg. 18.31; Ezra 6.3; Neh. 13.11; Isa. 2.2; Tob. 14.4, 5; Bar. 3.24), while in the NT it is used to refer to people – presenting them as the dwelling place of God (Heb. 3.6) – makes such a reading of 1 Peter viable.[265]

261. Donald Juel, *Messianic Exegesis: Christological Interpretation of the Old Testament in Early Christianity* (Philadelphia: Fortress, 1988) 108, uses 1 Peter 4.13-16 as an example of what he calls the 'democratization' of the messianic promise of Isa. 11.2 – 'And the Spirit of the Lord shall rest upon him' (cf. *Tg. Isa.* 11.2). This ought to be understood not as a replacement of the earlier Davidic promises but an expansion to a national level through the new covenant theology with Jesus as messiah. The promises that belonged to the messiah/king now rightfully belong to the new Israel community. In this case, 1 Peter 4.14 is associated with Ps. 89.50-51 by means of the verb ὀνειδίζεσθε (ὀνειδος in Ps. 89.50-51).

262. Juel, *Messianic Exegesis*, 109.

263. Thurén, *Argument*, 206.

264. Thurén, *Argument*, 176-7; cf. also Lohmeyer, *Temple*, 65ff. The house metaphor (בית) is capable of many different usages and meanings in the biblical context, primarily those that refer to the nation of Israel or the reign of David. A threefold function of the temple in the OT can be delineated as follows: It is the 'house' (οἶκος) where God rules, where he judges, and where one worships him. This is very similar to the threefold function of the concept of God's βασιλεία.

265. Otto Michel, 'οἶκος', *TDNT* 5.127. A variant οἶκος κυρίου τοῦ θεοῦ occurs in 1 Chron. 22.1, still in reference to the temple, while related term οἶκος κυρίου occurs also in reference to the temple in Ezra 3.6; Zech. 8.9; and Ezek. 44.4.

With most commentators agreeing that Ezek. 9.1-6 forms the likely background for 1 Pet. 4.14-17,[266] it is significant to note that Ezekiel constantly uses the term οἶκος to refer to both the people (2.5-8; 3.1, 4-7, 17, 24; 4.3-6; 5.4; 6.11; 8.17; 9.9; 11.5, 15; 44.6, etc.) and the sanctuary (8.14, 16; 9.3, 6-7; 10.4, 18, 19; 11.1, etc.).[267] Both the people and the structure are οἶκος making the interpretation of 1 Peter's reference to the 'temple-community' that much more convincing.[268]

It may be the case that in Ezek.l 9.1-6 οἶκος is used primarily for the sanctuary structure (and not for the people) making the theme of 'judgment *proceeding* from the sanctuary' the essential point of connection with 1 Pet. 4.14-17. Nevertheless, that the people are in view in Ezek. 9.1-6 is made clear by the announcement that the judgment began with the elders who stood in front of the temple (τῷ οἴκῳ).[269] In Ezek. 9.6 we see judgment being pronounced on the nation of Israel, beginning (ἄρχομαι) in the precinct of the sanctuary.[270] Elliott has argued that τῶν ἁγίων should be understood as reference to the elders rather than to the sanctuary so that the phrase τῶν ἁγίων μου ἄρξασθε should be interpreted as 'begin with my holy ones' rather than 'begin with my sanctuary'. However, either rendering would retain credence for our claim given that even the judgment on the elders happens within the temple precincts.[271]

Furthermore, it is also true of Ezekiel in general that judgment begins with the people of God (Ezek. 5.8, 10, 15; 7.8; 11.9; 18.30; 24.14; 36.19), followed

266. Other OT parallels for 1 Pet. 4.17 include Jer. 25.29 (LXX 32.29) and Mal. 3.1-4. The Jeremiah passage has a verbal correspondence with 1 Pet. 4.17 – the verb ἄρχομαι ('begin') is used in both passages to indicate the commencement of God's judgment on the people. Apart from that correspondence, there hardly is any other connection except the shared theme of judgment. Mal. 3.1-4 has been shown also to have a number of verbal and conceptual connections to 1 Pet. 4.17 including God's cleansing judgment on the temple, described as a 'fiery' judgment (cf. πῦρ Mal. 3.2 and πυρός– 1 Pet. 1.6-7; πυρώσις– 4.12) and a purification judgment that begins with the Levites before the destruction of the wicked (Mal. 3.5-6). While Malachi does indeed provide connections that are viable, it is still not convincing as the primary background for this passage. For one thing, the significant phrase οἶκος τοῦ θεοῦ is missing in Malachi. Cf. Johnson, 'Fire on God's House: Imagery from Malachi 3 in Peter's Theology of Suffering (1 Pet. 4:12-19)', *JETS* 29 (1986) 291.

267. While Philo also combines the terms for house and temple, these are for him only allegorical interpretations or illustrations of the mind. In *De Praemis et Poenis*, 123, he states that 'in truth the wise man's mind is a palace (τα βασιλεια) and a house of God (οικος του θεου). This it is which is declared to possess personally the God who is the God of all. This again is the chosen people (λαος εχαιρετος), the people not of particular rulers but of the one and only true ruler, a people holy even as he is holy.'

268. Selwyn, *First Peter*, 291.

269. Fransen, 'Homélie', 28–38; Dennis E. Johnson, 'Fire', 285–94; Achtemeier, *1 Peter*, 315–16. The MT has לפני ('in front of', 'before') which LXX translates as ἔσω ('within', 'inside'). Just as in 1.25, 1 Peter retains the elements adjacent to his OT passages here by using the phrase οἴκου τοῦ θεοῦ from Ezek. 9.6. Cf. Schutter, *Hermeneutic*, 79.

270. Elliott, *Home*, 243.

271. See Dubis, *Woes*, 152, for argument against Elliott's view.

by judgment on other nations (Ezek. 25–32). This thematic pattern of judgment is not unique to Ezekiel and can be seen in Isa. 3.13-14; 10.11-12; Jer. 46.28; Hab. 1.12; Mal. 3.1-5; 4.1; Zech. 13.7-9; *T. Benj.*10.10. The Mishnah (*m. Abot* 4.22) makes it clear that, 'It is [God] that shall judge ... You shall hereafter give account and reckoning before the King of Kings, the Holy One, blessed be he.' In *T. Benj.* 100.8-9, the connection to the judgment of other nations is made explicit: 'For the Lord judges Israel first for the wrong she has committed and then he shall do the same for the other nations.'[272] And just as Hab. 1.2 understood the suffering of the Israelites caused by the Babylonians as part of God's judgment, in 1 Pet. 4.17 the suffering of the believers in the hands of outsiders is understood as part of this eschatological judgment.[273]

Acknowledging the pervasiveness of the general theme of judgment *beginning* in the 'house of God' – both in the OT and in Second Temple Jewish literature – it is likely that the author of 1 Peter did not have a specific passage in mind but rather a recurrent theme. Indeed, the mere fact that the other passages alluded to are also premised on the temple gives the perspective a broader scope of understanding than would have been easily grasped by the audience of 1 Peter.[274] That both Mal. 3.1-5 and Ezek. 9.6 locate the judgment in the temple simply builds a stronger case for understanding 1 Pet. 4.17 as clearly referring to the temple rather than simply the 'household' (i.e. people of God). It leaves little doubt that the impression that 1 Peter has in mind is that of the 'temple-community' (2.5) with which God's judgment is to begin. With the 'new Israel', this judgment is envisioned as the national judgment that precedes the national eschatological restoration reminiscent of the OT prophetic messages and also true of the teaching of Jesus.[275]

272. This could also be understood as a case of *qal wahomer*: if judgment starts in the temple, the most holy of places, how much more the judgment of those outside.

273. *Dubis, Woes*, 149.

274. Schutter's extensive argument for Ezek. 9.6 (*Hermeneutic*, 154–66) as the primary background is well taken. However, the interpretation of the temple imagery is not entirely dependent on a precise identification of a specific OT passage since the primary theme of judgment beginning with God's house is evidenced elsewhere in Jewish writings as we saw earlier.

275. Sanders, *Jesus*, 95–119, proffers the argument that Jesus' message did not foresee a national judgment since the imminent national eschatological restoration was incompatible with expectation of a national judgment. So for Sanders, Jesus' belief in national judgment was simply the shared understanding with others that some Jews would be excluded from Israel's restoration. With Wright, *Victory*, 182–6, 326–36, the place of the final national judgment recedes even further. For Wright, Jesus' message of eschatological restoration proclaims the end of the exilic national judgment. However, Scot McKnight, *A New Vision for Israel: The Teaching of Jesus in National Context* (Grand Rapids: Eerdmans, 1999) 9–13, 138–49, asserts that Jesus viewed national judgment as an integral part of his message. See also Bryan, *Judgement*, 1–6, who primarily argues that the two aspects are so integrally entwined in Jesus' message that it is virtually

But why should the judgment begin in God's 'house/temple/people', i.e. the Christians, if they have not manifested rebellion and disobedience that brought judgment to the literal temple? The answer to this is found in 4.1 – 'Since therefore Christ suffered in the flesh, arm yourselves also with the same intention (for whoever has suffered in the flesh has finished with sin).' Suffering for being Christian is purificatory for 1 Peter (4.13) and would deal with the sinful nature. The model left by Christ is one of suffering and it has eschatological ramifications; 'so that you may also be glad and shout for joy when his glory is revealed' (4.13b). To be true Christians is to expect suffering: for by so doing we are equipped to live victorious lives over sin (4.2). Paradoxically, suffering becomes the mark of true faith and purity for the believers.

4.8. *Temple and The Restoration of 'Israel' (1 Pet. 5.10)*

Ὁ δὲ θεὸς πάσης χάριτος, ὁ καλέσας ὑμᾶς εἰς τὴν αἰώνιον αὐτοῦ δόξαν ἐν Χριστῷ Ἰησοῦ, ὀλίγον παθόντας αὐτὸς καταρτίσει, στηρίξει, σθενώσει, θεμελιώσει

A message of hope and restoration is what 1 Peter 5.10 promises to the 'exiles in Dispersion': that the suffering that they are undergoing is not going to be long since God will 'restore, establish, strengthen and found' them. Contrary to what many have understood these verbs to describe, i.e. only reprieve from the present moment of suffering of 1 Peter's audience,[276] Mark Dubis has recently argued persuasively for an understanding of fulfillment of eschatological hope and glory in this section.[277]

For Dubis, these verbs represent future eschatological works primarily because the verse reflects an exile/restoration motif. This motif also is present in the immediately preceding verse (5.9) which presents the picture of the believers as scattered throughout the world (cf. 1.1).[278] For Dubis, they

---

unthinkable that one would function without the other. While Jesus utilizes the traditions of national judgment, his revisionist approach to the same forced a 're-conceptualization of national restoration', since it did not view Roman rule as the ultimate hurdle of the restoration.

276. Dubis, *Woes*, 53-6. *Contra* Beare, *First Peter*, 207; Martin Luther, 'The Catholic Epistles' (ed. Jaroslav Pelikan, *Luther's Works*, vol. 30; St. Louis: Concordia, 1967) 143; Goppelt, *1 Peter*, 365; Marshall, *1 Peter*, 218–19; Edward Clowney, *The Message of 1 Peter: The Way of the Cross* (The Bible Speaks Today; Downers Grove, Ill.: InterVarsity Press, 1988).

277. Dubis, *Woes*, 54–5.

278. Dubis, *Woes*, 54ff. The shepherd motif in 1 Pet. 2.25 also reflects the eschatological regathering of the children of Israel with God as the Chief Shepherd. Combining imagery of the shepherd from Isa. 53.6 and Ezek. 34, 1 Pet. 5.10 makes the assertion that – in contrast to the faithlessness of the rulers of Israel – God himself (or Jesus the Messiah) will gather the scattered sheep and care for them (ἐπίσκοπον τῶν ψυχῶν ὑμῶν).

conjure memories of the exile of the children of Israel in Babylon. This makes the term ὀλίγος significant because it is understood as a soon-to-be-fulfilled expectation. In the LXX, at least five out of the seven occurrences of ὀλίγος are used in exile/restoration contexts.[279] These are references to the period in which the Israelites were to be in exile before the Lord would redeem and restore them.[280]

The location of the passage at the end of the epistle also comports well with prophetic genre, of which 1 Peter is heir (1.10-12), which typically announced judgment (1 Pet. 4.14-17), and then ended with promises of restoration.[281] While Goppelt's view that the prayer of 1 Pet. 5.10 summarizes the purpose of the entire letter may be plausible, his interpretation of the passage as an explanation of the *present state* of the Petrine audience is challenged by Dubis on the grounds of the *futuristic* orientation of the verbs.[282] These two seemingly opposed aspects may be reconciled by Michaels when he reasons that the 'victory described is future and eschatological [even though] the process by which it comes to realization is already underway'.[283] It is in this light that the temple imagery of 1 Peter has to be understood, as both a present reality and a future expectation.

Such expectation, expressed both in present and future terms, while also found in Qumran, provides a distinctive element to1 Peter's eschatological spin-offs. The significant difference is that for 1 Peter, this 'spiritual house' is the eschatological temple, while for the Qumran community the eschatological temple is yet anticipated, and seems to be a physical temple even though that is not clear.[284] And while like the Qumran community 1 Peter's interpretation and application of the temple imagery is eschatologically driven, he considers the present time to be the *eshaton* only in relation to the person of Jesus Christ.

---

279. 2 Chron. 14.10; 24.24; 1 Macc. 3.18; 7.28; Sir. 32.8. Adjectival adverb ὀλίγον is used in the LXX to translate the Hebrew מעט עובד even though μικρὸν is more commonly preferred.

280. Dubis, *Woes*, 55.

281. With Ezekiel 9.6 as the most likely background to the reference in 1 Pet. 4.17, it is important to point out that there is a message of hope even in the midst of the pronouncement of judgment by YHWH in Ezekiel. A promise is given by the prophet that, despite the judgment and exile, YHWH would remain in the midst of the people as their 'sanctuary' while they are in exile (Ezek. 11.16): 'Therefore say: Thus says the Lord GOD: Though I removed them far away among the nations, and though I scattered them among the countries, yet I have been a sanctuary to them for a little while (μικρός) in the countries where they have gone.' While this passage may have some connection to 1 Peter's assurance to his readers about suffering for 'a little time' – ὀλίγον ἄρτι (1.6-7), Shuzo Fujita, 'Temple Theology of theQumran Sect and the Book of Ezekiel: Their Relationship to Jewish Literature of the Last Two Centuries BC (Th.D. thesis, Princeton Theological Seminary, 1970), 323, has found no Jewish literature in the last two centuries BCE where the verse was referenced. This, nevertheless, does not necessarily deny the perspective held by many Jews of the time that God was still with them in exile, especially reflected in those biblical books like Daniel and Esther whose protagonists were 'Diaspora Jewish' characters.

282. Goppelt, *Typos*, 152; Dubis, *Woes*, 126.

283. Michaels, *1 Peter*, 302–3. Cf. also Sanders, *Jesus*, 77–90.

284. 11QTemp 29.9-10.

124   *Temple, Exile and Identity in 1 Peter*

Therefore, for him, virtually all the focal points of Judaism, i.e. the law, temple, and scripture, have to be understood and interpreted in light of their ultimate fulfillment in the person of Jesus Christ and only subsequently to the 'temple-community'.[285]

The end visualized in 1 Pet. 5.10 is the 'eschatological glory' that will characterize the believers in the *eschaton*.[286] This is not to deny that an element of a secondary reference to God's current activities among the audience of 1 Peter is also in the author's mind. Rather, the primary understanding is eschatological, especially since this verse also forms something of an *inclusio* for the entire letter which started also with reference to the 'suffering for a little while' that the audience was facing (1.6-7).

Dubis' analysis becomes even more significant for us as he argues that the rebuilding so envisioned by these four future indicatives (καταρτίσει, στηρίξει, σθενώσει, θεμελιώσει) is of the devastated Israel and its temple.[287] The rebuilding of the temple is central to the rebuilding of the nation and a key component of the restoration from exile (Isa. 66). Since 1 Peter already has transferred the Jewish expectations of the temple to the believers through Jesus, then the image of the restored temple envisioned in the OT is seen here to be awaiting fulfillment in the people. While the temple now undergoes God's judgment/purification (4.17), its ruins, the suffering people, will soon be restored/re-established.[288] Therefore, simultaneously, the temple in 1 Peter is being rebuilt (2.5) while also looking forward to being restored and established.

A significant term that lends credence to such an interpretation is the architectural term θεμέλιος which, as we noted earlier, was deliberately edited out of the Isaianic quote in 1 Pet. 2.4-9, but now is curiously inserted in this list of indicatives.[289] Given that it typically means 'to lay a foundation' and is frequently used in the LXX in reference to laying the foundation of the temple (1 Kgs 5.17; 6.37; 2 Chron. 8.16; Isa. 44.28; Hag. 2.18; Zech. 4.9; 8.9) – and even though it is a verb in 5.10 (in the sense of 'found' or 'establish') rather than a noun ('a foundation') – its inclusion in the text at this point is peculiar. It recalls the building motif in 2.5, which, as we have argued in this study, is representative of temple imagery. And given that 1 Peter has been shown to be drawing extensively from Isaiah 40–66, the most likely background for the concept θεμέλιος is probably Isa. 44.28.[290] This is the only explicit reference to the rebuilding of the temple (τὸν οἶκον τὸν ἅγιόν μου θεμελιώσω) found in this section of Isaiah and aligns well with the themes in 1 Pet. 5.10 and with the 'idea of exile'. To the Petrine believers

---

285. Cohen, *Maccabees*, 127ff.

286. Dubis, *Woes*, 56. The four indicatives in 5.10 anticipate this future expectation.

287. *Dubis, Woes*, 54.

288. Dubis, *Woes*, 55.

289. 1 Peter's omission of the same word in 2.4-10 may have been his emphasizing the identity of Christ as the 'cornerstone' (ἀκρογωνιαῖον) rather than the 'foundation' (θεμέλιός).

290. McKelvey, *New Temple*, 11 n. 2.

are the promises of Israel's eschatological restoration fully applied and transferred. [291]

Thus, 5.10, once again, reaffirms our claim about the underlying significance of temple imagery in the mind of 1 Peter, allowing connections of the believers' identity with temple imagery to be made by the author. While it is expected that the audience would follow the trail that leads to the understanding that 1 Peter seeks to explicate, there is also the possibility that the audience may not have fully appropriated the imagery. Nevertheless, as shown in this reading, the passage's linkage to the temple imagery is pertinent to a better understanding of the overall message of 1 Peter.

4.9. Conclusion

In this chapter we have endeavored to establish the significance of the temple imagery in 1 Peter by highlighting its utilization in the different sections of the letter. The historical development of the sanctuary structure plays a significant role in paralleling the literary structure of the epistle of 1 Peter, moving from the concept of the tabernacle to that of the temple and its different phases of construction, judgment and restoration. And for the community – as an embodiment of the royal/holy priesthood – maintaining holiness becomes a requirement reminiscent of ancient Israel's failed function as a priesthood to the nations. Purity and holiness also incorporate eschatological ramifications since the eschatological 'temple-community' envisioned in 1 Peter is understood to fulfill all Jewish eschatological expectations.

We have maintained that temple imagery incorporates the concepts of exile, judgment and restoration providing the cultic language by which 1 Peter addresses the concerns of identity and alienation with which his audience was struggling. The temple imagery provides the means not only to assure the believers of the presence of God in their midst, but also to affirm their current reality as the eschatological birth-pangs of the climactic consummation that is at hand. Consequently, the perception of their cause of suffering is reconfigured with 1 Peter making it clear that their suffering is not necessarily the result of sin or shortcoming on their part but – as with the temple of old – it is a reflection of the eschatological judgment of God that must begin with the purging of God's house. Suffering is not a judgment unto condemnation but a purification for the heavenly inheritance stored up for them and a confirmation that they are truly walking in the footsteps of their Messiah. The wise thing is to persevere, for if this is how it is for the believers, imagine how much worse it is for those who are not (4.18).

---

291. Dubis, *Woes*, 56.

Temple imagery also provides the premise for the hope that the readers so desperately seek during this period of suffering. While judgment is sure to start with God's house (4.14), there is hope for restoration (5.10). Much in the same way that the temple was restored in the OT (even though not satisfactorily), so now there is a promise of the eschatological glory that awaits the faithful. This hope is guaranteed in the work of Christ on the cross, who becomes the model the believers must now emulate. It is their nature as a 'spiritual house' that fully affirms the permanent presence of God in their midst, enabling them to persevere through all the tests and trials knowing God is glorified through them and will strengthen them to bear it all.

The overarching mindset in the Second Temple period that felt tension between the role of the rebuilt temple and the idealized expectations of a sanctuary built by God finds reconciliation in 1 Peter. The physical temple is replaced by the person of Jesus and through him the believers as λίθοι ζῶντες become building blocks for the new 'sanctuary' – the eschatological 'temple'.[292] The prevalent Jewish expectation of a religio-political messiah who would restore the glory of the physical temple (*1 Enoch* 79.36; 89.16; *Tg. Isa.* 53) (or replace it with a heavenly one that could not be defiled - Philo, *QE* 2.85; 4Q400–4Q405; *3 Enoch*; *Tg. Isa.* 6.3) finds a new *modus vivendi* in the person of Jesus – the Messiah – and, through him, the believers who corporately make up the 'new temple'.[293]

Yet this is no mere 'spiritualization' of the concrete OT counterpart, for in the Jewish mindset the antonym of 'spiritual' is not 'material' or 'legal' but *un-* or *non-*spiritual.[294] In this regard, it is an eschatological realization of a greater magnitude of fulfillment that contrasts an eschatological outlook that finds its fulfillment in the person of Christ with the other eschatological expectations current within Judaism.[295]

---

292. Cerfaux, 'Sacerdotium', 5–39. Building on texts gathered by Gottlob Schrenk, 'ἱεράτευμα', *TDNT* 3.249-51, Cerfaux identified two emphases of *kingship/royalty* and *priesthood* as the two marks of God's people. In relation to *kingship/royalty* emphasis, he perceived a messianic hope especially in the history of the nation of Israel where the hope was alive. On the idea of *priesthood*, he found a 'spiritualistic' exegesis of Alexandrian Judaism with emphasis on apocalyptic idealization of Law and *cultus*.

293. Goppelt, *Typos*, 136–57. It is more persuasive to understand the use of the OT images as typological rather than simply 'spiritualization' in which case they cease to have any physical form. In typology the essence remains the same even after change of form. In this regard Goppelt maintains that just as in the other means of grace in the OT 'the Temple too is set aside by the fulfillment that has been given to the church' (146). He can say this because in both cases it is the presence of God that sets apart both the Temple and the church, yet rests more fully in the person of Christ who is the ultimate revelation of God. And so he states that all the 'typological replacement of the redemptive gifts of the first covenant people rests in Christ' (148).

294. F. Gavin, *The Jewish Antecedents of the Christian Sacraments* (London: SPCK, 1928) 13. The author of 1 Peter is clearly of a Jewish origin judged, partly, by his extensive use of the OT. On the author's Jewishness see Schutter, *Hermeneutic*.

295. Ackroyd, *Exile*, 254.

Chapter 5

IMPLICATIONS AND CONCLUSIONS

5.1. *Introductory Remarks: Temple Imagery and the Central Themes of 1 Peter*

Different scholars highlight different themes in 1 Peter, making it difficult to find any level of consensus on the matter. For example, on the one hand, L. T. Johnson identifies the central themes of 1 Peter as follows: Faith and hope in God; Baptism; Imitation of the suffering Jesus; and Church as God's house.[1] On the other hand, Ralph Martin assumes the trinitarian formula (1.2) as basis of the theological themes of the epistle when he categorizes them as God – parent creator; Christ – his person and achievement; the Holy Spirit; and the Christian community – its problems and responses.[2]

In spite of this, some consensus exists concerning suffering as the overarching concern of the epistle of 1 Peter. The epistle is intent on explaining to the readers the premise of their current suffering (1.7), the right and wrong reasons for suffering (2.11-25; 4.12-19), the extent of suffering (1.6-7; 4.12), and the length of the period of suffering (1.6; 5.10). Overall, the current suffering of the readers is given a Christian eschatological τέλος by 1 Peter: It is a purification for the approaching final judgment and a partaking of the sufferings of the Messiah (1.18-22). The overall concern about suffering is addressed in light of the language of hope, holiness, identity, and judgment which, in turn, provide for our purposes the primary themes of the epistle which we will explicate in relation to 1 Peter's eschatological emphasis.

5.2. *Suffering, A Sign of The End Times: Suffering, Temple, and Eschaton*

Believers have become the new sacred space by virtue of their relationship with Jesus, and by the same token they should expect to suffer by virtue of this same

---

1.   Luke Timothy Johnson and Todd Penner, *The Writings of the New Testament* (Minneapolis: Augsburg Fortress, 1999), 435-38. It is interesting to note the vocabulary which, though reflected in the general presentation of the epistle, does not appear in 1 Peter, including church (ἐκκλησία), Israel, covenant (διαθήκη), disciples (μαθηταί).

2.   Andrew Chester and Ralph P. Martin, *New Testament Theology: The Theology of the Letters of James, Peter and Jude* (Cambridge: Cambridge University Press, 1994) 104–30.

relationship with Jesus. As we have seen, the current suffering of the believers addressed in 1 Peter is to be understood as performing two functions: First, it is a cleansing and purification of the believers in light of the fact that they are the 'new temple' and are thus the new residence of God (1.6-7). Second, it is part of the eschatological judgment of God which must begin within the 'house of God' (4.14-17).[3] Both are closely related as the purification that is necessitated by the speedily approaching *eschaton*.[4]

This suffering would be short-lived since the end is expected with the soon approaching revelation of Christ (1.6 – ὀλίγον ἄρτι ... ἐν ἀποκαλύψει Ἰησοῦ Χριστοῦ and 4.17 – ἐν ἀποκαλύψει Ἰησοῦ Χριστοῦ). With the preposition ἐν, the ἀποκαλύψις is here used in the temporal sense, i.e. 'at the time of the revelation of Jesus Christ'. While there is reference to when it will happen (i.e. ἐν καιρῷ ἐσχάτῳ) no time frame is given in this verse. However, in the verse just prior to this, the encouragement offered is based on the fact that the 'multitudes of sufferings' (ποικίλοις πειρασμοῖς) being experienced will not last long (ὀλίγον ἄρτι). In this regard then, the time frame is to be understood as one that anticipates a not too distant future. The present painful situation that the believers are experiencing is not to last beyond a protracted period of time with a foreseeable *terminus*.

Such expectation is also reitersted in 4.5-7, where the coming judgment is said to be fast approaching. In fact, the judge is said to be already standing at the door ready to come and judge everyone, both the living and the dead (4.5). In 4.7, it restates forthrightly that the end of all things is near (Πάντων δὲ τὸ τέλος ἤγγικεν) marking the anticipated καιρῷ ἐσχάτῳ of v. 5, that will precipitate the judgment that would commence with the arrival of the judge. While earlier in the letter the fiery trial (1.6, 7) that the readers were facing was equated to purification, 4.17 introduces a second element where suffering is equated to the judgment that is being ushered in by the end times. Suffering then is understood to be symptomatic of the times, a sign that the *eschaton* is near, and that is why the believers should persevere, knowing that their reward would be great (1.4).

In relation to the temple imagery – in the same way that 1 Peter joins the community to Christ resulting in the construct the 'temple-community' – believers must also partake in the sufferings of Christ, bearing the same marks of the 'living stone' (2.4) to whom they are now joined and in whom

---

3.	Selwyn, *First Peter*, 300, speaks of this understanding as a 'first installment of the last judgment'.

4.	Brox, *Petrusbrief*, 24–34. For Brox, the audience is unknown to the author personally. However, while there is no direct indication in the letter about any personal anecdotes that might betray a personal relationship between the author and his audience, there is no need to postulate a complete lack of personal relationship between them. Also, the epistle was written as an encyclical (1.1) and not as a personal letter, making it intentionally general but not impersonal. (Cf. also Chester and Martin, *Theology*, 88.)

they have their identity. Thus, it should come to them as no surprise that if Jesus suffered they too must suffer (4.1). Nonetheless, the promise is also given that in the same way that Jesus was made 'alive in the spirit' (3.18) so too the believers can look forward to their being made alive by God's spirit (4.6). In essence, 1 Peter simply says to his readers to expect to suffer if they are genuinely part of the construct whose cornerstone is Christ (2.7), knowing that their suffering is not in vain (4.1, 12-19).[5]

5.3. *Faith and Hope in God*

The primary purpose for writing the epistle is given by the author as a παράκλησις ('encouragement' or 'exhortation' – 5.12) to an audience that was experiencing trials (1.6) and testings (4.12). The premise for the exhortation is the 'hope' (ἐλπις – 1.13; 3.5; 3.15) built on the resurrection of Jesus Christ. The encouragement is twofold – one, to call them to perseverance in light of the resultant suffering and, two, give hope to those who are downcast and on the verge of giving up (2.12; 4.4-7) due to the same said sufferings.[6]

The suffering was being experienced at three levels: First was the fact that the believers were at odds with the society around them (1.6; 3.13-14; 4.4, 12-16; 5.9-10). Second, their social status was now in question given their conversion to a new religion (1.3; 2.10; 4.4). Third, the age-old questions of why good people have to suffer and whether God would actually do something about it now, rather than later (1.6; 2.19; 4.12).[7] 1 Peter's solution is spelled out along these three lines with the author basing his encouragement upon the promised messianic blessing now made accessible through Jesus Christ (1.18-19). First, the believers have to maintain positive conduct even in the face of persecution following the example of their Lord Jesus with whom they will share the glory (4.13). Second, the fear of losing their social status is replaced by a new identity as the 'new Israel', the 'spiritual house' and the 'new priesthood' (2.4-10). Third, 1 Peter offers theodicy as explanation of God's mysterious plan for the creation.[8] Ultimately, it is God, through the work of Christ, who will be victorious and vindicate the believers. Indeed,

---

5.   Johnson and Penner, *Writings*, 438. The partial quotation of Isa. 53.5 'by his wounds we are healed' in 1 Pet. 2.18 is the result of the Christological influence of the Isaianic suffering servant on the early Christian ethos.

6.   Chester and Martin, *Theology*, 88. Lohmeyer, *Temple*, 99, 'The Temple at Jerusalem was regarded as God's house among His people; this eschatological *basileia* is the holy place of all who will be God's guests and children. The prototype fellowship that was found in the Old Testament is completely taken over into the "new" House of God. This kingdom means for it truly a *consummare* and *elevare* a "destroying and building again".'

7.   Chester and Martin, *Theology*, 89.

8.   Chester and Martin, *Theology*, 90.

suffering for the name of Christ simply confirms that the believers are doing the right thing and that the spirit of God rests in them (4.14)

5.4. *Hope and Restoration of Israel*

Norbert Brox proffers that a clear train of thought governed by 'hope' forms the composition theme of the epistle of 1 Peter, though not in any strict pattern.[9] Schutter wants to include on top of this 'God's call to holiness' as a significant theme that governs the epistle's composition: 'As with the triad of "fear", "faith", and "hope" in 1.17-21, so "brotherly love" may represent a fourth attempt to translate what it means to be holy, resulting in a point of contact between 1.22 and 1.17-21, where he began the list.'[10] In this regard hope is intricately connected to conduct and purity.

The attitude of purity and holiness as a marker of a minority group or a sectarian tendency for resisting the encroachment of the larger society is well developed in the writings of the Qumran community. However, hope in 1 Peter needs also to be understood in light of the 'idea of exile' and the 'New Exodus'. The hope so reflected is essentially one of anticipation for the *restoration of Israel*. The four elements identified by Sanders as common to the future hope in Jewish understanding, i.e. restoration of the twelve tribes (1.1), conversion of Gentiles (2.12; 4.6-7), renewed purified temple (2.4-10) and purity both in morals and in worship (1.15, 22; 2.12; 3.1, 16) all find particular emphasis in 1 Peter[11] – 1 Peter refers to the believers as the ἐκλεκτοῖς clearly identifying them with Israel.[12] Given that perhaps the majority of the believers are Gentile converts fulfills the second expectation. The temple imagery (2.4-10) reformulates the 'spiritual temple' in light of the person of Jesus Christ, and 1 Peter calls on the believers not only to exercise 'upright conduct' (ἀναστροφὴ - 1.15; 2.12; 3.1, 16) but to base their conduct on the holiness of God ("Αγιοι ἔσεσθε, ὅτι ἐγὼ ἅγιος εἰμι' – Lev. 11.11 quoted in 1.16) calling them to emulate that holiness in all the spheres of their lives (1.15).[13]

The hope that 1 Peter talks about is couched in Jewish understanding that anticipated an eschatological manifestation of the outworking of God that would restore, renew, re-gather, and reestablish the nation of Israel but now encompasses a new dimension with the incarnation and the anticipated return of Jesus Christ (1.13).[14] As Ackroyd points out, 'It is evident that the new age

9.   Brox, *Petrusbrief*, 73.
10.   Schutter, *Hermeneutic*, 53–4.
11.   Sanders, *Judaism*, 289–90.
12.   Achtemeier, *1 Peter*, 69: 'In 1 Peter, the language, and hence the reality of Israel pass without remainder into the language and hence the reality of the new people of God.'
13.   Sanders, *Jesus*, 98.
14.   Sanders, *Jesus*, 98. The point of re-gathering, and the temple, as heralding the restoration of Israel are based on the understanding that, 'it is *Jesus who is to be positively connected with the hope for Jewish restoration*' (emphasis original).

anticipated by both the exilic and the restoration thinkers did not materialize. To that extent there is always therefore an element of deferment, and the same point may be noted in the thinking of New Testament times concerning the *parousia*.'[15] At the same time, 1 Peter is also redefining Israel, the temple, and the nature of the restoration.

Just as the exilic period was a time of testing for the Jewish community, where the formulation of a unique identity transpired, so too is the current state of the Petrine community as it faces its own 'exile' (1.1, 17).[16] The hope of the eschatological fulfilment of these expectations is premised on the anticipated ἀποκάλυψις of Jesus Christ, the *parousia*. It is this eschatological hope (ἐλπις) that shaped the spiritual conduct (ἀναστροφή) of the matriarchs who in turn have become the example for the community (3.5). The reality of this hope though for the Petrine community is not simply one that lies in the future but it is a hope that is alive – living hope (ἐλπίδα ζῶσαν) – having been guaranteed by Jesus Christ through his resurrection from the dead (1.3), and is now appropriated or made available to the believers through the 'new birth' – ἀναγεννήσας (cf. 4.6).

We have here then the 'already/not yet' Petrine eschatology. Though its fullness is still anticipated – since it presently lies in heaven awaiting to be revealed by God at the appointed time (1.4 - ἐν καιρῷ ἐσχάτῳ) – it also is presently being experienced as the 'living hope' that is shaping the community's life. Indeed, for 1 Peter, these are the ἐσχάτου τῶν χρόνων ('end of time' – 1.20) anticipating the final consummation (1.4). This hope is in God – even as it is premised on Jesus Christ – who performed the work of raising Jesus from the dead, through the Spirit, guaranteeing our hope (1.21). That hope, in turn, solidifies the anticipated glorious life of the believers which would be wrought by the same Spirit (4.6). This makes sense of the active role of the Spirit in 1 Peter (1.2, 21; 3.18; 4.6) indicative of the understanding that this is the expected eschatological outpouring of the Spirit that was perceived by some to be missing in the second temple (*b.Yoma* 9b).[17]

Furthermore, the hope of restoration that played out annually in the festival of the Passover is also reflected in 1 Peter. In this festival the exodus event not only provided a reminder of God's past salvation, but anticipated God's future salvation.[18] For 1 Peter, this expectation finds its fulfillment in the person

15. Ackroyd, *Exile*, 253.

16. Paul Hanson, 'The World of the Servant of the Lord in Isaiah 40-55', in Bellinger and Farmer, *Suffering Servant*, 9-22.

17. Heinz-Wolfgang Kuhn, *Enderwertung und gegenwartiges Heil* (SUNT 4; Göttingen: Vandenhoeck & Ruprecht, 1966) 137.

18. Cf. *m. Pesah* 10.5: 'In every generation a person is duty-bound to regard himself as if he personally has gone forth from Egypt ...', which reflects the necessity to *actualize* the exodus experience for every subsequent generation so that it is not simply fossilized in the past but it is experienced in the present. Passover meals would have offered a time to discuss the participants'

of Jesus Christ who has become the 'lamb without spot or blemish' (ἀμνοῦ ἀμώμου καὶ ἀσπίλου) of the Passover.[19] The exodus motif also finds expression in 1 Peter's metaphor of pilgrimage used to define the Petrine community's ongoing spiritual journey (1.1, 17; 2.11). This resonates with the recitation of the events of the exodus from Egypt during Passover and, also, with the fact that pilgrimage to Jerusalem during Passover for the Jews in the Dispersion had grown to have special significance, precipitating the emotive anticipation of the restoration hope and buoying eschatological speculation.[20]

Further still, the language of 'inheritance' (κληρονομία – cf. LXX Ps. 105.11, Israel's promised possession) is clearly a continuation and amplification of the exodus theme even as the inheritance is eschatological and equated with salvation (1.5, 7, 9). This hope of salvation (eschatological restoration of Israel) is what the prophets of old sought to find out about with limited success since it was really for the benefit of those who now find themselves living in the end times (1.10-12).[21] The collective hope for the salvation of God to which the OT prophets gave themselves so diligently, albeit unsuccessfully (in terms of realization of the revelation), is now fulfilled in the eschatological community of faith.[22] Even the angels to whom the prophets directed their inquiry as to the mysteries of God (Ezek. 40–48; Daniel; Zech. 1.9; 4 Ezra 4.1; Rev 17.1;

anticipation of 'a new deliverance, hope for change, and awareness of a deeper significance to the rituals' (Brunson, *Psalm 118*, 70 n. 205).

19.   See also Jn 1.29, 36; and 1 Cor. 5.7 where the same idea is expressed.

20.   Gerhard Kittel, *Theological Dictionary of the New Testament*, vol. V (trans. Geoffrey W. Bromiley; Grand Rapids: Eerdmans, 1965) 898: 'With [the Passover's] recollection of the deliverance from Egypt it awakened the national feelings and hopes of the coming redemption.'

21.   Selwyn, *First Peter*, 258–68, was the first to comprehensively argue that the prophets mentioned in 1 Pet. 1.10-12 are NT prophets rather than OT. This position has not attracted any adherents in spite of Duane Warden's ('The Prophets of 1 Peter 1.10-12', *RestQ* 31 [1989] 1–12) spirited defense. Julian Price Love, 'The First Epistle of Peter', *Int* 8 (1954) 63-87, argued for both NT and OT prophets as the point of reference in these verses. However, it is widely held by the majority of commentators that these are OT rather than NT prophets. Especially decisive is the fact that these prophets are said to have borne witness to Christ beforehand (προμαρτυρόμενον). Cf. Achtemeier, *1 Peter*, 108; Kelly, *Peter and Jude*, 59; Windisch, *Briefe*, 54; Spicq, *Saint Pierre*, 55; Michaels, *1 Peter*, 41.

22.   The two terms applied to the activity of the prophets (ἐξηραύνησαν, ἐραυνῶντες) mean basically the same thing and function as hendiadys putting an emphasis on the persistence and thoroughness of the search. See Daniel Arichea, 'God or Christ? A Study of Implicit Information', *BT* 28 (1977) 412–18, 415. Hamerton-Kelly, 'Temple', 9–10, is of the opinion that the two opposing perspectives, i.e. those who wanted to rebuild and those who were opposed to the building of the second temple, were divided between those who anticipated an eschatological temple built by God (as per Ezekiel) versus those of the priesthood (Deuteronomic tradition) who longed for a sanctuary to resume the priestly cult. The latter won and established the second temple. But the former promulgated the apocalyptic worldview and the eschatological temple, which 1 Peter perceives as fulfilled in the person of Jesus, and the Petrine community.

21.9) are here portrayed as also seeking to find out this mystery of God.[23] Such language bolsters the community's self-identity as the 'new Israel' of God in whom are fulfilled the OT promises.[24]

Ultimately, eschatological hope was symbolized in the anticipation of the renewal or reconstitution of the temple in Jerusalem/Zion (Isa. 66.18). With the replacement of the physical temple with the 'spiritual' (2.4-10), 1 Peter understands the reign of God that brings to an end the state of 'exile' for Israel as having been inaugurated in the death and resurrection of Jesus Christ (3.18). Jesus is a central piece of the new temple for he is the 'elect cornerstone' (ἀκρο γωνιαῖον ἐκλεκτὸν) which holds the building together and gives it stability, a part of the rejected foundation stone that the Lord laid down in 'Zion' for the construction of God's house (2.6).

Having been ransomed (λυτρόω) through the precious blood of Christ – the Passover lamb who is without spot or blemish (1.18-19) – the believers' response is to be one of grateful obedience (1.20-25). This ransom language clearly connotes restoration, a setting free that makes possible the return from 'exile'.[25] With such an understanding suffering ceases to be perceived negatively – the result of sin – and instead is positively appropriated as a purification process (1.6-7; 2.11-12).

Furthermore, these references, allusions, and echoes of the exodus motif also find expression and interpretation in Isa. 40–55. The themes of 'girding of loins' (Exod. 12.11 in 1 Pet. 1.13), dwelling as exiles (Exod. in 1 Pet. 1.1; 2.11), the need for ransom (Exod. 15.13; 24 in 1 Pet. 1.18, and the Paschal lamb without blemish (Exod. 12.5 in 1 Pet. 1.18-20) are echoed in the imagery of Isa. 43.14-21 and in Hosea 2.[26] Isaiah and Hosea reformulate the Sinai covenant in light of the new captive state of the Jewish people. The Babylonian exile experience is interpreted in light of the earlier exodus experience, both to maintain the hope for restoration and to call the people to holiness as the basic motivating principles of their relationship to God.

With a discernible 'Past–Present–Future' matrix ('Exodus–Exile–Apocalyptic'), 1 Peter formulates the concept of 'spiritual house', 'royal priesthood' and 'the holy people' (2.4-10) as designated by the appropriation of the *terminus technicus* – 'exiles' (1.1, 17; 2.11). Adaptation of the motif of

---

23.   Michaels, *1 Peter*, 48: 'The notion that some heavenly mysteries are hidden even from the angels who dwell in heaven is found both in Jewish apocalyptic literature (e.g., *1 Enoch* 16.3, *2 Enoch* 24.3) and in the NT (e.g. Mark 13:32, and by implication Eph 3:10 ... This tradition exists in apocalyptic literature alongside that of the "interpreting angel" who explains God's mysteries to a prophet or seer.'

24.   Jean-Claude Margot, *Les Epîtres de Pierre* (Geneva: Labor et Fides, 1960) 25, points out the continuity of the divine revelation that was begun in the OT and now finds its fulfillment in the NT.

25.   Jonsen, 'Moral', 97.

26.   Jonsen, 'Moral', 97 n. 12.

a 'New Exodus' and 'a counter temple theme' allows for articulation of the anticipated eschatological redemption that finds fulfillment in the person of Jesus Christ.[27]

Streams of OT traditions are adopted and adapted by 1 Peter in his development of the 'idea of exile'.[28] It is the idealization of the event by recasting subsequent adversities in terms of the exile, that made the 'idea of exile' so pertinent to the self-reclamation of the people of God. The 'idea of exile' becomes a heuristic paradigm through which 1 Peter interprets the present situation of his audience, recasting the hope for the future that he seeks to establish for his 'exiled' community. By combining the concepts of exile with the saving work of Jesus Christ, 1 Peter is able to articulate a most unique and encouraging word for its audience.

5.4.1. *Hope and the Fiery Testing*

The phrase πυρὸς δὲ δοκιμαζομένου ('purifying fire') which 1 Peter 1.6-7 uses to explain the experience of its audience (cf. 4.12) echoes the exile experience as it finds parallels in at least three OT passages – Isa. 48.10; Zech. 13.9; Mal. 3.3. All three texts are exilic (or post-exilic) and all use the language of πυρός to describe the Babylonian exile as a purifying process for the believers which, unlike the metallurgic process of producing perishable gold, produces imperishable results of being established as God's people (Ps. 65[66].10; Ps. 16[17].3; Prov. 17.3; Sir. 2.1-6; 1QS 8.4).[29] If indeed Isa. 48.10 is in the back of the author's mind at this stage, then an appeal could be made to the larger context of Isa. 48 which suggests an understanding of God doing a new thing in Israel (48.6-8) – restoration from exile.[30]

Even more enchanting is Zech. 13.9, which presents an intriguing connection if only by the sheer amount of vocabulary correspondences between the two passages (πῦρός, δοκιμάζω, χρυσίον). The picture in Zechariah is, once again, that of the Babylonian exile as a refining fire. However, the refining here is limited to only a portion of Israel – one third – following the judgment on the Shepherds (13.7-8). This portion is probably a reference to the exiles who, following their 'purification', would be ready to be used by God. Zechariah's allusion to the 'covenant formula' – They will call on my name, and I will answer them. I will say, 'They are my people'; and they will

---

27.   Wright, 'Dialogue', 254: 'Sometimes those visions of days of old included the hope for a revived monarchy. Exodus, temple, kingship: a powerful combination. There is plenty of evidence that a large number of Jews in the period roughly 100 B.C. to A.D. 140 embraced and acted on something like this vision. This was the context within which words like salvation meant what they meant.'

28.   Klyne Snodgrass, 'Streams of Tradition Emerging from Isaiah 40:1-5 and their Adaptation in the New Testament', *JSNT* 8 (1980) 24–45.

29.   Elliott, *1 Peter*, 343.

30.   In Mal. 3.3 it is the coming Messiah who would cleanse and purify the sons of Levi only, while in Zech. 13.9 God purifies all the remnants.

say, 'The LORD is our God' — reflected in 1 Peter's allusion to Hos. 2.23 ('Once you were not a people, but now you are God's people; once you had not received mercy, but now you have received mercy'; cf. also Isa. 51.11 – 'You are my people'), in 1 Pet. 2.10, also enhances the likelihood of this assumption.

These passages deal with the theme of exile, with the judgment as a purifying process that refines the exiles confirming their status as still the elect community of YHWH.[31] The promise of restoration uttered echoes the 'covenant formula' and assures the people of God's commitment to rescue them and restore them to their covenant relationship, purity, the land, and temple.[32] By adopting a similar language of exile 1 Peter leaves little doubt in the mind of the readers that his conceptualization of them as the 'new Israel' places them in a similar path as that of 'old Israel' that would culminate with God's victorious act of redemption. Indeed, the promises that originally belonged to Israel now exclusively belong to the new Petrine eschatological community.

The sufferings of Christ are 'predicted' (προμαρτυρόμενον: 1 Pet. 1.10 – a *hapax*) recalling the suffering Servant-Messiah of Isa. 53 whose image has been variously translated either as a messianic individual or as a corporate identity of the nation of Israel. 1 Peter identifies the suffering servant with Jesus Christ whose own παθήματα were predicted in those of the Isaianic servant (2.22-24). Moreover, since the suffering of the believers is patterned after that of Christ they too are vicariously identified with the suffering servant (4.6). In 1 Pet. 4.13, it is the premise of eschatological rejoicing – 'But rejoice insofar as you are sharing Christ's sufferings (παθήμασιν), so that you may also be glad and shout for joy when his glory is revealed.'

Second, by identifying the Christian community with Israel, 1 Peter transfers all the conceptions of the exile wholly to the present condition of the believers, who not only are socio-political aliens,[33] but also are suffering 'alienation' by the mere virtue of being Christians.[34] Nevertheless, while 1 Peter maintains the identity of the Church with OT Israel, there are some significant modifications in the way the OT themes are applied. The national unity in the exile motif is replaced by the eschatological unity of the Church,[35] the national

31. See Rainer Albertz, 'Exile as Purification: Reconstructing the "Book of the Four"', in Paul L. Redditt and Aaron Schart, eds., *Thematic Threads in the Book of the Twelve* (BZAW 325; Berlin, New York: Walter de Gruyter, 2003) 232–51. Focusing on Hosea, Amos, Micah and Zephaniah he concludes that, being the product of a final redactor, '... the concept of purifying judgment constitutes the redactional chain of the whole composition' (240).

32. Ackroyd, *Exile*, 110–13.

33. Elliott, *Home*, 23-48. Feldmeier, *Fremde*.

34. E. Lohse, 'Paränese und Kerygma im 1. Petrusbrief', ZNW 45 (1954) 68–89; F. W. Beare, *The First Epistle of Peter* (Oxford: Blackwell, 3rd edn, 1970) 196; Wolff, 'Christ und Welt', 333–42; W. G. Kummel, *Introduction to the New Testament* (Nashville: Abingdon, 1975) 418; Furnish, 'Sojourners', 1–11.

35. Fishbane, *Text*, 129–30.

sanctuary of Israel is transformed into an eschatological spiritual sanctuary of the 'new Israel' (2.4-10) and the national hope for political restoration is reinterpreted in light of the Christian hope for eschatological redemption through the atoning sacrificial death of Jesus Christ (1.18-22). The suffering of 1 Peter's audience – the struggles with the world around them, their spiritual struggles to understand the presence of God in their suffering, and their concerns of identity – all have to do with their being in 'exile' (1.4, 7; 4.12).[36]

Third, the concept of exile is crucial not only in providing the backdrop to the entire letter of 1 Peter, but also in situating the author within the milieu of Jewish thinking that perceived the concept of exile as descriptive of the continuing state of subservience that had plagued Jewish people beyond the Babylonian exile. N. T. Wright envisions this particular 'exile' as encompassing not only the Jews in the dispersion, but also those in Palestine who, though technically not in 'exile', still continued to live under foreign domination.[37] Therefore, Wright maintains that the Second Temple Jewish community continued to look forward to the *eschatological* national restoration that would permanently get them out of 'exile'.[38] This is what spawned a mode of perception that anticipated a once-for-all eschatological resolution to the perennial subservient status of the Jewish nation – *eschatological apocalypticism*.[39]

Fourth, as we have noted above, while the term 'Diaspora' may be useful, it does not quite capture the negative elements that are associated with the concept of 'exile'. In 1 Peter the situation of the audience is shown to be so intense that one commentator has referred to the Petrine community (1.6-7; 4.12) as a 'besieged Christian community'.[40] Within such circumstances of persecution and suffering, the temptation would be isolation and disconnection from the larger society.[41] As a result, 1 Peter writes to encourage his audience

---

36. Indeed, as far as Chevallier ('Diaspora', 394) is concerned, the condition of exile is what characterizes all Christians everywhere and in every age: 'Actually, the concept of foreign residents defines for him [1 P] the common condition of all Christians because, for him, as he saw it, all Christians are in diaspora.'

37. Wright, *People*, 268–9.

38. Wright, *People*, 269. Gowan, 'Exile', 219: 'The main themes of the canonical OT history – the promise, the Exodus, the occupation of the land, the monarchy – were of no help in coping with the problems the apocalyptic writers faced. But the exile was not only actually responsible, historically, for some of them, it was also the kind of history that made sense theologically to people without security, living in an alien world even though it was their own country.'

39. Plöger, *Theocracy and Eschatology*; Hamerton-Kelly, 'Temple', 1–15; Knibb, 'Exile', 253–72; Gowan, 'Exile', 205–22. Cf. Dubis, *Woes*, 37–44.

40. Brox, *Petrusbrief*, 95: 'eine bedrängte Christenheit'. However, Brox does not perceive the state of suffering believers as a reality since for him it is the eschatological premise which provides the grounds for ethics and is thus not reflective of any early Christian situation (203). See also Thurén, *Argument*, 170 n. 255.

41. Wolff, 'Christ und Welt', 328.

to maintain a positive outlook in their Christian hope against the negative impulses that the surrounding society hurls at them. Their exodus is not toward isolation or retreat from the world but a movement into the world (2.12; 3.1).[42] It is primarily because of their state of 'exile' that these issues arise presenting the mental framework as perceived by the author, and expected to be comprehended at some level by his audience.

5.5. Imitation of the Suffering Christ

Jesus is consistently portrayed as one who suffers in 1 Peter (1.10, 19; 3.18; 4.1) providing the example (ὑπογραμμὸν) for the believers to emulate.[43] The believers are to follow in the footsteps of Christ who though reviled did not commit sin and 'no guile was found on his lips' (2.21-23). In the same manner that their connection to Christ makes them the 'spiritual house' of God, believers also partake of Christ's suffering by their connection to Christ (4.13). Even in passages clearly addressed to the household slaves and wives, one perceives the intent of the author to address the entire community (3.9), such that even the behavior of the husband in relation to the wife is related to the *cultus* by making the answer to prayer conditional on one's behavior (3.7; 4.7).

If, as noted above, 1 Peter is thoroughly eschatological – and even apocalyptic[44] – such an outlook seeks to mitigate the suffering which the recipients (and even possibly the author) of the epistle are undergoing due to their faith. Built on the author's christological understanding, the epistle exemplifies a strong sense of the immediacy of the eschatological consummation (1.3-10; 2.12; 3.16; 4.4-5; 4.12-19). This way, describing the readers' present suffering as a purifying process preceding the 'revelation (ἀποκάλυψις) of Jesus Christ' (1 Pet. 1.7), reflects a radical appropriation of an understanding that had its foundation in the preaching and suffering of Jesus Christ (Mt. 12.28; Mk 1.15; Lk. 10.9) and was anticipated in the exilic prophets.

1 Peter's primary concern is the way the believers will conduct (ἀναστροφή) themselves (1 Pet. 1.15; 2.12, 3.1, 16) in light of the eschatological expectation (1 Pet. 4.12) since theirs has to be conduct that is geared toward those on the outside as a tool of evangelization (3.1) and as an antidote or a foil to any false accusations that may be levied (2.12).[45] Command to obedience is not just 1

---

42.   Kohler, 'Communauté ', 2; Chevallier, 'Diaspora', 395.

43.   Selwyn, *First Peter*, 296. A *hapax* in the NT, ὑπογραμμὸν appears only in 2 Macc. 2.28 with the sense of 'imprint' or 'visible evidence'.

44.   Robert Leslie Webb, 'The Apocalyptic Perspective of First Peter' (Th.M. thesis, Regent College, 1986). Cf also Kee, *Understanding*, 335; Dubis, *Woes*, 37–44.

45.   Cf. Mt. 5.16, 'let your light shine before others, so that they may see your good works and give glory to your Father in heaven'.

Peter's personal advice, it is the will of God for the believers (2.15; 4.2) and is for the Lord's sake (διὰ τὸν κύριον – 2.13). Therefore, 1 Peter's concern is with a fundamental change in behavior commensurate with the realization of the onset of the eschatological reality (1.13-14) which would soon usher in the swift return of the Lord (4.7-11).[46] That is why the *imitatio Christi* is the basis of their behavior, for that assures them not only that they are on the right track but that they are continuing the work that their Lord began when he was in the world (2.21-23).

As a sign of how seriously they have to take this conduct, 1 Peter appropriates the warning from Ezekiel (9.6) concerning the judgment that would accompany the Lord's return. This judgment, like that of Ezekiel, is to commence in God's own house (4.14-17). For this reason, the call to holiness (1.16) gains greater urgency for the readers of 1 Peter since it is not simply an injunction on how to live a life dedicated to God – it is that and more. Call to holiness, then, is to prepare for the inevitable and imminent eschatological judgment (3.14, 17).

5.6. Holiness, Temple and Christian Suffering

The concern with holiness and purity is a reflection of a minority community struggling to survive in the midst of a dominant group:[47] 'The priestly concerns about separation, purity, and "quarantine" of the "holy seed" reveal a community responding to serious perceptions of social pressure and subordination.'[48] This attitude is clearly present in 1 Peter as the audience is encouraged to maintain a life of holiness premised on a classic levitical passage that equates God with holiness (1.16 = Lev. 11.11). As a minority group, maintaining holiness means aligning themselves with God who is overall more powerful than the majority.[49] It is a counter assertion – in light of their marginalized position in the larger society – in order to stake a claim to greater honor by aligning themselves with the greater power, God, who will ultimately judge the world (1.17-18). So 1 Peter can encourage his readers that, in spite of the evidence to the contrary, in reality, true honor belongs to God who, in turn, has power and dominion over worldly rulers and authorities (2.16-17).

---

46.   Van Unnik, *Sparsa Collecta*, 91.

47.   קדשׁ with its etymology of separation, is inherent in the injunction from Lev. 11.44, 45 quoted in 1 Pet. 1.16.

48.   Smith-Christopher, 'Impact', 33.

49.   Smith-Christopher, 'Impact', 34: Éduoard Cothenet, 'Les orientations actuelles de l'exégèse de la première lettre de Pierre', in Charles Perrot *et al.*, eds., *Études sur la Première Lettre de Pierre: congrès de L'ACFEB, Paris 1979* (Paris: Les Edition, du Cerf, 1980) 21: 'The term *peirasmos* (1.6; 4.12) convenient for hazing, humiliation, and such negative labeling, in fact exposed the minority nature of the Christians.'

Lohmeyer, in putting some perspective to the centrality of holiness and temple in relation to suffering within Jewish thinking, states that:

> The Jewish cult necessitated ... the idea and the fact of eschatological fulfillment ... Holiness meant, in a historical sense and in faith, life pure and undisturbed: sin therefore meant for individual and nation, for city and country, hunger and need and suffering and death. The Temple in Jerusalem had to be the place which not only resolved the tangle of oppression and suffering mysteriously and yet immovably, but also overcame them with the cleansing power of the holy God.[50]

However, a major distinction exists between 1 Peter's re-appropriation of the temple imagery and the role of the Jerusalem temple as highlighted by Lohmeyer. Israel's sin and disobedience are the primary culprit in the suffering related to the destruction of the Jerusalem temple. In contrast the suffering experienced in 1 Peter is not as a result of sin necessarily, even though sin could be partly attributed (2.20; 3.17; 4.15), but because of their faith in Jesus Christ (2.19; 3.1, 13-17; 4.14). Suffering is also an imitation of the Lord who suffered (4.13) and an assurance that one would partake of the glory of Christ at his revelation.

Holiness also is linked to the fact that the believers now compose the 'new priesthood'. Maintenance of purity and holiness characterize the undergirding responsibility of the priests in the OT sanctuaries and, consequently, the new priesthood of 1 Peter has a responsibility to God not only to be obedient, but also to maintain purity.

For the OT priest, purity was not only a cultic requirement but a prerequisite to the abiding of God's presence in their midst (Num. 5.1-4; Josh. 24.14-28; cf. Exod. 25.8-9). Therefore, by drawing on this OT element of purity, 1 Peter not only assures the believers of God's continued presence in their midst, but also grounds their faith in obedience and hope.

By creating the concept of the community as the 'spiritual house', 1 Peter removes the age-old conundrum of the presence of God – immanence and transcendence of God. This he achieves via the appropriation of the trinitarian conception (1.3). The believers are a 'spiritual house' through Christ (2.5), are indwelt by the Spirit of God and of glory (4.14) and have put their trust in God the judge of all (1.17; 2.12). God's presence is guaranteed, for even death cannot separate the believer from the presence of God (4.5). The divine mystery is revealed in full in Christ and fulfills the functions of the temple as the place for revelation, the sacrifices of God, the presence of the Spirit of God and the eschatological expectation of the manifestation of the glory of God on earth.

---

50. Lohmeyer, *Temple*, 97–9.

APPENDIX

Literary Structure of 1 Peter: A Proposal

The literary structure of 1 Peter continues to be a focus of contention. The primary concern seems to be whether the letter is a composite or not.[1] Richard Perdelwitz was the first to suggest that the letter consisted of a baptismal homily to newly baptized Christians with primarily two layers: a main layer 1.3–4.11 which was anticipating suffering, to which had been joined second layer (a brief word of comfort) consisting of 1.1-2; 4.12–5.14 which had been sent to Christians in Asia Minor already undergoing persecution.[2] Subsequently, different possibilities in regards to the structure of the epistle have been suggested including a baptismal hymnic structure,[3] a sermonic structure or even a midrash on Ps. 34.[4] It is important to point out that it is sermonic elements of the letter that have prompted some to identify 1 Peter as a Paschal homily[5] or as a homiletic midrash.[6] Overwhelmingly, though, the integrity of 1 Peter as a genuine letter has been affirmed.[7]

1.   See the extensive discussion in Martin, *Metaphor*, 135–275. See also the discussion in Achtemeier, *1 Peter*, 59ff. He perceives the emerging consensus as the recognition that 'far from being a composite work, the letter must rather be seen as a literary unity'. Cf. Also Schutter, *Hermeneutic*, 19ff.

2.   Richard Perdelwitz, *Die Mysterienreligion und das problem des 1. Petrusbriefes* (Religionsversuche und vorabeiten 11/3; Giessen: Töpelmann, 1911). He argues that the reference to the ὀλίγον ἄρτι in 1 Pet. 1.6-7 anticipates a future persecution yet to start, while the πυρώσει πρὸς πειρασμὸν ὑμῖν of 4.12 identifies the persecution as unquestionably real. (Cf. Cross, *Liturgy*, 28–41.) However, this argument for many scholars has not been convincing. Both references assume a state of persecution that is best understood as current, even if the full force of it is yet anticipated.

3.   Boismard, 'Liturgies'.

4.   Bornemann, 'Taufrede?', 143-65, and Snodgrass, 'Affinities', 97–106.

5.   Cross, *Liturgy*. Cross, basing his arguments on Melito of Sardis' *On Pascha*, argues that the framework of the letter of 1 Peter is generally laid out in line with the liturgy of the Jewish Paschal ceremony. He finds connection between the word for suffering (πάσχω) used in 1 Peter with the 'Passover' (πάσχα) which allows 1 Peter to juxtapose these two in a play of words. The suffering then is to be understood as not actual but 'mystical' in unity with Christ. John H. Elliott, '"1 Peter, Its Situation and Strategy": A Discussion with David Balch', in Talbert, *Perspectives on 1 Peter*, 61-8, and *idem.*, 'Hellenization/Acculturation in 1 Peter', in Talbert, *Perspectives on 1 Peter*, 79–102, have since shown the social reality of the audience in 1 Peter to be a critical element to understanding the situation of the audience.

6.   Schutter, *Hermenuetic*, 85ff.

7.   See the thoroughly extensive and helpful analysis done by Martin, *Metaphor*, 41–79. Cf. also Elliott, *1 Peter*, 7–12.

Michaels identifies two markers that according to him divide the letter into three parts. These are the use of the vocative ἀγαπητοί ('Beloved') with asyndeton in 2.11 and 4.12, dividing the letter into three sections – 1.1–2.10; 2.11–4.11; and 4.12–5.14. Michaels identifies a concentric structure of the development of themes in the letter with each section, to some degree, anticipating the next.[8] The first section deals with the identity of the people which rests on their experience of salvation (1.5, 9-10; 2.3b) and rebirth (1.3, 22-23; 2.2-3). The second shifts from the identity of the people to their consequent responsibility in a hostile world. And the third section combines a plea for faithfulness in the midst of 'fiery ordeal' and admonition to mutual love, hospitality and ministry by the church community and the elders. While we maintain some differences with Michaels' analysis, we agree with him that the letter does exhibit a progressive development of themes.

The structure we have developed, in Diagram 1 below, is based on both conceptual and verbal correspondences that we perceive to highlight temple/sanctuary imagery in the epistle of 1 Peter as a thematic motif. It provides what we consider a more specific outline of the thought frame of 1 Peter even as he pursues the issues that concern him in the epistle. It is further proof of the cogency of a skillful writer whose presentation reflects a strong affinity to the temple and its imagery. It also maintains what has been lately perceived as the 'emerging consensus' that 1 Peter is a literary unity rather than a composite.[9]

If the concern for conduct and defection is the twin purpose of the writing of 1 Peter as has been suggested, then 1 Peter's reinterpretation of the temple is significant in communicating God's assured presence among the concerned believers.[10] Temple/sanctuary imagery provides not only a linguistic framework with which to address the author's concerns but also the mental picture with which to show not only the immanence of God, but also the association of the faithfulness of God in relation to the imminent eschatological consummation (1 Pet. 1.8; 4.14-17). The temple as the visible manifestation of the immanence of God in Israel evokes, in the minds of the readers, a specific understanding of God's presence in their midst, especially when applied by the author to their state of suffering and persecution.

According to our proposed outline, a parallel can be drawn between the OT tabernacle and temple in the history of Israel and 1 Peter. The first chapter of 1 Peter primarily reflects the tabernacle imagery in the language of blood sprinkling as sacrifice that it employs (Exod. 24; Num. 19). The second chapter then combines the two images of temple and tabernacle in the description of the believers as 'living stones' being built into a 'spiritual house', producing

8.   Michaels, *1 Peter*, xxxiv–xl.
9.   Achtemeier, *1 Peter*, 61.
10.   Martin, *Metaphor*, 274.

what we would call a mobile temple (2 Chron. 5; 1 Kgs 8). The third chapter, which extends into the fourth chapter, deals with the ethics of the temple especially as it relates to the place of prayer. The second half of the fourth chapter reflects the *Šekinah* presence in the same way that the cloud came down upon the tabernacle (Exod. 25) and the temple (1 Kgs 8; 2 Chron. 7.1) at their dedication, and the subsequent destruction of the temple (Ezek. 9). The last chapter reflects the restoration of the temple (Isa. 44.28).

Diagram 1

Chapter 1	Chapter 2	Chapter 3 –	Chapter 4:12 –	Chapter 5
Tabernacle imagery	Temple and tabernacle merge	4:11 Ethics and temple holiness	19 Šekinah presence and judgment in/of the temple	Temple restoration
–'Exodus/Exile' (1:1, 17-25) – Sacrifice and ῥαντισμὸν αἵματος Ἰησοῦ Χριστου (1:2b)	– People as the mobile temple (2:4-10) – Dispersion (2:12-25).	– ἀγνὴν ἀναδ τροφὴν – holy conduct (3:1) – προσευχάς (3:7; 4:7) – Noah's Ark as sign of warning for disobedience and of hope for salvation.	(4:14, 17) – ἧς δόξης καὶ τὸ τοῦ θεοῦ πνεῦμα – κρίμα ἀπὸ τοῦ οἴκου τοῦ θεοῦ	– καταρτίσει, στηρίξει, σθενώσει, θεμελιώσει (5:10)

BIBLIOGRAPHY

Abel, F. M., *Les Livres des Maccabées*. Paris: Editions du Cerf, 1948.

Abernathy, David, Exegetical Considerations in 1 Peter 2:7-9, *Notes on Translation* 15 (2001): 24–39.

Achtemeier, Paul J., *1 Peter: A Commentary on First Peter*. Hermeneia; Minneapolis: Fortress Press, 1996.

——, 'John H. Elliot, 1 Peter: An Appreciation', *Biblical Theological Bulletin* (2002): 150–4.

Ackroyd, Peter R., *Exile and Restoration: A Study of Hebrew Thought of the Sixth Century B.C.* Philadelphia: Westminster, 1968.

——, 'Isaiah 36-39: Structure and Function', in *Von Kanaan bis kerala. Festschrift J. P. M. Van der Ploeg*. AOAT 211; Neukirchen-Vluyn: Neukirchener Verlag, 1982.

Agnew, F. H., '1 Peter 1:2 – An Alternative Translation', *Catholic Biblical Quarterly* 45 (1983): 68–73.

Alexander, P., '3 (Hebrew Apocalypse of) Enoch: A New Translation and Introduction' in J. H. Charlesworth, ed., *The Old Testament Pseudepigrapha*. Garden City, NY: Doubleday, 1983.

Alon, Gedalia, 'The Bounds of Levitical Cleanness', in Gedalia Alon, ed., *Jews, Judaism and the Classical World*. Jerusalem: Magnes Press, 1977.

Altmann, A., ed., *Biblical Motifs, Origins and Transformation*. Study and Texts of the Philip L. Lown Institute of Advanced Judaic Studies 3; Cambridge, Mass.: Harvard University Press, 1966.

Avraham, G., ed., *Israel's Apostasy and Restoration: Essays in Honor of Ronald K. Harrison*. Grand Rapids: Baker, 1987.

Balch, David L., *Let Wives Be Submissive: The Domestic Code in 1 Peter*. SBLMS 26; Atlanta: Scholars Press, 1981.

Baltensweiler, H. and B. Reicke, eds. *Neues Testament und Geschichte: Historisches Geschehen und Deutung im Neuen Testament: Oscar Cullmann zum 70. Geburstag*. Tübingen: Mohr [Siebeck], 1972.

Bammel, Ernst and C. F. D. Moule, eds., *Jesus and the Politics of His Day*. Sheffield: Sheffield Academic Press, 1984.

Banks, Robert, ed., *Reconciliation and Hope: New Testament Essays on Atonement and Eschatology presented to L. Morris on his 60th Birthday*. Exeter: Paternoster Press, 1974.

Barker, Margaret, *The Gate of Heaven: The History of the Temple in Jerusalem*. London: SPCK, 1991.

Barstad, Hans M., *A Way in the Wilderness: The 'Second Exodus' in the Message of Second Isaiah*. JST 12; Manchester: Manchester University Press, 1989.

Bartchy, S. Scott, *Mallon Chresai: First Century Slavery and the Interpretation of 1 Corinthians 7:21*. SBLDS 11; Missoula, Mont.: Society of Biblical Literature, 1973.

———, 'Slavery (Greco-Roman)', *Anchor Bible Dictionary*. Garden City, NY: Doubleday, 1988.

Bauer, Walter, *Greek English Lexicon of the New Testament and Other Early Christian Literature*. 2nd edn, ET, ed. W. F. Arndt and F. W. Gingrich; rev. F. W. Gingich and F. W. Danker. Chicago: University of Chicago Press, 1979.

Baumgarten, J. M., *Studies in Qumran Law*. Leiden: Brill, 1977.

———, 'Sacrifice and Worship among the Jewish Sectarians of the Dead Sea (Qumran) Scrolls', *Harvard Theological Review* 45 (1953).

Beare, Francis Wright, *The First Epistle of Peter: The Greek Text with Introduction and Notes*. 3rd edn; Oxford: Blackwell, 1970.

Bell, Jr., Albert, *Exploring the NT World*. Nashville, Tenn.: Thomas Nelson, 1998.

Bellinger, Jr., William H. and William R. Farmer, eds., *Jesus and the Suffering Servant: Isaiah 53 and Christian Origins*. Harrisburg, Pa.: Trinity Press International, 1998.

Ben-Yashar, M., 'Noch zum Miqdaš'ĀDĀM in 4QFlorilegium', *Review de Qumran* 10 (1981): 586–7.

Bergsma, John Sietze, 'The Jubilee: A Post-Exilic Priestly Attempt to Reclaim Land?', *Biblica* 84/2 (2003): 225-46.

Best, E., *1 Peter*. NCB; London: Oliphants, 1971.

———, '1 Peter and the Gospel Tradition', *New Testament Studies* 16 (1970): 95–113.

———, 'I Peter II. 4-10: A Reconsideration', *Novum Testamentum* 11 (1969): 270–93.

Bevere, Allan, *Sharing in the Inheritance: Identity and the Moral Life in Colossians*. JSNTSup 226; Sheffield: Sheffield Academic Press, 2003.

Bigg, Charles, *Epistles of St. Peter and St. Jude*. ICC; New York: Charles Scribner's Sons, 1922.

Biran, Avram, ed., *Temples and High Places in Biblical Times: Proceedings of the Colloquium in Honor of the Centennial Hebrew Union College – Jewish Institute of Religion, Jerusalem, 14–16 March 1977*. Jerusalem: Nelson Glueck School of Biblical Archeology of Hebrew Union College – Jewish Institute of Religion, 1981.

Black, Matthew, *The Book of Enoch or 1 Enoch: A New English Edition*. Leiden: E. J. Brill, 1985.

Blinzler, Joseph, "IERATEYMA: Zur Exegese von 1 Petr 2.5 u 9', in *EPISKOPUS: Festschrift für Kardinal Michael von Faulhaber*. Regensburg: F. Pustet, 1949.

Blinzler, Joseph, O. Kuss and F. Mußner, eds., *Neutestamentliche Aufsätze: Festschrift für Professor Josef Schmid zum 70. Gerburstag.* Regensburg: Friedrich Pustet, 1963.

Boismard, M. -E., 'Liturgies Baptismale dans Pierre (1re Épître)', in *Supplement au Dictionnaire de la Bible,* Louis Pirot et André Robert, eds. Paris: Letouzey & Ane, 1966.

Bornemann, W., 'Der erste Petrusbrief – eine Taufrede des Silvanus?' *ZNW* 19 (1920): 143–65.

Brett, Mark G., ed., *Ethnicity and the Bible.* Leiden: Brill, 1996.

Brown, Colin, ed., *The New International Dictionary of New Testament Theology.* 3 vols. Grand Rapids: Zondervan, 1967–78.

Brown, Raymond, *Introduction to the New Testament.* New York: Doubleday, 1997.

Brown, Raymond, J. A. Fitzmyer and J. Murphy-O'Connor, eds., *The Jerome Biblical Commentary.* Englewood Cliffs, NJ: Prentice-Hall, 1968.

Brownlee, Harold W., 'The Jerusalem Habakkuk Scroll', *Bulletin of the American School of Oriental Research* 112 (1948): 6–18.

———, *The Midrash Pesher of Habakkuk.* Missoula, Mont.: Scholars Press, 1979.

Brox, Norbert, *Der erste Petrusbrief.* EKKNT; Zurich: Benziger, 1979.

Brueggemann, Walter, *Hopeful Imagination: Prophetic Voices in Exile.* Philadelphia: Fortress, 1986.

———, 'Preaching to Exiles', *Journal for Preachers* 16 (1993): 3–15.

Brunson, Andrew, *Psalm 118 in the Gospel of John.* WUNT 2 Reihe 158; Tübingen: Mohr Siebeck, 2003.

Bryan, Steven, *Jesus and Israel's Traditions of Judgement and Restoration.* Cambridge: Cambridge University Press, 2002.

Butler, J., 'Grace and Suffering: A Study in 1 Peter', *Notes on Translation* 10 (1996): 58–60.

Calvin, John, *Institutes of Christian Religion,* II.17. Edinburgh: n. p., 1874.

Caquot, André, Mireille Hadas-Lebel, and Jean Riaud, eds., *Hellenica et Judaica: Hommage à V. Nikiprowetzky.* Leuven–Paris: Peters, 1986.

Casey, Maurice, 'Where Wright is Wrong: A Critical review of N. T. Wright's Jesus and the Victory of God', *Journal for the Study of the New Testament* 69 (1998): 95–103.

Cerfaux, Lucien, 'Regale Sacerdotium', *Revue des sciences philosophique et theologique* 28 (1939): 5–39.

Charles, R. H., *The Ethiopic Version of the Book of Enoch Edited from Twenty-Three MSS Together with the Fragmentary Greek and Latin Versions.* Oxford: Oxford University Press, 1906.

———, *The Ethiopic Version of the Hebrew Bible of Jubilees.* Oxford: Oxford University Press, 1895.

Charlesworth, James H., ed., *The Old Testament Pseudepigrapha I: Apocalyptic Literature and Testaments.* 2 vols.; New York: Doubleday, 1985.

Chester, Andrew, and Ralph P. Martin, *New Testament Theology: The Theology of the Letters of James, Peter and Jude*. Cambridge: Cambridge University Press, 1994.

Chevallier, Max-Alain, Condition et vocation des chrétiens en diaspora: Remarques exégétiques sur la 1er Épître de Pierre, *RSR* 48 (1974): 387–98,

Chilton, Bruce, *The Isaiah Targum*. The Aramaic Bible, vol. 11; Wilmington, Del.: Michael Glazier, 1987.

Churgin, Pinkhos, 'The Period of the Second Temple: An Era of Exile', [Hebrew] *Horeb* 8 (1944): 1–66.

Clowney, Edward, *The Message of 1 Peter: The Way of the Cross*. The Bible Speaks Today; Downers Grove, Ill.: InterVarsity Press, 1988.

Cohen, A., *Psalms*. Soncino Books of the Bible; London: Soncino, 1945.

Cohen, Shaye J. D., *From Maccabees to the Mishnah*. Philadelphia: Westminster Press, 1987.

Cole, Alan, *The New Temple: A Study in the Origins of the Catechetical 'Form' of the Church in the New Testament*. London: Tyndale, 1950.

Collins, John Joseph, *Daniel: With an Introduction to Apocalyptic Literature*. FOTL 20: Grand Rapids: Eerdmans, 1984.

Collins, John J., 'Jerusalem and the Temple in Jewish Apocalyptic Literature of the Second Temple Period', *International Rennert Guest Lecture Series* 1 (1998).

———, *Between Athens and Jerusalem: Jewish Identity in the Hellenistic Diaspora*. 2nd edn; Grand Rapids: Eerdmans, 2000.

Coloe, Mary, *God Dwells with Us: Temple Symbolism in the Fourth Gospel*. Collegeville, Minn.: Liturgical Press, 2001.

Congar, Marie-Joseph, *The Mystery of the Temple*. Philadelphia: Fortress, 1968.

Coppens, Joseph, 'The Spiritual Temple in the Pauline Letters and its Background', *Studia Evangelica* 6 (1973): 53–66.

Cothenet, Édouard, 'Le réalisme de l'espérance chrétienne selon 1 Pierre', *New Testament Studies* 27 (1981): 564–72.

———, Les Orientations actuelles de L'Exégèse de la Première Lettre de Pierre, in Charles Perrot, ed., *Études sur la Première Lettre de Pierre: congrès de L'ACFEB, Paris 1979. Paris: Les Éditions du Cerf, 1980*.

Cross, Frank Leslie, *1 Peter: A Paschal Liturgy*. London: Mowbray, 1954.

———, 'The Council of Yahweh in Second Isaiah', *Journal of Near Eastern Studies* 12 (1953).

Cross, Frank Moore, *Canaanite Myth and Hebrew Epic*. Cambridge, Mass.: Harvard University Press, 1973.

———, *The Ancient Library of Qumran and Modern Biblical Studies*. Garden City, NY: Doubleday, 1958.

Cryer, Frederick H. and Thomas L. Thompson, eds., *Qumran between the Old and the New Testaments*. Sheffield: Sheffield Academic Press, 1998.

Cullmann, Oscar, *The Johannine Circle: Its Place in Judaism, Among the Disciples of Jesus and in Early Christianity*. London: SCM Press, 1975.

——, 'L'opposition contre le Temple de Jerusalem, motif commun de la theologie johannique et du monde ambiant', *New Testament Studies* 5 (1958-9): 157–73.

Dalton, William Joseph, 'So that your Faith may also be your hope in God (1 Peter 1:21)', in Robert Banks, ed., *Reconciliation and Hope: New Testament Essays on Atonement and Eschatology presented to L. Morris on his 60th Birthday*. Exeter: Paternoster Press, 1974, 262–74.

——, *Christ's Proclamation to the Spirits: A Study of 1 Peter 3.18–4.6*. AnBib 23; Rome: Pontifical Biblical Institute, 1965.

Danker, Frederick W., '1 Peter 1:24–2:17 – A Consolatory Pericope', *ZNW* 58 (1967): 93–102.

Davids, Peter H., *The Book of 1 Peter*. NICNT; Grand Rapids: Eerdmans, 1990.

Davies, Philip R., *In Search of Ancient Israel*. Sheffield: Sheffield Academic Press, 1992.

——, 'The Ideology of the Temple in the Damascus Document', *Journal of Jewish Studies* 33 (1982): 287–301.

Davies, W. D. and David Daube, *The Background of the New Testament and Its Eschatology*. Cambridge: Cambridge University Press, 1964.

Deissmann, Adolf, *Light from the Ancient East: The New Testament Illustrated by Recently Discovered Texts of the Graeco-Roman World*, trans. Lionel R. M. Strachan. New York: George H. Doran, 1927.

Derrett, J. Duncan M., 'The Stone that the Builders Rejected', *Studia Evangelica* 4 (1968): 180–6.

Deterding, Paul E., 'Exodus Motifs in First Peter', *Concordia Journal* 7 (1981): 58-65.

Dever, William G., 'Will the Real Israel Please Stand Up? Archeology and Israelite Historiography: Part 1', *Bulletin of the American School of Oriental Research* 297 (1995): 61-80.

Dillmann, August, *Das Buch Henoch: Übersetzt und erklärt*. Leipzig: F. C. W. Vogel, 1853; repr. New York: Unger, 1955.

Dimant, Devorah, 4QFlorilegium and the Idea of the Community as Temple, in A. Caquot, M. Hadas-Lebel and J. Riaud, eds., *Hellenica et Judaica: Hommage à Valentin Nikiprowetzky*. Leuven and Paris: Peeters, 1986, 165–89

Dodd, C. D., *According to Scripture: The Sub-structure of New Testament Theology*. London: Nisbet, 1952.

Dubis, Mark, *Messianic Woes in First Peter: Suffering and Eschatology in 1 Peter 4:12-19*. New York: Peter Lang, 2002.

Earl, Richard, *Reading 1 Peter, Jude and 2 Peter: A Literary and Theological Commentary*. Macon, Ga.: Smyth and Helwys, 2000.

Edersheim, Alfred, *The Temple: Its Ministry and Services as they were at the Time of Jesus Christ*. London: F. H. Revell, 1874.

Eichrodt, W., *The Theology of the Old Testament*. Philadelphia: Westminster Press, 1961.

Elliott, John H., *1 Peter: A New Translation with Commentary*. AB; Garden City, NY: Doubleday, 2001.

——, 'Book Review of Reinhard Feldmeier's *Die Christen als Fremde*', CBQ 56/4 (1994): 792–3.

——, 'Peter, First Epistle of', *Anchor Bible Dictionary*. New York: Doubleday, 1992, 5:269–78

——, *A Home for the Homeless: A Sociological Exegesis of 1 Peter, Its Situation and Strategy*. Philadelphia: Fortress, 1981.

——, *The Elect and the Holy: An Exegetical Examination of 1 Peter 2:4-10 and the Phrase* βασίλειον ἱεράτευμα. NovTSup; Leiden: Brill, 1966.

Evans, Craig A., 'Aspects of the Exile and Restoration in the Proclamation of Jesus and the Gospels', in James M. Scott, ed., *Exile: Old Testament, Jewish and Christian Conceptions*. Leiden: Brill, 1997, 305–12.

Evans, Craig A. and Shemaryahu Talmon, eds., *The Quest For Context and Meaning: Studies in Biblical Intertextuality in Honor of James A. Sanders*. Leiden: Brill, 1997.

Fatehi, Mehdad, *The Spirit's Relation to the Risen Lord in Paul: An Examination of Its Christological Implications*. WUNT 2 Reihe 128; Tubingen: Mohr Siebeck, 2000.

Feldmeier, Reinhard, *Der Erste Brief des Petrus*. THNT 15/1; Leipzig: Evangelische Verlagsanstalt, 2005.

——, *Die Christen als Fremde: Die Metapher der Fremde in der antiken Welt, in Urchristentum und im 1. Petrusbrief*. WUNT 64; Tübingen: J. C.B. Mohr Siebeck, 1992.

Fishbane, Michael, *Biblical Interpretation in Ancient Israel*. Oxford: Clarendon, 1985.

——, *Text and Texture: Close Readings of Selected Biblical Texts*. New York: Schocken Books, 1979.

Fitzmyer, J. A., 'The Dead Sea Scrolls and the New Testament after Thirty Years', *Theology Digest* 29 (1981): 357–8.

Flusser, David, 'Two Notes on the Midrash on 2 Sam vii', *Israel Exploration Journal* (1959): 99–109.

——, The Dead Sea Sect and Pre-Pauline Christianity, in C. Rabin and Y. Yadin, eds., *Aspects of the Dead Sea Scrolls*. Scripta Hierosolymintana 4; Jerusalem: Magnes, 1958, 215–66.

Forster, Raymond S., *The Restoration of Israel: A Study of Exile and Return*. London: Darton, Longman and Todd, 1970.

Fransen, Irénée, 'Une homélie chrétienne: La première Epître de Pierre', *Bible et vie chrétienne* 31 (1960): 28–38.

Freedman, D. N., *The Unity of the Hebrew Bible*. Ann Arbor: University of Michigan Press, 1991.

Freedman, Louis H., and John R. Levison, eds., *Josephus' Contra Apionem*. Leiden: Brill, 1996.

Furnish, Victor, 'Elect Sojourners in Christ: An Approach to the Theology of First Peter', *Perkins Journal* 28 (1975): 1–11.

García Martínez, Florentino, 'The Temple Scrolls', *Near Eastern Archeology* 63/3 (2000): 172–4.

García Martínez, Florentino, and Eibert J. C. Tigchelaar, *The Dead Sea Scrolls: Study Edition*. 2 vols.; Grand Rapids: Eerdmans; and Leiden: Brill, 1997.

Garnet, Paul, *Salvation and Atonement in the Qumran Scrolls*. WUNT 3; Tubingen: Mohr-Siebeck, 1977.

Gärtner, Bertil, *The Temple and the Community in Qumran and the New Testament: A Comparative Study in the Qumran Texts and the New Testament*. Cambridge: Cambridge University Press, 1965.

Gaston, Lloyd, *No Stone On Another: Studies in the Significance of the Fall of Jerusalem in the Synoptic Gospels*. Leiden: E. J. Brill, 1970.

Gavin, F., *The Jewish Antecedents of the Christian Sacraments*. London: SPCK, 1928.

Goldberg, A. M., *Untersuchungen über die Vorstellung von der Schekhinah in der frühen rabbinischen Literatur*. SJ 6; Berlin: de Gruyter, 1969.

Goldingay, John. E., *Daniel*. WBC 30; Dallas, Tx.: Word Books, 1989.

Goldstein, Horst, *Paulinische Gemeinde im ersten Petrusbrief*. SBS 80; Stuttgart: Katholisches Bibelwerk, 1975.

Goldstein, J. A., *I Maccabees: A New Commentary with Introduction and Commentary*. AB; Garden City, NY: Doubleday, 1976.

———, *II Maccabees: A Translation With Introduction and Commentary*. AB; Garden City, NY: Doubleday, 1983.

Goppelt, Leonhard, *A Commentary on 1 Peter*. Grand Rapids: Eerdmans, 1993.

———, *Typos: The Typological Interpretation of the Old Testament in the New*. Grand Rapids: W. B. Eerdmans, 1982.

Gordon, R. P., 'The Targumists as Eschatologists', in *Congress Volume: Göttingen, 1977*. VTSup 29; Leiden: E. J. Brill, 1978.

Gottwald, Norman. K., *Studies in the Book of Lamentations*. London: SCM Press, 1954.

———, *The Tribes of Yahweh*. New York: Maryknoll, 1979.

Gowan, Donald E., 'The Exile in Jewish Apocalyptic', in *Scripture in History and Theology: Essays in Honour of J. Coert Rylaarsdam*, ed. Arthur L. Merrill and Thomas W. Overholt. Pittsburgh, Pa.: Pickwick, 1977, 205–22.

Green, W. S., ed., *Approaches to Ancient Judaism*, II. Chico, Calif.: Scholars Press, 1980.

Gruen, Eric S., *Diaspora: Jews amidst Greeks and Romans*. Cambridge, Mass.: Harvard University Press, 2002.

Gundry, Robert H., '*Verba Christi* in 1 Peter: Their Implications Concerning the Authorship of 1 Peter and the Authenticity of the Gospel Tradition', *NTS* 13 (1967): 336–50.

———, 'Further *Verba* on *Verba Christi* in First Peter', *Biblica* 55 (1974): 211–32.

Gutmann, Joseph, 'The Strange History of the Kapporet Ritual', *Zeitschrift für die alttestamentliche Wissenschaft* 112 (2000): 624–6.

Hamerton-Kelly, Robert G., 'The Temple and the Origins of Jewish Apocalyptic', *Vetus Testamentum* 20 (1970): 1–15.

Hanson, Stig, *Unity of the Church in the New Testament: Colossians and Ephesians*. ASNU 14; Uppsala: Almquist & Wiksells, 1946.

Haran, Menahem, 'Temple and Community in Ancient Israel', in Michael V. Fox, ed., *Temple in Society*. Winona Lake: Eisenbrauns, 1988, 17–25.

Harris, J. Rendall, *Testimonies*. Cambridge: Cambridge University Press, 1916.

Hawthawne, G. and Otto Betz, eds., *Tradition and Interpretation in the New Testament*. Grand Rapids: Eerdmans; and Tübingen: Mohr, 1987.

Hayes, John H. and J. Maxwell Miller, eds., *Israelite and Judean History*. Philadelphia: Westminster Press, 1977.

Hays, Richard, *Echoes of Scripture in the Letters of Paul*. New Haven: Yale University Press, 1989.

Hegemann, Harald, 'The Diaspora in the Hellenistic Age', in W. D. Davies and Louis Finkelstein, eds., *The Cambridge History of Judaism*. 3 vols.; Cambridge: Cambridge University Press, 1999.

Hertzberg, Hans-Wilhelm, *Gottes Wort und Gottes Land*. Göttingen: Vandenhoeck & Ruprecht, 1965.

Higgins, A. J. B., *New Testament Essays for T. W. Manson, 1893-1958. Sponsored by Pupils, Colleagues and Friends*. Manchester: Manchester University Press, 1959.

Hill, David., '"To Offer Spiritual Sacrifices …" (1 Peter 2:5): Liturgical Formulations and Christian Paraenesis in 1 Peter', *JSNT* 16 (1982): 45–63.

———, 'On Suffering and Baptism in 1 Peter', *Novum Testamentum* 18 (1976): 181–9.

———, *Greek Words and Hebrew Meaning*. SNTSMS 5; Cambridge: Cambridge University Press, 1967.

Hillyer, Norman, 'Rock-Stone Imagery in 1 Peter', *Tyndale Bulletin* 22 (1971): 68–73.

Holloway, Steven W. and Lowell K. Handy, eds., *The Pitcher is Broken: Memorial Essay for Gösta W. Ahlström*. JSOT 190; Sheffield: Sheffield Academic Press, 1995.

Holzmeister, U., *Commentarius in epistulas SS. Petri et Judea, I Epistula Prima S. Petri*. Cursus Scripturae Sacrae III 13; Paris: Lethielleux, 1937.

Horbury, William, ed., *Templum Amicitiae: Essays on the Second Temple Presented to Ernst Bammel*. Sheffield: Sheffield University Press, 1991.

Horbury, William, W. D. Davies, and John Sturdy, eds., *The Cambridge History of Judaism*. 3 vols.; Cambridge: Cambridge University Press, 1999.

Hort, F. J. A., *The First Epistle of St. Peter I.1–II.17*. London: Macmillan, 1898.

Iwry, Samuel, 'Was there a Migration to Damascus? The Problem of ישראל שבי', *Eretz-Israel* 9 (1969): 86–8.

Janssen, Enno, *Juda in Exilzeit: ein Beitrag zur Frage der Entstehung des Judentums*. FRLANT 69; Gottingen: Vandenhoeck & Ruprecht, 1956.

Jaubert, A., 'La notion d'Alliance dans les judaïsme aux abords de l'ère chrétienne', in *Patristica Sorbonensia*. Paris: Éditions du Seuil, 1963.

Jenson, Philip Peter, *Graded Holiness: A Key to the Priestly Conception of the World*. JSOTSup 106; Sheffield: Sheffield Academic Press, 1992.

Jobes, Karen H., *1 Peter*. BECNT; Grand Rapids: Baker Books, 2005.

Jobes, Karen H., and Moisés Silva, *Invitation to the Septuagint*. Grand Rapids and Carlisle: Eerdmans and Paternoster, 2000.

Johnson, Dennis E., 'Fire on God's House: Imagery from Malachi 3 in Peter's Theology of Suffering (1 Pet. 4:12-19)', *Journal for the Evangelical Theological Society* 29 (1986): 285–94.

Johnson, Luke Timothy, and Todd Penner, *The Writings of the New Testament*. Minneapolis: Augsburg Fortress, 1999.

Jonsen, Albert R., 'The Moral Theology of the First Epistle of St. Peter', *Sciences Ecclésistiques* 16 (1964): 93–106.

Juel, Donald, *Messianic Exegesis: Christological Interpretation of the Old Testament in Early Christianity*. Philadelphia: Fortress, 1988.

——, *Messiah and Temple: The Trial of Jesus in the Gospel of Mark*. Missoula, Mont.: Scholars Press, 1977.

Kaplan, Abraham, 'Identity and Alienation: Zionism For the West', in Étan Levine, ed., *Diaspora: Exile and the Contemporary Jewish Condition*. New York: Steimatzky, 1986, 327–52.

Käsemann, Ernst, *The Wandering People of God: An Investigation of the Letter to the Hebrews*, trans. Ray A. Harrisville and Irving L. Sandberg. Minneapolis: Augsburg, 1984.

Kee, Howard Clark, *Understanding the New Testament*. 5th edn; Englewood Cliffs: Prentice-Hall, 1983.

——, 'The Testaments of the Twelve: A New Translation and introduction' in *The Old Testament Pseudepigrapha I: Apocalyptic Literature and*

Testaments, ed. James H. Charlesworth. 2 vols.; New York: Doubleday, 1985.

Keener, Craig. *A Commentary on the Gospel of Matthew*. Grand Rapids: Eerdmans, 1999.

Kelly, J. N. D., *The Epistles of Peter and Jude*. BNTC; London: Adam & Charles Black, 1969.

Kittel, Gerhard and G. Friedrich, eds., *Theological Dictionary of the New Testament*, trans. Geoffrey W. Bromiley. 10 vols.; Grand Rapids: Eerdmans, 1964–76.

Klein, Michael, 'The Translation of Anthropomorphisms in the Targumim', in *Congress Volume, Vienna 1980* VTSup 32; Leiden: E. J. Brill, 1981, 162–77.

Klein, Ralph W., *Israel in Exile: A Theological Interpretation*. Philadelphia: Fortress, 1979.

Klinzing, Georg, *Die Umdeutung die Kultus in des Qumrangemeinde und im Neuen Testament*. SUNT 7; Göttingen: Vandenhoeck & Ruprecht, 1971.

Knibb, Michael A., 'The Exile in the Literature of the Intertestamental Period', *Heythrop Journal* 17/3 (1976): 253–72.

——, *The Qumran Community*. Cambridge: Cambridge University Press, 1987.

Knight, Douglas A., 'Foreword' to the Scholars Press edition of *Prolegomena to the History of Israel* by Julius Wellhausen. Atlanta, Ga.: Scholars Press, 1994.

Koester, Craig, *The Dwelling of God: The Tabernacle in the Old Testament, Intertestamental Jewish Literature and the New Testament*. CBQMS 22; Washington, D.C.: Catholic Biblical Association of America, 1989.

Kohl, Israel, *The Messiah before Jesus: The Suffering Servant of the Dead Sea Scrolls*. Berkeley: University of California Press, 2000.

Kohler, M.-E., 'La Communauté chrétienne selon la première Épître de Pierre', *Revue de théologie et Philosophie* 114 (1982): 1–21.

Kuhn, Heinz-Wolfgang, *Enderwertung und gegenwartiges Heil*. SUNT 4; Gottingen: Vandenhoeck & Ruprecht, 1966.

Kummel, W. G., *Introduction to the New Testament*. Nashville: Abingdon, 1975.

Kuschke, A., *Verbannung und Heimkehr*. Tübingen: J. C. B. Mohr, 1961.

Lacocque, André, 'The Liturgical Prayer in Daniel 9', *Hebrew Union College Annual* 47 (1976): 119–42.

Lanci, John R., *A New Temple for Corinth: Rhetorical and Archeological Approaches to Pauline Imagery*. SBL 1; New York: Peter Lang, 1997.

Lane, William L., *Hebrews 1–8*. WBC 47A; Dallas Tx.: Word Books, 1991.

——, *Hebrews 9–13*. WBC 47B; Dallas Tx.: Word Books, 1991.

Lapham, F., *Peter: The Myth, the Man and the Writings*. Sheffield: Sheffield Academic Press, 2003.

LaVerdiere, Eugene A., 'Covenant Theology in 1 Peter 1:1–2:10', *The Bible Translator* 42 (1969): 2907–16.

Lea, Thomas, 'How Peter Learned the Old Testament', *Southwestern Journal of Theology* 22 (1980): 96–102.

Lee, Pilchan, *The New Jerusalem in the Book of Revelation: A Study of Revelation in Light of its Background in Jewish Tradition.* WUNT 2 Reihe 129; Tübingen: Mohr Siebeck, 2001.

Lestringant, Pierre, *Essai sur l'unité de la révélation biblique.* Paris: Editions 'Je sers', 1942.

Levenson, Jon D., 'The Temple and the World', *Journal of Religion* 64 (1984): 275–98.

Levine, Étan, ed., *Diaspora: Exile and the Contemporary Jewish Condition.* New York: Steimatzky, 1986.

Levine, Lee I., ed., *The Synagogue in Later Antiquity.* Philadelphia: American Schools of Oriental Research, 1987.

Levinskaya, Irina, *The Book of Acts in its Diaspora Setting.* Book of Acts in its First Century Setting 5; Grand Rapids: Eerdmans; and Carlisle: Paternoster, 1996.

Levison, John R., 'Did the Spirit Withdraw from Israel', *New Testament Studies* 43 (1997): 35–57.

———, 'The Debut of the Divine Spirit in Josephus's *Antiquities*', *Harvard Theological Review* 87 (1994).

Lichtenberger, Hermann, 'Atonement and Sacrifice in the Qumran Community', in W. S. Green, ed., *Approaches to Ancient Judaism*, II. Chico, Calif.: Scholars Press, 1980, 159–71.

Lincoln, A. T., *Paradise Now and Not Yet: Studies in the Role of the Heavenly Dimension in Paul's Thought With Special Reference to his Eschatology.* SNTSMS 43; Cambridge: Cambridge University Press, 1981.

Lindars, Barnabas, *New Testament Apologetic.* London: SCM Press, 1961.

Lodahl, Michael E., *Shekinah Spirit: Divine Presence in Jewish and Christian Religion.* New York: Paulist Press, 1992.

Lohfink, Norbert, 'Die Priesterschrift und die Geschichte', in *Congress Volume: Göttingen, 1977.* VTSup 29; Leiden: E. J. Brill, 1978.

Lohmeyer, Ernst, *Lord of the Temple: A Study of the Relation between Cult and the Gospel*, trans. Stewart Todd. Richmond: John Knox Press, 1962.

Lohse, E., 'Paränese und Kerygma im 1. Petrusbrief', *Zeitschrift für die neuetestamentliche Wissenschaft* 45 (1954): 68–89.

Longenecker, Richard, *The Christology of Early Jewish Christianity.* London: SCM Press, 1970.

Longman III, Tremper, and Daniel G. Reid, *God is a Warrior.* Studies in Old Testament Biblical Theology; Grand Rapids: Zondervan, 1995.

Luther, Martin, *Werke in Auswahl*, vol. IV. Berlin: W. de Gruyter, 1935.

Lyle, Emily, ed., *Sacred Architecture in the Traditions of India, China, Judaism, and Islam*. Edinburgh: Edinburgh University Press, 1985.

Maier, Johann, *The Temple Scroll: An Introduction, Translation and Commentary*. JSOTSup 34; Sheffield: JSOT Press, 1985.

Manns, Frederic, "'La maison où réside l'Esprit".1 P 2,5 et son arrière-plan juif', *Studii biblici franciscani liber annus* 34 (1984): 207–24.

Marcus, Joel, *The Way of the Lord: Christological Exegesis of the Old Testament in the Gospel of Mark*. Louisville, Ky..: Westminster John Knox Press, 1992.

Margot, Jean-Claude, *Les Epîtres de Pierre*. Geneva: Labor et Fides, 1960.

Marshall, I. Howard, *1 Peter*. Downers Grove, Ill. and Leicester: InterVarsity Press, 1991.

Martin, Dale, *Slavery as Salvation: The Metaphor of Slavery in Pauline Christianity*. New Haven and London: Yale University Press, 1990.

Martin, Troy W., *Metaphor and Composition in 1 Peter*. SBLDS 131; Atlanta, Ga.: Scholars Press, 1992.

McCartney, Dan G., 'λογικός in 1 Peter 2,2', *Zeitschrift für die neutestamentliche Wissenschaft* 82 (1991): 128–32.

——, 'The Use of the Old Testament in the First Epistle of Peter'. Ph.D. diss., Westminster Theological Seminary, 1989.

McKelvey, Robert J., *The New Temple: The Church in the New Testament*. London: Oxford University Press, 1969.

——, 'Christ the Cornerstone', *New Testament Studies* (1962): 352–9.

McKnight, Scot, *1 Peter*. NIV Application Commentary; Grand Rapids: Zondervan, 1996.

——, *A New Vision for Israel: The Teaching of Jesus in National Context*. Grand Rapids: Eerdmans, 1999.

McNamara, Martin, *Targum Neofiti 1: Genesis*. The Aramaic Bible, 1A; Collegeville, Minn.: Liturgical Press, 1992.

——, *Targum and Testament. Aramaic Paraphrases of the Hebrew Bible: A Light on the New Testament*. Grand Rapids: Eerdmans, 1972.

Melito of Sardis, *On Pascha*, ed. and trans. Stuart George Hall. Oxford Early Christian Texts; Oxford: Clarendon Press, 1979).

Merrill, Arthur L. and Thomas W. Overholt, eds., *Scripture in History and Theology: Essays in Honour of J. Coert Rylaarsdam*. Pittsburgh, Pa.: Pickwick, 1977.

Metzger, Bruce., *A Textual Commentary on the Greek New Testament*. Stuttgart: Deutsche Bibelgesellschaft, 1994.

Meyers, Carol L., and Eric M. Meyers. *Haggai, Zechariah 1–8*. AB, 25B; Garden City, NY: Doubleday, 1987.

——, *Zechariah 9-14*. AB 25C; Garden City, NY: Doubleday, 1993.

Michaels, J. Ramsey, 'Eschatology in 1 Peter 3:17', *New Testament Studies* 13 (1967), 394–401.

——, *1 Peter*. WBC 49; Waco, Tx.: Word Publishers 1988.

——, 'Review of Troy Martins, *Metaphor and Composition in 1 Peter*', *Journal of Biblical Literature* 112 (1993).

Migne, J.-P., *Patrologia Graeca*. Paris: Migne, 1857–66, vol. 85.

Milik, J. T., *The Books of Enoch, Aramaic Fragments of Qumran Cave 4*. Oxford: Oxford University Press, 1976.

Miller, Donald, *Upon This Rock: A Commentary on 1 Peter*. Princeton Theological Monograph Series 34; Allison Park, Pa: Pickwick Publications, 1993.

Moule, C. F. D., 'Sanctuary and Sacrifice in the Church of the New Testament', *Journal of Theological Studies* 1 (1950).

——, 'Some Reflections of the Stone Testimonia in Relation to the Name of Peter', *New Testament Studies* 2 (1955/6): 56–9.

Muller, P.-G. and W. Stegner, eds., *Kontinuität und Einheit: Fur Franz Mussner*. Freiburg: Herder, 1981.

Murphy-O'Connor, Jerome, 'The Essenes and Their History', *Revue biblique* 81 (1974): 215–44.

Nauck, W., 'Freude in Leiden, Zum Problem einer urchristlichen Verfolgungstradition', *Zeitschrift für die alttestamentliche Wissenschaft* 46 (1955): 68–80.

Neusner, Jacob, *Understanding Seeking Faith: Essays on the Case of Judaism*, vol. I. Atlanta, Ga.: Scholars Press, 1986.

——, 'History and Structure: The Case of Mishnah', *Journal of the American Academy of Religion* 45 (1977): 161–92.

——, *The Idea of Purity in Ancient Judaism*. Leiden: Brill, 1973.

Neusner, Jacob, Ernest S. Frerichs, Peder Borgen, and Richard Horsley, *The Social World of Formative Christianity and Judaism*. Philadelphia: Fortress Press, 1988.

Neusner, Jacob, William S. Green, and Ernest Frerichs, eds., *Judaisms and Their Messiahs at the Turn of the Christian Era*. Cambridge: Cambridge University Press, 1987.

Neve, Lloyd, *The Spirit of God in the Old Testament*. Tokyo: Seibunsha, 1972.

Newman, C. C., ed., *Jesus and the Restoration of Israel: A Critical Assessment of N. T. Wright's* Jesus and the Victory of God. Downer's Grove: Inter-Varsity Press, 1999.

Newsom, Carol, 'Merkabah Exegesis in the Qumran Sabbath Shirot', *Journal of Jewish Studies* 38 (1987): 11–30.

——, *Songs of the Sabbath Sacrifice*. Harvard Semitic Studies 27; Atlanta: Scholars Press, 1985.

Newton, Michael, *The Concept of Purity at Qumran and in the Letters of Paul*. Cambridge: Cambridge University Press, 1985.

Nickelsburg, George W. E., *Ancient Judaism and Christian Origins: Diversity, Continuity, and Transformation*. Minneapolis: Fortress Press, 2003.

——, *1 Enoch 1*. Minneapolis: Fortress Press, 2001.

——, *Jewish Literature between the Bible and the Mishnah: A Historical and Literary Introduction*. London: SCM Press, 1981.

Nötscher, F., 'Heiligkeit in den Qumranschriften', *Review de Qumran* 6 (1960): 161–81.

Oded, Bustenay, 'Judah and the Exile', in *Israelite and Judean History*, ed. John H. Hayes and J. Maxwell Miller. Philadelphia: Westminster Press, 1977.

Olson, Vernon Solomon, 'The Atonement in 1 Peter'. Th.D. diss., Union Theological Seminary, 1979.

Osborne, T. P., 'L'utilisation des citations de l'Ancien testament dans la première épître de Pierre', *Theologie de Louvain* 12 (1981): 64–77.

———, 'Guidelines for Christian Suffering in 1 Peter: A Source-Critical and Theological Study of 1 Peter 2:21-25', *Biblica* 64 (1983): 381–408.

Otto, Michel, *Studies of the Jewish Background of the New Testament*. Assen: Van Gorcum, 1969.

Parfitt, Tudor, *The Lost Tribes of Israel: The History of a Myth*. London: Weidenfeld & Nicolson, 2002.

Parker, David C., 'The Eschatology of 1 Peter', *Biblical Theological Bulletin* 24/1 (1994): 27–32.

Perdelwitz, Richard, *Die Mysterienreligion und das Problem des 1. Petrusbriefes*. Religionsversuche und Vorarbeiten 11/3; Giessen: Töpelmann, 1911.

Perrot, Charles, *et al.*, eds., *Études sur la Premiere Lettre de Pierre: congrès de L'ACFEB, Paris 1979*. Lectio Divina 102; Paris: Les Editions du Cerf, 1980.

Peterson, David, 'Zechariah's Vision: A theological Perspective', *Vetum Testamentum* 34 (1984): 195–206.

Pirot, Louis and André Robert, eds., *Supplement au Dictionnaire de la Bible*. Paris: Letouzey & Ane, 1966.

Plöger, Otto, *Theocracy and Eschatology*, trans. S. Rudman; Richmond, Va.: John Knox, 1968.

Prigent, Pierre, *Les Testimonia dans le Christianisme primitif. L' Épître de Barnabe I – XVI et ses sources*. Paris: Études Bibliques, 1961.

Rabin, C. and Y. Yadin, eds., *Aspects of the Dead Sea Scrolls*. Scripta Hierosolymintana 4; Jerusalem: Magnes, 1958.

Redditt, Paul L., *Haggai, Zechariah, Malachi*. NCBC; London: Marshall Pickering, and Grand Rapids: William B. Eerdmans, 1995.

Redditt, Paul L. and Aaron Schart, eds., *Thematic Threads in the Book of the Twelve*. BZAW 325; Berlin and New York: Walter de Gruyter, 2003.

Reiser, Marius, 'Die Eschatologie des 1 Petrusbriefs'. in *Weltgericht und Weltvollendung: Zukunftsbilder im Neuen Testament*, ed. Hans-Josef Klauck. Quaestiones Disputatae 150; Freiburg: Herder, 1994, 164–81.

Rendtorff, Heinrich, *Getrostes Wandern: Eine Einführung in den ersten Brief des Petrus*. Die Uhrchristliche Botschaft 20; Hamburg: Furche, 1951.

Rendtorff, Rolf, *Ersten, was man sät: Festschrift Klaus Koch*. Neukirchen-Vluyn: Neuchirchener Verlag, 1991.

———, 'Zur Komposition des Buches Jesajas', *VT* 34 (1984) 295–320.

Ritschl, Albrecht, *Die christliche Lehre der Rechtfertigung und Versöhnung*. Bonn: Adolf Marcus, 1899.

Rogers, Jr., Cleon L. and Cleon L. Rogers III, eds., *The New Linguistic Exegetical Key to the Greek New Testament*. Grand Rapids: Eerdmans, 1998.

Runia, D. T., 'How to Read Philo', *Nederlands Theologisch Tijdschrift* 40/3 (1986): 185–98.

Russell, Ronald, 'Eschatology and Ethics in 1 Peter', *Evangelical Quarterly* (1975): 78–84.

Safrai, Shmuel and M. Stern, *The Jewish People in the First Century*. 2 vols.; Philadelphia: Fortress, 1974.

Sanders, E. P., *Judaism: Practice and Belief, 63 BCE– 66 CE*. London: SCM Press; and Philadelphia: Trinity Press International, 1994.

———, *Jesus and Judaism*. Philadelphia: Fortress, 1985.

Schäfer, Peter, *Die Vorstellung vom heiligen Geist in der rabbinischen Literatur*. SANT 28; Munich: Kösel, 1972.

Scharlemann, Martin, 'Why the Kuriou in 1 Pet. 1 25?', *Concordia Theological Monthly* 3/5 (1959): 354.

Schiffman, Lawrence. H., ed., *Archeology and History in the Dead Sea Scrolls*. Sheffield: JSOT Press, 1990.

———, *Sectarian Law in the Dead Sea Scrolls: Courts, Testimony, and the Penal Code*. BJS 33; Chicago: Scholars Press, 1983.

Schulz, S., *Neutestamentliche Ethik*. Zurich: Theologischer Verlag, 1987.

Schüssler Fiorenza, Elisabeth, *In Memory of Her: A Feminist Theological Reconstruction of Christian Origins*. New York: Crossroad, 1994.

———, 'Cultic Language in Qumran and in the New Testament', *Catholic Biblical Quarterly* 38 (1976): 159–77.

Schutter, William L., *Hermeneutic and Composition in 1 Peter*. Tubingen: J. C. B. Mohr, 1989.

Schwartz, Daniel R., *Studies in the Jewish Background of Christianity*. Tübingen: J. C. B Mohr, 1992.

———, Introduction: On the Jewish Background of Christianity, in *Studies in the Jewish Background of Christianity*. Tübingen: Mohr, 1992, 5.

———, 'The Three Temples of 4QFlorilegium', *Revue de Qumran* 10 (1979): 83–91.

Scott, James M., ed., *Exile: Old Testament, Jewish and Christian Conceptions*. Leiden: Brill, 1997.

Seitz, Christopher R., 'The Divine Council: Temporal Transition and New Prophecy in the Book of Isaiah', *Journal of Biblical Literature* 109/2 (1990): 229–47.

Seland, Torrey, *Strangers in the Light: Philonic Perspectives on Christian Identity in 1 Peter*. Biblical Interpretation Series 76; Leiden: Brill, 2005.

——, 'The "Common Priesthood" of Philo and 1 Peter: A Philonic Reading of 1 Peter 2:5, 9', *Journal for the Study of the New Testament* 57 (1995): 87–119.

Selwyn, E. G., *The First Epistle of St. Peter*. London: Macmillan, 1946; repr., Grand Rapids: Baker Books, 1987.

Senior, Donald, 'The Conduct of Christians in the World (2:11-3:12)', *Review Expositor* 79 (1982): 427–33.

Sevenster, Gerhard, 'Het-Koning- en Priestershap de Gelovigen in Het Nieuwe Testament', *Neue theologische tijdschrift* 13 (1958): 301–17.

Shimada, Kazuhito, 'Is 1 Peter Dependent on Ephesians? A Critique of C. L. Milton', *Annual of the Japanese Biblical Institute* 17 (1991): 77–106.

——, 'The Christological Creedal Formula in 1 Peter 3:18-22 Reconsidered', *Annual of the Japanese Biblical Institute* 5 (1979): 154–76.

Smith, Daniel L., *The Religion of the Landless: The Social Context of the Babylonian Exile*. Bloomington, Ind.: Meyer Stone, 1989.

Smith-Christopher, Daniel L., *A Biblical Theology of Exile*. Minneapolis: Fortress Press, 2002.

——, 'Reassessing the Historical and Sociological Impact of the Babylonian Exile (597/587–539 BCE)', in James M. Scott, ed., *Exile: Old Testament, Jewish and Christian Conceptions*. Leiden: Brill, 1997, 7–36.

——, ed., *Text and Experience: Toward a Cultural Exegesis of the Bible*. Sheffield: Sheffield Academic Press, 1995.

Snodgrass, Klyne, '1 Peter II.1-10: Its Formation and Literary Affinities', *New Testament Studies* 24 (1977): 97–106.

——, 'Streams of Tradition Emerging from Isaiah 40:1-5 and their Adaptation in the New Testament', *Journal for the Study of the New Testament* 8 (1980): 24–45.

Soards, Marion, '1 Peter, 2 Peter, and Jude as Evidence of a Petrine School'. *ANRW* 2:25: Part 5, Principat 2:25. Berlin: Walter de Gruyter, 1988.

Sokolowski, F., 'The Real Meaning of Sacral Manumission', *Harvard Theological Review* 47 (1954): 173–81.

Spicq, Ceslas, 'La Iᵃ Petri et le témoignage évangélique de saint Pierre', *Studia Theologica* 20 (1966) 37–61.

——, *Les Épîtres de Saint Pierre*. Paris: J. Gabalda & Cie, 1966.

Steck, O. H., *Das apokryphe Baruchbuch: Studien zu Rezeption und Konzeption 'kananischer' Überlieferung*. Göttingen: Vandenhoeck & Ruprecht, 1993.

Stegemann, Ekkehard W., and Wolfgang Stegemann, *The Jesus Movement: A Social History of Its First Century*, trans. O. C. Dean, Jr.; Minneapolis: Fortress, 1999.

Swarup, Paul N. W., 'An Eternal Planting, a House of Holiness: The Self Understanding of theDead Sea Scroll Community', synopsis of a Ph.D. Thesis, University of Cambridge, 2002, in *Tyndale Bulletin* 54/1 (2003): 151–6.

Sweeney, James, 'Jesus, Paul and the Temple: An Exploration of some Patterns of Continuity', *Journal of the Evangelical Theological Society* 46 (2003): 605–31.

Talbert, Charles H., ed., *Perspectives on 1 Peter*. NABPR Special Series 9; Macon, Ga.: Mercer University Press, 1986.

Talmon, Shemaryahu, 'Waiting for the Messiah: The Spiritual Universe of the Qumran Covenanters', in *Judaisms and Their Messiahs at the Turn of the Christian Era*, ed. Jacob Neusner *et al*. Cambridge: Cambridge University Press, 1987, 97–137.

The Targum of the Minor Prophets, translated with Critical Introduction, Apparatus, and Notes by Kevin J. Cathcart and Robert P. Gordon. Wilmington, Del.: Michael Glazier, 1989.

Taylor, N. H., 'Jerusalem and the Temple in Early Christian Life and Teaching', *Neotestamentica* 33/2 (1999): 445–61.

Testuz, Michel, *Les Idées religieuses du livre des Jubilés*. Geneva: E. Droz, 1960.

Thiede, Carston, *Simon Peter, From Galilee to Rome*. Exeter: Paternoster Press, 1986.

Thiering, Barbara, 'Mebaqqer and Episkopos in the Light of the Temple Scroll', *Journal of Biblical Literature* 100 (1981): 58–74.

Thompson, T. L., *The Origin Tradition of Ancient Israel 1: The Literary Formation of Genesis and Exodus 1-23*. Sheffield: Sheffield Academic Press, 1987.

Thurén, Lauri, *Argument and Theology in 1 Peter: The Origins of Christian Paraenesis*. JSNTSup 114; Sheffield: Sheffield Academic Press, 1995.

Tiller, Patrick A., *A Commentary on the Animal Apocalypse of 1 Enoch*. Society of Biblical Literature/Early Judaism and Its Literature 4; Atlanta, Ga.: Scholars Press, 1993.

Towner, W. Sibley, *Daniel: A Bible Commentary for Teaching and Preaching*. Interpretation; Atlanta: John Knox Press, 1984.

VanderKam, James C., *The Dead Sea Scrolls Today*. Grand Rapids: Eerdmans, 1994.

———, *Enoch and the Growth of an Apocalyptic Tradition*. Washington, D.C.: Catholic Biblical Association of America, 1984.

Vanhoye, Albert, 'L'Epître (1 P 2,1-10): La maison spirituelle', *Assemblées du Seigneur* 43 (1964): 16–29.

van der Ploeg, J., ed. *La Secte de Qumrân et les Origines du Christianisme. Communication aus IXes Journées bibliques Louvain, Sept. 1957*. Paris: Desclée De Brouwer, 1959.

Van Seters, John, *In Search of History: History and Historiography in the Ancient World and the Origins of Biblical History*. New Haven: Yale University Press, 1983.

van Unnik, Willem Cornelius, *Das Selbstverständnis der jüdischen Diaspora in der hellenisch-römischen Zeit*. AGJU 17; Leiden: Brill, 1993.

———, *Sparsa Collecta: The Collected Essays of W. C. van Unnik*. NovTSup 30; Leiden: Brill, 1980.

———, 'The Redemption in 1 Peter 1:18-19 and the Problem of the First Epistle of Peter', in *Sparsa Collecta: The Collected Essays of W. C. van Unnik*. NovTSup 30; Leiden: Brill, 1980.

Vermes, Geza, *Scripture and Tradition in Judaism*. SPB 4; Leiden: Brill, 1961.

Verseput, D. J., 'The Davidic Messiah and Matthew's Jewish Christianity', *SBL Abstracts and Seminar Papers* 34 (1995): 105–16.

Villiers, J. L., 'Joy in Suffering in 1 Peter', *Neotestamentica* 9 (1975): 64–86.

Vincent, Jeanne-Francoise, Raymond Verdier and Daniel Dory, eds., *La Construction Religieuse de Territoire*. Paris: Ed. l'Harmattan, 1995.

von Schlatter, Adolf. *Petrus und Paulus nach dem ersten Petrusbrief*. Stuttgart: Calwer Vereinsbuchhandlung, 1937.

Wacholder, Ben Zion, *The Dawn of Qumran: The Sectarian Torah and the Teacher of Righteousness*. Monographs of the Hebrew Union College 8; New York: Ktav, 1983.

Walton, John, Victor H. Matthews, and Mark W. Chavalas, eds., *The IVP Bible Background Commentary: Old Testament*. Downers Grove, Ill.: IVP, 2000.

Warden, Duane, 'The Prophets of 1 Peter 1:10-12', *Restoration Quarterly* 31 (1989): 1–12.

Watts, Rikki E., 'Consolation or Confrontation: Isa. 40-55 and the Delay of the New Exodus', *Tyndale Bulletin* 41/1 (1990): 31–59.

Webb, Robert Leslie, 'The Apocalyptic Perspective of First Peter'. Th.M. Thesis, Regent College, 1986.

Weinberg, Joël, *The Citizen-Temple Community*. Sheffield: Sheffield Academic Press, 1992.

———, 'Der *'am hā'āres* des 6.-4. Jh. v. u. Z.', *KLIO* 22 (1974): 325–35.

———, 'Das Beit Avot im 6-4 Jh. v.u.Z.', *Vetus Testamentum* 23/4 (1973): 400–14.

Weitzman, Steve, 'Allusion, Artifice, and Exile in the Hymn of Tobit', *Journal of Biblical Literature* 115 (1996): 49–61.

Wellhausen, Julius, *Prolegomena to the History of Israel*. London: A & C Black, 1885; repr., Grand Rapids: Baker, 1993.

Wenschkewitz, Hans, 'Die Spiritualisierung der Kultusbegriffe Temple, Priester und Opfer im Neuen Testament', *Angelos* 4 (1932): 70–230.

Wentling, Judith, 'Unraveling the Relationship Between 11QT, and the Eschatological Temple and the Qumran Community', *Revue de Qumran* 14 (1989–90): 61–73.

Westermann, Claus, *Isaiah 40-66*. OTL; Philadelphia: Westminster, 1969.

Wiarda, Timothy, *Peter in the Gospels: Pattern, Personality and Relationship*. WUNT 2 Reihe 127; Tübingen: Mohr Siebeck, 2000.

Windisch, Hans, *Die katholischen Briefe.* Tübingen: J. C. B. Mohr [Paul Siebeck], 1930.

Wintermute, O. S., 'Jubilees: A New Translation and Introduction', in *Old Testament Pseudepigrapha*, vol. II, ed. James H. Charleswoth. Garden City, NY: Doubleday, 1985, 35–142.

Wire, Antionette, Review of John H. Elliott, *A Home For the Homeless: A Sociological Exegesis of 1 Peter, Its Situation and Strategy,* and David L. Balch, *Let Wives Be Submissive: The Domestic Code in 1 Peter. Religious Studies Review* 10/3 (1984): 209–16.

Wise, Michael O. *et al., Methods of Investigation of the Dead Sea Scrolls and the Khirbet Qumran Site: Present Realities and Future Prospects.* ANYAS 722; New York: The New York Academy of Sciences, 1994.

Wolff, Christian, 'Christ und Welt in 1. Petrusbrief', *Theologische Literaturzeitung* 100 (1975): 334–42.

Wolfson, Harry Austyn, *Philo: Foundations of Religious Philosophy in Judaism, Christianity, and Islam,* 2 vols. Cambridge, Mass.: Harvard University Press, 1947.

Wright, N. T., In Grateful Dialogue: A Response, in C. C. Newman, ed., *Jesus and the Restoration of Israel: A Critical Assessment of N. T. Wrights* Jesus and the Victory of God. Downers Grove, Ill.: Inter-Varsity Press, 1999, 252–61.

——, *Jesus and the Victory of God.* Christian Origins and the Question of God 2. Minneapolis: Fortress, 1996.

——, *The New Testament and the People of God.* Christian Origins and the Question of God 1. Minneapolis: Fortress, 1992.

Yadin, Y., *The Temple Scroll,* 3 vols. Jerusalem: Israel Exploration Society, 1977.

——, *The Scroll of the War of the Sons of Light against the Sons of Darkness,* trans. B. and C. Rabin. Oxford: Clarendon Press, 1962.

Zimmer, Robert G., 'The Temple of God', *Journal of the Evangelical Theological Society* 18 (1975): 41–6.

Zimmerli, Walther, *Gottes Offenbarung: Gesammelte Aufsätze zum Alten Testament.* Munich: Chr. Kaiser, 1963.

INDEX OF REFERENCES

INDEX OF AUTHORS